ROUTLEDGE LIBRARY EDITIONS: ISRAEL AND PALESTINE

Volume 3

FACTS AND FABLES

T0332276

FACTS AND FABLES
THE ARAB–ISRAELI CONFLICT

CLIFFORD A. WRIGHT

Routledge
Taylor & Francis Group

LONDON AND NEW YORK

First published in 1989

This edition first published in 2015
by Routledge
2 Park Square, Milton Park, Abingdon, Oxon, OX14 4RN

and by Routledge
711 Third Avenue, New York, NY 10017

Routledge is an imprint of the Taylor & Francis Group, an informa business

British Library Cataloguing in Publication Data
A catalogue record for this book is available from the British Library

ISBN: 978-1-138-89267-5 (Set)
eISBN: 978-1-315-69513-6 (Set)
ISBN: 978-1-138-90362-3 (Volume 3)
eISBN: 978-1-315-69675-1 (Volume 3)
Pb ISBN: 978-1-138-90366-1

Publisher's Note
The publisher has gone to great lengths to ensure the quality of this reprint but points out that some imperfections in the original copies may be apparent.

Disclaimer
The publisher has made every effort to trace copyright holders and would welcome correspondence from those they have been unable to trace.

Facts and Fables: The Arab–Israeli Conflict

Clifford A. Wright

Kegan Paul International

London and New York

First published in 1989 by
Kegan Paul International Limited
PO Box 256, London WC1B 3SW

Distributed by
John Wiley & Son Ltd
Southern Cross Trading Estate
1 Oldlands Way, Bognor Regis
W. Sussex PO22 9SA, England

Routledge, Chapman and Hall Inc.
29 West 35th Street
New York, NY 10001,
USA

The Canterbury Press Pty Ltd.
Unit 2, 71 Rushdale Street
Scoresby, Victoria 3179
Australia

Produced by Worts-Power Associates

Set in 10 on 12 pt Times Roman
by Wessex Typesetters
(Division of The Eastern Press Ltd)
Frome, Somerset
and printed in Great Britain by
Dotesios Printers Ltd
Trowbridge, Wiltshire

ISBN 0 7103 0294 0

Contents

Contents

Maps

The Growth of 'Eretz Israel': Fulfillment of the Zionist Mission (Maps 12 to 18)

Appendices

To my mother Helen DeYeso Wright
and my father Harold I. Wright

Acknowledgements

This book began as an attempt to update a 1978 work by John Reddaway, the former Director of the Council for the Advancement of Arab–British Understanding. It quickly became clear that an entirely new book was in the offing. But I am deeply indebted to David Watkins, Mr Reddaway's successor, for granting me permission to utilize large portions of *Commentaries on Recurrent Themes of Zionist Propaganda about Palestine* and for encouraging me to write this book.

Reading early drafts of other people's writings is a tiresome and taxing chore so I would especially like to thank Professors Zachary Lockman and Walid Khalidi of Harvard University, Donald Wagner, Jim Paul, Tamara Kohn, Khalil Nakhleh and John Mahoney for their comments and criticisms of the various drafts of the manuscript.

I would also like to thank Joseph Schecla, Director (USA) of the International Organization for the Elimination of All Forms of Racial Discrimination and Dr Roselle Tekiner of Eckerd College, Florida, for permission to use portions of her paper, 'Jewish Nationality Status as the Basis for Institutionalized Racism in Israel'; Eric Alterman of the Institute for Independent Social Journalism for permission to use portions of Joy Bonds, et al., *Our Roots are Still Alive: the Story of the Palestinian People*; Philip Mattar, Associate Editor of the *Journal for Palestine Studies* for permission to use portions of Uri Davis and Walter Lehn's 'And the Fund Still Lives: the Role of the Jewish National Fund in the

Determination of Israel's Land Policies', *Journal of Palestine Studies*, 28, Summer 1978; Mavis E. Pindard of Faber and Faber Publishers and David Hirst for permission to use scattered paragraphs from his book, *The Gun and the Olive Branch: the Roots of Violence in the Middle East*; P. A. Barlow of Longman Group Ltd and Henry Cattan for permission to paraphrase portions of Mr Cattan's book, *Palestine and International Law*; Patricia Walsh and Susan Ziadeh of the Association of Arab–American University Graduates and Sheila Ryan for permission to rely on portions of *Palestine is, but Not in Jordan*.

I would also like to thank David Yates of Americans for Middle East Understanding for invaluable help in researching the maps used; Joe Stork, Editor of *MERIP Middle East Report* for his assistance in allowing me to search through MERIP's photograph archive; and Nubar Hovsepian for his help with the manuscript. Since I do not read Arabic or Hebrew I would like to thank the person who wishes to remain unnamed for helping in the translation of sources from those languages. Thanks should also go to the helpful librarians at Widener Library at Harvard University. A special thank you goes to Nancy Campbell for her advice and friendship.

Finally, I wish to thank John F. Mahoney, Executive Director of Americans for Middle East Understanding, Inc. and its board of directors for their grant which contributed to making this book a reality, and the board of directors of the American Middle East Peace Research Institute.

Clifford A. Wright
Cambridge, Massachusetts
December 1988

Introduction

The Arab–Israeli conflict is one of the most protracted, confusing and heated political struggles of our time. For 100 years Palestinian Arabs and Zionist Jews have contested the same land. It is not a simple territorial dispute but a dispute involving claims emanating from a different conceptual basis. The foundation of the Jewish claim to the land is rooted in the Bible. The Palestinian claim is based on historical permanence and residence, i.e. they are the natives of this land.

The Arab–Israeli conflict is also uniquely dangerous as the most likely point of contact should a superpower conflagration occur. The conflict is notably immune to outside intervention. No conflict in the world today elicits such strong emotional involvement not only from participants but also from distant observers.

The conflict is primarily about land but it is also an ideological struggle between two peoples which involves a score of myths and fables. Fables are most often created to serve a political purpose and all nationalisms have their own myths and falsehoods. Unfortunately, fables limit understanding about causes and reasons for events. They arise sometimes as a result of ignorance but, mostly, as a result of propaganda. Images are constructed which shape not only public opinion but the parameters of political discourse. For several decades the popular image of the Palestinian has been as terrorist and of Israel as the bastion of Western democracy. The images are reinforced through television, for example, in the startling contrast so often seen between the incoherent rambling of a Palestinian spokesman whose poor English communicates little and the articulate American immigrant to Israel speaking of the 'pioneering spirit'. Israel, described as a Western democracy, is usually placed in the setting of a 'sea of Muslims'. Meanwhile the Arab is often portrayed as exotic, irrational, unreasonable, lecherous, hysterical, vicious and lacking decency. Discourse has been constrained by the images conveyed by these fables.

The myths and legends that have been assumed as reality have been appropriated by one side and cast a shroud around any deeper understanding of the conflict. Rather than dispel obscurity, recourse by pundits and commentators to wide generalizations such as the 'Arab tendency to terrorism', 'Arab penchant for exaggeration', 'anti-Semitism', 'intransigence' and 'senseless violence' contribute heavily to the general confusion. This popular view is reflected at the governmental level as well as in the Fourth Estate. A myopic policy at the government level was evident during the Palestinian Uprising in early 1988. By the time US Secretary of State, George Schultz, arrived in the Middle East to propose a peace initiative 100 Palestinians (half of whom were children) had been killed. Hundreds of thousands of Palestinians were demonstrating in the West Bank against Israeli occupation and for the Palestine Liberation Organization as their sole representative. In this climate, Schultz declared that the PLO could not participate in any negotiations and that their Observer Mission to the United Nations would be forced to close. The press too, takes for granted that the Arabs start all the wars, that the Arabs and Jews have been eternal enemies, that Arabs are inherently war-like and fight peace and that the Palestinian refugee problem is of their own making. Few Western observers find these kind of assumptions questionable, at least on the psychological level. The Palestinians who are exiled are called Palestinians yet it is denied that they come from anywhere. This ideological shroud consists of over a dozen myths that recur whenever the Arab–Israeli conflict is under discussion and especially when it heats up as during the Uprising in 1988. They permeate the media, the government as well as popular sentiment. It is interesting to observe that some of these myths have been questioned by Israeli scholars themselves, and even publicly discussed in Israel, but never reported in the West.

These fables have been exposed in one place or another. Even so, given US sympathy with Israel and the intensity of prejudices, all accounts and documentation coming from Arabs have been treated with the greatest suspicion. Needless to say, propaganda surrounding the struggle has developed into an art.

This book is the first of its kind in that it attempts to take the demystification process into the arena of popular politics, but uses extensive documentation. It is hoped that the demystification process will eventually extend back again into the realm of the university and, more importantly, into political planning. I have avoided using Arab sources whenever Zionist sources were available. My hope is that this book might break down the suspicion from which the Arab narrative, whether oral history or scholarly research, often suffers, so that in the future we can listen to the Palestinian – and believe the story.

I have not endeavored to address every issue relevant in the Arab–Israeli conflict. There are some major questions and many minor ones which have been omitted. For instance, I do not discuss the issues revolving around the activities of the Grand Mufti of Jerusalem, Muhammed Amin al-Husayni, during the Second World War nor the prickly question of the status of Jerusalem, nor the claim that the Palestinians sold their land to the Jews. This book focuses on the major fables, those which recur countless times, from official pronouncements to newspaper editorials. I refer the reader to Philip Mattar's *The Mufti of Jerusalem: Al-Hajj Amin Al-Husayni and the Palestinian National Movement* on the Grand Mufti, to Henry Cattan's *The Question of Jerusalem* concerning Jerusalem and to Walter Lehn and Uri Davis's *The Jewish National Fund* on the land question.[1] I examine each belief or claim on its own merit. For example, although I personally believe the argument from divine right (chapter 15) is nonsense I treat it seriously. This book is about what I believe to be the seventeen most important and most commonly held beliefs on the Arab–Israeli conflict.

Although I conceive the book as a primer the chapters are structured in no particular order of importance; I have, however, attempted to group them logically. Each chapter recounts a common belief and explores the argument and evidence. The Palestinians themselves are the topic of the first chapter simply because it is of the utmost interest when one party to a conflict (Israel) devotes such extraordinary effort not only to defeating and destroying their enemy, the Palestinians, but also to denying their existence or importance.

The second, third and fourth chapters expand on chapter 1 to solve some of the mystery of why a nation would pack its bags and leave its home, turn its country over to its antagonists – all as a result of 'radio broadcasts'. Who are these Palestinian refugees, how many of them are there? For several decades the public has heard about the miracle of Israel. What is this 'miracle' and what do the Palestinians want?

The next three chapters deal with core issues: terror, democracy and Zionism. Chapters 8, 9 and 10 examine the questions of the practice of democracy in Israel, the situation on the West Bank and Gaza, and Israeli conceptions and efforts towards peace.

Chapters 11–17 are historical chapters that can be read first. In fact, I have organized the book so that one could start at the back and read chapter 1 last.

At the end of every chapter I have recommended readings that are particularly noteworthy for all or some aspect of the chapter.

The most important question the reader might have after reading this book is whether peace is possible in the Middle East between Arabs and Jews. Recent events from 1982 onwards might lead one to believe, ever increasingly, that peace is distant. My assembled arguments do not encourage any easy or dreamy solutions. An opening for peace may arise from a bold and unpredictable new consciousness on the part of both Israelis and Palestinians. Perhaps the unique statements by two former hawks, one Israeli and one Palestinian, in early 1988 is a sign that a new plateau is being reached. Yehoshafat Harkabi, the former head of Israeli military intelligence, wrote that Israel must negotiate with the Palestine Liberation Organization (PLO) while Bassam Abu Sharif, the press spokesman of PLO chairman Yasser Arafat and a former politburo member of the radical Popular Front for the Liberation of Palestine, wrote in the *New York Times* that the PLO wants peace with Israel, did not seek its destruction and was willing to sit down with Israel and work towards peace.[2] Both men were roundly criticized within their own communities for their respective positions and statements but the thing to remember is that precedence is important.

By the end of 1988, this precedent setting development expanded to a full-fledged diplomatic breakthrough when Arafat, in an address to the UN General Assembly on 13 December 1988, recognized Israel's right to exist, renounced terrorism and invited

Israel to make peace with the Palestinians. The United States recognized the PLO and began talks with Arafat. This historic breakthrough does not change history as described in the following chapters; it creates a new chapter and question.

The question of what becomes of Zionism and Palestinian nationalism once peace is negotiated is yet another interesting question and one which will have to be the subject of a future book.

Notes to Introduction

1. Mattar, Columbia University Press, 1988; Cattan, Third World Centre for Research and Publishing, 1980; and Lehn and Davis, Kegan Paul International, 1988.
2. Yehoshafat Harkabi, *Israel's Fateful Decisions*, trans. Lenn Schramm, Harper and Row, 1988, p. xvi; and Bassam Abu Sharif, *New York Times*, 22 June 1988.

Chapter 1

The Palestinians

Until recently most Zionists have claimed that the Palestinians do
not exist or that they are simply part of the Arab world with no
distinct identity. The Zionist slogan, first coined by Israel Zangwill,
a founder of Zionism, that Palestine was 'a land without people,
waiting for a people without land', captured this denial of the
Palestinian people.[1]

The concept represented by this slogan is maintained even today
in Israel where the Palestinians who are Israeli citizens are officially
known as the 'Arabs of Israel'. Zionists have maintained this
position in one form or another, over the years, because they
contend that the Arab–Israeli conflict amounts to the stubbornness
of the Arab states to recognize Israel rather than to the grievances
of a people, namely the Palestinians, who were dispossessed in
order that Israel might exist.

Zionists today, especially those who live in Israel, have come
to grant that there are Palestinians, mainly because the enormous
effort to subjugate them has drawn the world's attention and
demonstrated to even the most myopic Zionist that it is not a
mirage throwing rocks at Israeli occupation troops. But although
granting that they exist as persons Zionists deny that the Palestinians exist as a nation.

Another Zionist claim suggests that since the Palestinians consider themselves Arabs, part of the Arab nation and have called for Arab unity they therefore do not have a separate existence as Palestinians.

What are the Facts?

The famous Jewish philosopher, Hannah Arendt, once said that if Israel could not come to terms with the central fact of its existence, the dispossession of the Palestinians, then it would degenerate into a small warrior tribe such as Sparta.[2] She understood that the success of Zionism *necessarily* meant the dispossession of the Palestinians.

The existence of the Palestinians constitutes a perennial and stark reminder that the Zionist enterprise has a fundamental moral flaw. As the pro-Zionist British historian Christopher Sykes said, 'This was indeed the whole problem of Palestine: it was inhabited.'[3]

The earliest Zionist colonialists in Palestine knew that the land they were settling was inhabited. Some chose to ignore this 'minor' problem while others tried to overcome it. Many Zionists, as with most Europeans of the late nineteenth century, agreed with Theodor Herzl's characterization of Arab Palestine, and for that matter all the Arab world, as a 'plague-ridden blighted corner of the Orient' to which the Jews would 'bring cleanliness, order and the well-distilled customs of the Occident'.[4]

Herzl, the father of Zionism, believed that the native Palestinians would resist the takeover of their country and therefore he recommended that they be dealt with through 'assured supremacy', a euphemism for brute force and military superiority.[5] Herzl wrote that military power was an essential component of his strategy and that, ideally, the Zionists should acquire the land of their choice by armed conquest.[6]

As for the already existing and native Arabs living in Palestine, the site of Zionist territorial desires, the Zionists should 'try to spirit the penniless population across the border'. The process of dispossession must be done 'discreetly and circumspectly', Herzl advised.[7] In fact, in 1901 Herzl tried, unsuccessfully, to obtain a charter from the Ottoman Turkish rulers to establish a Jewish colonization association in Palestine which would have had the right to deport the native Palestinians.[8]

Seven decades later, the Zionists continued their refusal to recognize the Palestinians, let alone their 'rights'. Prime Minister Golda Meir of Israel, in all seriousness, claimed that 'there was no such thing as Palestinians'.

> *There was no such thing as Palestinians.*
>
> Golda Meir, Prime Minister of Israel
> London *Sunday Times*, 15 June 1969.

Today, the twin claims, that the Palestinians don't exist and that Palestine was empty, are maintained in one form or another.

This denial of the Palestinians is a wholesale dehumanization of a people. In 1982, Prime Minister Menachem Begin described the Palestinians, in a speech in the Knesset, as 'two-legged beasts'.[9]

Former Israeli Army Chief of Staff Raphael Eitan likened the Palestinians to drugged cockroaches.[10] In July 1981 the Israeli Air Force bombed an apartment building in a residential neighborhood of Beirut killing 300 Palestinians civilians; not a single Israeli leader dissented or expressed a hesitation about the morality of this act.

During the Palestinian Uprising in early 1988, Defense Minister Yitzhak Rabin announced a new policy towards the Palestinians on the West Bank and Gaza, one of 'force, power, and blows'. Civilians, mostly children, were rounded up by the Israeli forces and beaten indiscriminately. Although the policy of beatings was condemned by the US State Department it continued unabated.[11]

By the 1980s only ardent Zionists denied or degraded the existence of the Palestinians. The world community overwhelmingly recognized the Palestinian people and their right to national self-determination. The United Nations General Assembly passed a resolution in 1975 establishing a Committee on the Exercise of the Inalienable Rights of the Palestinian People and declared 29 November to be a day of international solidarity with the Palestinian people.

Who, then, are the Palestinians?

Palestine has been continuously inhabited since the dawn of history. From Ottoman sources it can be estimated that, by 1850, more than half a million people lived in Palestine. Of this Palestinian population, 80 percent were Muslim, 10 percent Christian and 7 percent Jews.[12]

By 1914 the British estimated Palestine's population at 689,272 of whom no more than 60,000 or 9 percent were Jews.[13] The most accurate census at that time was the 1922 census conducted by the British. Of the total of 757,182, 78 percent were Muslim, 10 percent were Christian, 11 percent were Jewish. Seventy-five percent of the Jews were Europeans and their offspring.[14] About 10,000 or 1 percent were classified as 'other'. The census also did not count the nearly 50,000 Bedouin Palestinians in the Negev desert.

The British conducted a second census in 1931. Of the more than 1,000,000 people, 73 percent were Muslim, 9 percent were Christian. Because of Jewish emigration from Europe the Jewish population in Palestine constituted a significant minority of 17 percent. After 1931 the British only provided estimates of the population.

The last official estimate was in 1947 which gave a population of 1,908,775 (61 percent Muslim, 8 percent Christian and 31 percent Jewish). The Jews had increased their share in the population from 11 percent in 1922 to 31 percent in 1947.

The increase in the Jewish population was the result of massive immigration. The share of the Palestinian population, on the other hand, decreased from over 90 percent in 1922 to less than 70 percent in 1947, although the actual number had increased in that period from 673,000 to 1,319,000. The latter figure is probably low since the Palestinian population was under-enumerated in the 1931 census and the Bedouin population was assumed, by British census officials, to have remained unchanged. Arab immigration into Palestine amounted to 40,500 people between 1922 and 1945.[15]

There is, however, a difficulty from which the Zionist dares not avert his eyes, though he rarely likes to face it. Palestine proper has already its inhabitants.

Israel Zangwill
The Voice of Jerusalem, London, 1920, p. 88.

Did these Arabs consider themselves, and did others consider them, to be Palestinians?

Palestine's geographic location, its physical characteristics, and, partly as a result of these, its history, distinguish it from surrounding regions.[16] It would, therefore, be surprising if its inhabitants had not responded in their own distinct way to their particular circumstances and developed into a people distinguishable from, but not without close affinities with, their neighbors.

To be a nation means, generally, to share a language and, to the people concerned, to feel an intimate attachment to a homeland, perceiving their past, present and future to be inextricably linked with the land they hold dear. It is also usual for other communities to acknowledge the separate status of that people's land. Did the area which became the British Mandate of Palestine signify nothing more to its inhabitants, or to others, than the areas which surround it? Was it perceived to be nothing other than the southern part of Syria or a part of the larger Arab world?

The Arabic name for Palestine, Filastin, was derived from the Latin Palaestina, the name given by the Romans to Judea after the last Jewish revolt in AD 132–35. The Latin name, in turn, was derived from Philistia, the name given to the area by the ancient Philistines. Palaestina was divided into three units: Palaestina Prima (the West Bank of today and the southern part of the eastern side of the Jordan valley), Palaestina Secunda (the Jordan Valley, eastern and central Galilee and the northern part of the eastern side of the Jordan valley) and Palaestina Tertia (the southern part of Transjordan, the Negev and Sinai).

When the Arabs arrived they retained (as they usually did elsewhere) the administrative organization of the territory of Palestine as it had been under the Romans and later the Byzantines. The Arabs named the territory Djund Filastin (military district of Palestine).

In 1517 the Ottoman Turks conquered Palestine and divided its area into three districts. In the late nineteenth century, still under the Ottoman Turks, the area of Palestine which was to come under British rule and later be known as 'mandated Palestine', included the *sanjak* (sub-province) of Jerusalem and two *sanjaks* of the *vilayet* (province) of Beirut. After 1887 the Jerusalem *sanjak*, because of its significance for the monotheistic religions, was administered directly from Constantinople (Istanbul) as though it were a full province (see map 1).

The Israeli scholar Y. Porath has demonstrated that 'at the

Map 1 Ottoman Palestine

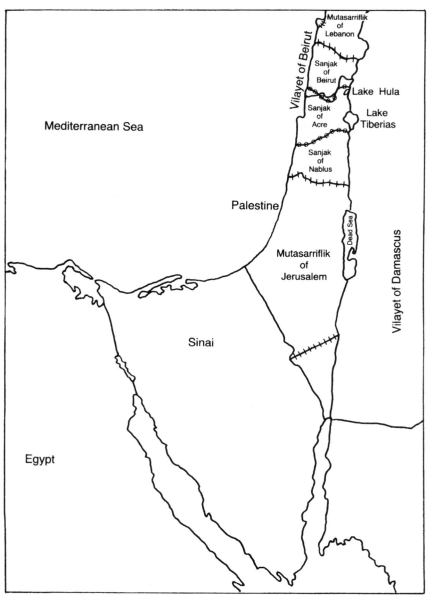

Shown with 1917 Ottoman jurisdictional boundaries and boundaries of British Mandate 1922–48.

—————— British Mandate boundaries.

+++++ }
−○○○○− } Ottoman boundaries.

end of the Ottoman period the concept of *Filastin* was already widespread among the educated Arab public, denoting either the whole of Palestine or the Jerusalem Sanjak alone'.[17]

Zionists who deny the existence of the Palestinians, or 'Palestine', claim that when the Western Powers, after the First World War, laid down the modern frontiers of the Middle East they did so entirely arbitrarily. The facts show that, in establishing the boundaries of 'mandated Palestine' where they did, the Western Powers implicitly recognized the reality of Palestine as an area of special significance whose residents were a people distinguishable from their neighbors. Equally revealing, Palestine was also recognized as a distinct area by tourists. Baedeker's famous guidebook, published in 1876, was entitled *Palestine – Syria*. Herzl himself, in his correspondence with the Ottoman Sultan Abdul Hamid, referred to 'Palestine' and neither seems to have been confused by the term.

When we have settled the land, all the Arabs will be able to do about it will be to scurry around like drugged cockroaches in a bottle.

Raphael Eitan, Israeli Chief of Staff
New York Times, 14 April 1983.

The boundaries then established for Palestine by the Western Powers after the First World War enhanced the already existing unity of the area. Evidently the Palestinians and others did regard pre-British Mandate Palestine as a distinct area, as something much more than a part of Syria or the Arab world.

In short, the Palestinians recognized it as their homeland, and others recognized it to be so. It hardly needs stating that these facts alone would be enough on which to base the conclusion that Palestine's residents regarded themselves, and were regarded by others, as Palestinians. But what other evidence is there to support this conclusion? Two categories of evidence demonstrate the existence of a Palestinian nation before and during the Mandate. First, the Palestinian opposition to Zionism and, second, the opinions of outsiders.

[The Palestinians are] beasts walking on two legs.

Menachem Begin, Prime Minister of Israel in a speech to the Knesset,

quoted in Amnon Kapeliouk, 'Begin and the "Beasts",'
New Statesman, 25 June 1982.

The Palestinians opposed, from its inception in the 1880s, the immigration of European Zionists to Palestinian land for the purpose of colonization. As early as 1891 Palestinian leaders demanded that the Ottoman ruler of Palestine, Sultan Abdul Hamid II, forbid the acquisition of land titles by European Zionists in Palestine.[18]

The King-Crane Commission appointed by US President Woodrow Wilson submitted a report after the 1919 Versailles Peace Conference which said:

> If . . . the wishes of Palestine's population are to be decisive as to what is to be done with Palestine, then it is to be remembered that the non-Jewish population of Palestine – nearly nine-tenths of the whole – are emphatically against the entire Zionist program.[19]

America's allies refused to cooperate with the King-Crane Commission and its findings.

Shortly after this report a serious disturbance in Palestine occurred because of Arab disappointment at the non-fulfillment of the promises of independence made by the British during the First World War; the belief that the Balfour Declaration implied a denial of the right of self-determination; and fear that an increase in Jewish immigration would lead to the Arabs' economic and political subjection to the European Jews.[20]

Throughout the 1920s and 1930s disorders continued with a constant stream of representation to the British, who had been given the Mandate authority by the League of Nations in 1922.

Y. Porath, examining the Palestinian arguments, found two basic and recurring themes: the emphasis on their continuous occupation of the land and the presence of an Arab majority in Palestine.[21] He concludes:

> Both these arguments came close to the fundamental principle of the nationalist movements in Europe towards the end of the First World War, the 'rights of nations to self-determination.' That is to

say, a group of people speaking a common language, dwelling in unbroken territorial continuity and possessing a common consciousness of their unique historical development, constituted a nation and by virtue of this fact possessed the right of self-determination, which for the most part, was interpreted as meaning a right to have a state of their own.[22]

This sustained opposition to Zionism and sustained demand for independence cannot be dismissed as the isolated acts of individuals unrepresentative of their community as a whole. The Palestinians' actions and arguments were essentially nationalist and permeated all levels of their society.

That outsiders considered the Palestinians to be a separate people cannot be doubted. The most compelling evidence lies in Article 22 of the Covenant of the League of Nations which states:

Certain communities formerly belonging to the Turkish Empire have reached a stage in their development where their existence as independent nations can be provisionally recognized subject to the rendering of administrative advice and assistance by a Mandatory until such a time as they are able to stand alone.

The League of Nations Mandate for Palestine specifically entrusted Britain with giving effect to the provisions of the Article (see appendices 6 and 7).

Zionists also assert that the Palestinians regarded themselves as nothing more than a part of the broader Arab nation or, alternatively, as 'Syrians'. Certainly the Palestinians consider themselves to be part of the Arab world and identify closely with their neighbors. But that does not preclude their possession of a distinct Palestinian identity.

Without a doubt Palestinians have made appeals for Arab unity. But such unity was primarily sought in the hope that it would strengthen their hand in their struggle with Israel. Porath is quite explicit on this:

Resistance to Zionism was the prime motive force behind Palestinian nationalist activity; their relation to the question of Arab unity in its various manifestations was a function of the efficacy of the anti-Zionist struggle. When they were of the opinion that unity would help them in this struggle, they lean towards it (1919–20), but when they grew suspicious of the intentions of certain Arab nationalists from Syria with respect to Zionism, they dissociate themselves from them and tried to go it alone.[23]

Palestinians now number some 4.5 million persons. This figure is neither totally accurate nor simply unreliable. The fact that an accurate census of the Palestinians has been impossible is symptomatic of their plight. About 40 percent of the Palestinians live within Palestine, including 700,000 in pre-1967 Israel.

The most significant fact about the existence of the Palestinians has been not just their displacement as a result of the 1948 war, but their continual and systematic displacement. The Israeli invasion of Lebanon in 1982 was only the most recent episode that has forced the Palestinians ever further away from their homes now occupied by Israel (see appendix 19).

It is clear that the central issue in the Arab–Israeli conflict is the Palestinians. For this reason Israel has devoted enormous energy to expelling them from their homes, to stripping away their identity, and to denying their existence and importance for the resolution of the conflict. Israel refuses to talk not only to the Palestine Liberation Organization but to *any* representative Palestinian political entity.

Notes to Chapter 1

1. Israel Zangwill, 'The Return to Palestine', *New Liberal Review*, II, December 1901, p. 627.
2. Hannah Arendt, *The Jew as Pariah*, Grove Press, 1978, p. 187.
3. Christopher Sykes, *Crossroads to Israel 1917–1948*, Collins, 1965, p. 116.
4. Theodor Herzl, *The Complete Diaries*, Herzl Press and Thomas Yoseloff, 1960, I, p. 343.
5. Herzl, *The Jewish State: a Modern Solution to the Jewish Question*, Rita Searl, 1946, p. 29.

6. Herzl, *Gesammelte Zionistische Schriften*, Judischer Verlag, 1934–5, I, p. 114; II, pp. 50, 58, 78, 102; III, p. 526.
7. Herzl, *The Complete Diaries*, I, p. 88.
8. Adolf Bohm, *Die Zionistische Bewegung bis zum Ende des Weltkrieges*, Hozaah Ivrith, 1935, I, p. 706.
9. Quoted by the Israeli journalist Amnon Kapeliouk in 'Begin and the "Beasts",' *New Statesman*, 25 June 1982.
10. Raphael Eitan, Israeli Chief of Staff at the time, said in reference to the Palestinians living on the West Bank, 'When we have settled the land, all the Arabs will be able to do about it will be to scurry around like drugged cockroaches in a bottle.' *New York Times*, 14 April 1983.
11. *Jerusalem Post*, 22 January 1988.
12. Janet L. Abu-Lughod, 'The Demographic Transformation of Palestine' in Ibrahim Abu-Lughod, ed., *The Transformation of Palestine: Essays on the Origin and Development of the Arab–Israeli Conflict*, Northwestern University Press, 1971, p. 140. Estimating population in the Ottoman territories is notoriously inaccurate. Although Ottoman estimates put the population at half a million, other estimates (see appendix 2) show the population around 400,000.
13. Great Britain, *Census of Palestine 1922*, p. 142. See appendix 2 for slightly different estimates for 1912.
14. ibid.
15. Edward Hagopian and A. B. Zahlan, 'Palestine's Arab Population: the Demography of the Palestinians', *Journal of Palestine Studies*, III, 4, Summer 1974, p. 43.
16. The following discussion is adapted from Council for the Advancement of Arab–British Understanding, *Commentaries on Recurrent Themes of Zionist Propaganda about Palestine*, London: CAABU, n.d., pp. 5–7.
17. Y. Porath, *The Emergence of the Palestinian National Movement 1918–1929*, Frank Cass, 1974, pp. 8–9.
18. See Neville J. Mandel, *The Arabs and Zionism before World War I*, University of California Press, 1976.
19. Walter Laqueur and Barry Rubin, eds., *The Israel–Arab Reader: a Documentary History of the Middle East Conflict*, Penguin, 1984, p. 29.
20. Henry Cattan, *Palestine, the Arabs and Israel*, Longman, 1969, p. 17.
21. Porath, op. cit., pp. 39–41.
22. ibid., p. 41.
23. ibid., p. 63.

Recommended Reading

Joy Bonds, et al., *Our Roots are Still Alive: the Story of the Palestinian People*, Peoples Press, 1977.

Jonathan Dimbleby and Donald McCullin, *The Palestinians*, Quartet, 1979.

Sarah Graham-Brown, *Palestinians and Their Society 1880–1946*, Quartet, 1980.

The International Status of the Palestinian People, United Nations, 1979.

Walid Khalidi, *Before Their Diaspora: a Photographic History of the Palestinians 1876–1948*, Institute for Palestine Studies, 1984.

Khalil Nakhleh and Elia Zureik, eds., *The Sociology of the Palestinians*, St Martin's Press, 1980.

Edward W. Said, et al., *A Profile of the Palestinian People*, Palestine Human Rights Campaign, 1984.

Edward W. Said with Jean Mohr, *After the Last Sky: Palestinian Lives*, Pantheon, 1985.

Edward W. Said and Christopher Hitchens, *Blaming the Victims: Spurious Scholarship and the Palestinian Question*, New York and London: Verso, 1988.

Edward W. Said, *The Question of Palestine*, Times Books, 1979.

Rosemary Sayigh, *Palestinians: from Peasants to Revolutionaries*, Zed Press, 1979.

Chapter 2

Why Did the Palestinians Leave?

Israel and its supporters claim that the Palestinians left their homes in Palestine of their own accord, without harassment from Zionist military forces. The Palestinians left in 1948 primarily, the Zionists claim, because 'Arab leaders stimulated the Arab departure with frightening radio broadcasts because they wanted to arouse the Arab world into a holy war against the Jews'. They also claim that the Arabs 'fabricated atrocity stories' to terrify the Palestinians into leaving.[1]

Zionists claim that the Palestinians were asked to stay and live as citizens in the Jewish state but chose to leave, for whatever reasons, and therefore they have forfeited their rights to their land, and must bear responsibility for their plight.

Zionists also claim that United Nations resolutions do not recognize any right of return by the Palestinian refugees.

What are the Facts?

Not until 1961 did anyone in the Western world bother to check

13

the truth of the Zionist claims or ask the Palestinians themselves the reasons for their flight. There were more than 700,000 refugees; each and all had a story to tell about their expulsion, yet they were ignored. In 1959 a scholar at the American University of Beirut, Walid Khalidi, published original research documenting the systematic expulsion of the Palestinians by the Zionists.[2]

In 1961 the Irish journalist Erskine Childers spent several months retracing the evidence supplied by the Zionists in order to verify and establish the true story. Childers asked the Israeli authorities for the evidence supporting their claim. Israel was unable to produce any evidence that Arab radio broadcasts encouraged the Palestinians to leave their homes. He then examined the American and the British radio-monitoring records for all of 1948 and found that

> there was not a single order or appeal, or suggestion about evacuation from any Arab radio station inside or outside Palestine in 1948. There is repeated monitored record of Arab appeals, even flat orders, to the civilians of Palestine to stay put.

Childers also found considerable evidence that Zionist radio stations had been broadcasting *in Arabic* in 1948 urging Palestinians to leave their homes.[3] A Zionist participant in the expulsion of the Palestinians confirmed that Zionist radio stations broadcast in Arabic to frighten the Palestinians into leaving.[4]

Both the process of expropriation [of the Palestinians] and the removal of the poor must be carried out discreetly and circumspectly.

Theodor Herzl
The Complete Diaries, Herzl Press, 1960, I, p. 88.

Nevertheless, Zionists continue to repeat these claims and cite statements by Arab leaders allegedly confirming their point of view. It was discovered by Childers and others that the statements usually quoted are out of context, unsubstantiated or concoctions. For example, one of the earliest pieces of 'evidence' cited by Israel, and one that was very influential in turning much of Western public opinion against the Palestinians at an early stage, was a quotation by the Greek Catholic Archbishop of Galilee, George Hakim, that appears in virtually every piece of propaganda produced by Israeli or Zionist organizations around the world. The quotation, from a small Lebanese journal, *Sada al-Janub*, on 16 August 1948 reads:

> The refugees had been confident that their absence from Palestine would not last long; that they would return within a few days – within a week or two. Their leaders had promised them that the Arab armies would crush the Zionist gangs very quickly and that there would be no need for panic or fear of a long exile.

It will be noted that this statement does not, in fact, allege that the Arab leaders ordered Palestine civilians to evacuate. But when the Zionists use this quote after an assertion of their own that there were such orders the effect of the Archbishop's words appears to confirm these 'evacuation' orders.

Childers wrote to the Archbishop asking him to explain what actually happened and to comment on the Zionists' use of his comments. The Archbishop replied:

> There is nothing in this statement to justify the construction which many propagandists had put on it . . . At no time did I state that the flight of the refugees was due to the orders, explicit or implicit, of their leaders. On the contrary, no such orders were ever made by the military commanders, or by the Higher Arab Committee, or, indeed by the Arab League or Arab States. I have not the least doubt that any such allegations are sheer concoctions and falsifications . . . The truth is that the flight was primarily due to the terror with which the Arab population of Palestine were struck in consequence of atrocities committed by Jews.[5]

Contrary to the Zionist claim, the Arab Higher Committee did not issue orders for the Palestinians to leave 'to make room for Arab armies'. On record is a letter dated 8 March 1948 from the Arab Higher Committee which specifically asks the Arab governments to cooperate in preventing Palestinians from leaving the country.[6]

It was not realized at the time that the expulsion of the Palestinians was the result of a deliberate master plan, code named Plan Dalet, to clear out the Arab population from areas alloted to the Jewish state under the UN Partition Plan of 1947. Plan Dalet, which was formulated shortly after the UN decision, was preceded by other plans as early as May 1942. The Zionist leadership began preparations to convert the whole of Palestine into a Jewish state.[7] Zionist military planners began drawing up plans and by 1947 had mapped and catalogued information about every Palestinian village, its strategic character and importance.[8]

The central aim of Plan Dalet was 'control of the area given to us by the UN *in addition to areas occupied by us which were outside these borders* and the setting up of forces to counter the possible invasion of Arab armies'.[9]

Plan Dalet was directed against the existing Palestinian population. In the words of the official Zionist history, Palestinian villages that resisted 'should be destroyed . . . and their inhabitants expelled beyond the borders of the Jewish state'.[10] The Zionist strategy for Palestinian town-dwellers was similar: 'Palestinian residents of urban quarters which dominate access to or egress from the towns should be expelled beyond the borders of the Jewish state in the event of their resistance.'[11]

Areas lying outside the area of the proposed Jewish state, Palestinian towns and villages such as Qalqilyah, Tulkarm, Acre, Nazareth, Lydda, Ramleh, Bethlehem, Beit Jala, Hebron were to be put under siege and occupied. 'The inhabitants of Jaffa should be imprisoned within their municipal boundaries and not dare leave them.' All the villages between Tel Aviv and Jerusalem should be occupied. All the Palestinian quarters of West and East Jerusalem, as well as the environs of the city were to be conquered.[12]

The reason for the Zionist plan to expel the Palestinians results from the project of Zionism itself: to establish a Jewish state in Eretz Israel (Land of Israel). The goal was best summed up by Joseph Weitz, the administrator responsible for Jewish colonization, in 1940:

> Between ourselves it must be clear that there is no room for both people together in this country . . . The only solution is a Palestine . . . without Arabs. And there is no other way than to transfer the

Arabs from here to the neighboring countries, to transfer all of them; not one village, not one tribe, should be left.[13]

There is no other way than to transfer the Arabs from here [Palestine] to the neighboring countries, to transfer all of them; not one village, not one tribe, should be left.

Joseph Weitz, Jewish National Fund, administrator responsible for Zionist colonization
Davar, 29 September 1967 from *My Diary and Letters to the Children*, Massada, 1965, III, p. 293

The official Zionist history describes which methods of terrorism should be used to attack the Palestinians. Palestinian military and political leaders, those who financed them and those who incited them, 'e.g., journalists', were to be targets. The objective was to 'inflict physical harm' or 'liquidate them'. Terrorist bombs were to be placed in 'clubs, cafes, and other meeting places, communication centers, flour mills, water plants and other vital economic installations'.[14]

The latest evidence contradicting Zionist claims concerning the reasons for Palestinian flight comes from a recently discovered Zionist document outlining the result of their expulsion plans. The document is a report dated 30 June 1948, written by the Israel Defense Forces Intelligence Branch for the Israeli Prime Minister. The document was uncovered in the Hashomer Hatza'ir Archive by an Israeli researcher, Benny Morris. The report states that the Palestinian exodus was the result, primarily of three reasons:

1. Direct, hostile Jewish operations against Arab settlements.
2. The effects of hostile operations on nearby Arab settlements.
3. Operations of Zionist terrorist groups such as Menachem Begin's Irgun.[15]

The Israel Defense Force report goes on to say that 'without a doubt, hostile [Haganah] operations were the main cause of the movement of population'. The report concludes by saying that 'it is possible to say that at least 55 percent of the total of the exodus was caused by our [Haganah] operations and by their influence'.

To this the Intelligence Branch adds the effects of the operations of the 'dissident' Jewish organizations 'who directly [caused] some 15 percent . . . of the emigration'.

The Israeli report also contradicts standard Zionist propaganda concerning Arab radio broadcasts. It states that 'the Arab institutions attempted to struggle against the phenomenon of flight and evacuation'. It also says that the Arab states used radio broadcasts to *curb* the exodus not to encourage it.[16]

We shall try to spirit the penniless population [the Palestinians] across the border by procuring employment for it in the transit countries, while denying it any employment in our own country.

Theodor Herzl
The Complete Diaries, Herzl Press, 1960, I, p. 88.

Even today, contradicting their own official histories and the memoirs of their leaders, Zionist apologists and propagandists claim that Arab leaders stimulated the Palestinian exodus with 'frightening radio broadcasts'.[17]

In fact, Arab leaders, such as Fawzi al-Kawoukji, warned that 'Zionist agents are spreading defeatist news in order to cause . . . panic among the peaceful population.' He recommended in radio broadcasts for everyone to remain calm and to be 'cautious of battle reports spread by the enemy who wants to create panic among the population'.[18]

Other Arab leaders, such as King Abdullah of Jordan, admonished the Palestinians to

> defend yourselves if you are attacked. Do not murder old men or women or children. Be merciful and humane. Most Jews who are in Palestine undoubtedly want to live with you in peace and prosperity. Those who incite the Jews to aggression and evil [the Zionists] are the unfaithful and the aggressors.[19]

The Headquarters of the Arab army broadcast repeated announcements to the Palestinians not to leave and to defend their villages.[20]

The 'frightening radio broadcasts' that were broadcast came, in truth, from the Zionists. Harry Levin, a British Zionist, described them:

Nearby [in Jerusalem] a loudspeaker burst out in Arabic. *Haganah* broadcasting to civilian Arabs urging them to leave the district before 5:15 am. 'Take pity on your wives and children get out of this bloodbath . . . Get out by the Jericho road, this is still open to you. If you stay you invite disaster.'[21]

An Israeli reserve officer reveals just how deliberate were the broadcasts:

. . . as uncontrolled panic spread through all Arab quarters, the Israelis brought up jeeps with loudspeakers which broadcast recorded 'horror sounds'. These included shrieks, wails and anguished moans of Arab women, the wail of sirens and the clang of fire-alarms bells, interrupted by a sepulchral voice calling out in Arabic: 'Save your souls, all ye faithful: The Jews are using poison gas and atomic weapons. Run for your lives in the name of Allah.'[22]

That Plan Dalet was a deliberate plan to drive out the Palestinians has been admitted by former Israeli Foreign Minister Yigal Allon who was, in 1948, the head of the Palmach, the strike force of the Haganah. In describing the tactics used in the Galilee campaign he explained that, as the date of the final British withdrawal approached, the Zionists

. . . looked for means . . . to cause the tens of thousands of sulky Arabs who remained in the Galilee to flee . . . I gathered all of the Jewish muktars, who have contact with Arabs in different villages and asked them to whisper in the ears of some Arabs that a great Jewish reinforcement has arrived in Galilee and that it is going to burn all of the villages of the Huleh. They should suggest to these Arabs, as their friends, to escape while there is still time . . . The tactic reached its goal . . . wide areas were cleaned.[23]

Former Prime Minister Yitzhak Rabin's description of the conquest of Lydda (Lod), after the completion of Plan Dalet, was so damaging that portions of his memoirs were cut by the official Israeli censors. The censored version was leaked to the *New York Times* and published there (23 October 1979). Rabin wrote: 'We

19

walked outside, Ben-Gurion accompanying us. Allon repeated his question "What is to be done with the [Palestinian] population?" B.G. waved his hand in a gesture which said "Drive them out!"'

Plan Dalet went into effect during the first week of April 1948. Six major operations of the plan were launched and two of them, Operations Nachson and Harel, were designed to occupy and destroy the Palestinian villages along the whole length of the Jaffa-Jerusalem road, thus splitting in two the Palestinian state as allotted by the UN Partition Plan (see maps 10 and 11).

During these two operations the massacre at Deir Yassin occurred. While Haganah forces were in a battle at Castel, a village nearby, Irgun and Stern Gang[24] units massacred the inhabitants of Deir Yassin. The report of the Israel Defense Forces Intelligence Branch admitted that the massacre of 254 Palestinian men, women and children was 'a decisive accelerating factor' of the Palestinian exodus. An Israeli soldier present at Deir Yassin described how the Irgun gunmen 'shot everyone they saw in the houses, including women and children – indeed the commanders made no attempt to check the disgraceful acts of slaughter'.[25]

Zionist apologists claim that the Irgun and Stern Gang were dissident groups and that the main body of the Jewish forces, the Haganah, condemned the attack.[26] They fail to mention that on the same day as the massacre the Irgun was admitted to the Joint Command of the military with the Haganah. They also fail to mention that Zionist radio broadcasts at the time falsely, but cleverly, accused the Arabs of the massacre.[27]

Other, now forgotten, atrocities occurred. On 3 May 1948 seventy Palestinians were massacred by a battalion commanded by Moshe Kelman near the town of Ein az Zeitun.[28] On 12 May 1948 the Irgun massacred seven boys who refused to name the owners of weapons found in the town of Sabbarin.[29] In Lydda on 12 July 1948 Israeli troops, with orders to shoot at 'any clear target', massacred 250–400 Palestinians fleeing the fighting.[30] On 30 October Israeli soldiers entered the Christian village of Eilabun and, after discovering the bodies of two of their soldiers, the commander chose twelve boys who were executed in the streets of the village. The army then looted the village.[31] On the same day about seventy men were executed, women were raped in the village of Safsaf and ninety-four were blown up in a house in Saliha.[32]

Rarely mentioned is the massacre at Duwayma, a village between Hebron and the coast. An Israeli soldier, witness to the terror, described the carnage: 'They killed some eighty to one hundred Arabs, women and children. The children were killed by smashing their skulls with clubs.'[33]

By July 1948, when it was clear that the Palestinians were about to be defeated, the Israeli forces began to 'concentrate' the frightened and confused Palestinian populations into concentration centers for eventual transfer or removal out of the country. Yosef Vashitz, a high-ranking member of the Mapam Party, was disturbed enough about the concentration of Palestinians to write,

> this concentration is the most important act done with respect to the Arabs in the State of Israel. Here it will be decided whether the State of Israel will be a democratic state or a feudal state with medieval customs and Nuremberg laws.[34]

As early as 1882 Zionists contemplated taking Palestine through force of arms.

> The final purposes . . . are to take possession in due course of Palestine and to restore to the Jews . . . political independence. Furthermore it will be necessary to teach the young and the future generations the use of arms.[35]

In 1911, local Zionist leaders in Palestine were wondering how to get rid of the native Palestinian population.[36] Non-Jewish Zionists also submitted ideas on how to expel the Palestinians to make room for Jews. The British government's Peel Partition Plan suggested their removal.[37] David Ben-Gurion, in 1937, said that the Jews 'must expel Arabs and take their places'.[38] Avraham Ussishkin, the head of the Jewish National Fund, even thought that there was nothing immoral about transferring Arab families out of their country: 'It is the most moral [thing to do]. We will not be able to begin our political life in a state in which Arabs constitute 45% [of the population].'[39] Ex-US President Herbert Hoover called for the 'engineering' of the removal of the Palestinians to Iraq.[40]

Even today, the presence of 2,000,000 Palestinians in the area under Israel's control is both a deterrent against, and a stimulus for, the completion of Zionist plans to expel all Palestinians. According to Israeli General Aharon Yariv, former head of military intelligence, plans exist to take advantage of a future war situation as an opportunity to expel the remaining Palestinians.[41]

Chaim Weizmann, the first President of Israel, who supposedly had a reputation of being humanitarian, welcomed the exodus of the Palestinians as a 'miraculous simplification of Israel's task'.[42] In this revealing remark, Weizmann appears to overlook the extent to which this 'miracle' was man-made by acts of terror and atrocity.

By 15 May 1948, the day of Israel's declaration of independence, the Zionists had successfully expelled 400,000 Palestinians. After 15 May, their tactics became even more ruthless and explicit. Edgar O'Ballance, a British military historian, wrote:

> No longer was there any 'reasonable persuasion.' Bluntly the Arab inhabitants were ejected and forced to flee into Arab territory, as at Ramleh, Lydda and other places. Wherever the Israeli troops advanced into Arab country, the Arab population was bulldozed out in front of them.[43]

By December 1948 another 400,000 had been expelled.

We must do everything to ensure they [the Palestinian refugees] never do return.

David Ben-Gurion
in his diary, 18 July 1948, quoted in Michael Bar Zohar, *Ben-Gurion: the Armed Prophet*, Prentice-Hall, 1967, p. 157.

Zionists maintain that the various UN resolutions calling for the repatriation of the Palestinian refugees to their homes are not meant to be an unconditional right of return. But section 11 of UN Resolution 194 (see appendix 11), the relevant resolution, contradicts the Zionist argument. It states that the United Nations 'resolves that the refugees wishing to return to their homes . . . should be permitted to do so'. Section 5 of UN 194 does not alter or affect the meaning of this resolution.

The controversy about the reasons for the exodus of refugees has tended to obscure a basic question. Whatever the reasons for the flight of civilians in wartime, it does not affect the validity of their claim to return to their homes once the fighting has ceased.

The evidence of both the Zionists and their Palestinian victims shows that the major reason why the Palestinians left their homes was because of direct and hostile Zionist military operations against civilian and military targets in the hope of depopulating the land of Arabs.

The United Nations mediator, the Swedish Count Folke Bernadotte, later assassinated by the Zionists, summarized the reasons for the flight of the refugees in 1948 in these words: 'The exodus of Palestinian Arabs resulted from panic created by fighting in their communities, by rumors concerning real or alleged acts of terrorism, or explusion.'[44]

Notes to Chapter 2

1. Leonard J. Davis, *Myths and Facts 1985: a Concise Record of the Arab–Israeli Conflict*, Near East Report, 1984, p. 94. This book is a publication of the American–Israel Public Affairs Committee, the official lobby of Israel in the United States.
2. Walid Khalidi, 'The Fall of Haifa', *Middle East Forum*, XXXV, 7, 1959, pp. 22–32. Also see his 'Why Did the Palestinians Leave?', Arab Information Centre, Paper 3, London.
3. Erskine Childers, 'The Other Exodus', *Spectator*, London, 12 May 1961; reprinted in Walter Laqueur and Barry Rubin, eds., *The Arab–Israeli Reader: a Documentary History of the Middle East Conflict*, Penguin, 1984, Document 34.
4. Harry Levin, *Jerusalem Embattled: a Diary of the City under Siege, March 25, 1948 to July 18, 1948*, Gollancz, 1950, p. 160.
5. The Archbishop's letter dated 4 December 1958 to Erskine Childers is reprinted in 'The Wordless Wish: from Citizens to Refugees', in Ibrahim Abu-Lughod, ed., *The Transformation of Palestine: Essays on the Origin and Development of the Arab–Israeli Conflict*, Northwestern University Press, 1971, pp. 197–8.
6. Robert John and Sami Hadawi, *The Palestine Diary*, PLO Research Center, 1970, II: *1945–1948*, p. 384.
7. These plans came out of the meeting of Zionist leaders in Baltimore, Maryland in 1942 and became known as the Biltmore Program.
8. David Ben-Gurion, *Rebirth and Destiny of Israel*, Philosophical

Library, 1954, p. 239; Harry Sacher, *Israel: the Establishment of a State*, Clowes and Son, 1952, p. 217.

9. *Ourvot* [Battles of 1948] in Khalidi, ed., *From Haven to Conquest: Readings in Zionism and the Palestine Problem until 1948*, Institute for Palestine Studies, 1971, p. 39.

10. From Benzion Dinur, ed., *Sefer Toldot Ha-Haganah* (8 vols.), Zionist Library-Marakot, 1954–72), III, pp. 1472–5, appendix 48, pp. 1955–60. [*The Official History of the Haganah* unpublished in English.]

11. ibid.

12. ibid.

13. *My Diary and Letters to the Children*, Massada, 1965, II, p. 81 (in Hebrew).

14. Dinur, op. cit., pp. 1253–5, appendix 39, pp. 1939–43.

15. The Irgun was the underground terrorist organization led by Begin. It joined with the Haganah in 1948. The documentary history of Benny Morris, the diplomatic correspondent of the *Jerusalem Post*, was published as *The Birth of the Palestinian Refugee Problem, 1947–1949*, Cambridge University Press, 1988. Unfortunately, Morris's greatest weakness is that he deemed it unproductive to employ methods of oral historical research and, therefore, has few interviews with participants, Palestinian or Jewish. Morris's basic argument is that there was no overall preconceived plan of expulsion, yet his book is a documentation of expulsion. The reason for this seeming contradiction is that Morris never delves into the philosophy of Zionism which, for decades preceding the establishment of the state of Israel, conditioned Jews to understand that a Jewish state must be free of Arabs. Therefore, expulsion was a natural and logical outcome of the 1948 war since its roots are fundamental to the Zionist enterprise itself.

16. The document is titled 'The Emigration of the Arabs of Palestine in the Period 1/12/1947–1/6/1948', 30 June 1948 (t'nu'at ha'hagira shel arvi'yei eretz yisrael ba't'kufa 1/12/1947–1/6/1948). Mr Morris discovered the document in the private papers of Aharon Cohen, the former director of the Mapam Party's Arab Department, in the Hashomer Hatza'ir Archive in Givat Haviva, Israel. See Benny Morris, 'The Causes and Character of the Arab Exodus from Palestine: the Israel Defence Forces Intelligence Branch Analysis of June 1948', *Middle East Studies*, XXII, 1, January 1986, pp. 5–19.

17. Leonard J. Davis, *Myths and Facts 1985: a Concise Record of the Arab–Israeli Conflict*, Near East Report, 1984, p. 94.

18. Al-Inqaz, Arab Liberation Army Radio, clandestine, in Arabic, 24 April 1948, 6:00 a.m. E.S.T.; US Foreign Broadcast Information Service (FBIS), 'Daily Report: Middle East and North Africa', 26 April 1948, p. II–4.

19. Sharq al-Adna, Jerusalem, in Arabic, 4 May 1948, 11:00 a.m. E.S.T.; FBIS, 5 May 1948, p. II–1.

20. Al-Inqaz, Arab Liberation Army Radio, Damascus, in Arabic, 5 May 1948; FBIS, 6 May 1948, p. II–3.
21. Levin, op. cit., p. 160. The Haganah was the mainstream Jewish terrorist organization, out of which the Israeli army grew.
22. Quoted in David Hirst, *The Gun and the Olive Branch: the Roots of Violence in the Middle East*, Faber and Faber, 1977, p. 141.
23. Yigal Allon, *Ha Sepher Ha Palmach* (in Hebrew), II, p. 268, quoted in Khalidi, *From Haven to Conquest: Readings in Zionism and the Palestine Problem until 1948*, Institute for Palestine Studies, 1971, p. 42. Benny Morris in *The Birth of the Palestinian Refugee Problem* argues that Plan Dalet was not a deliberate plan of expulsion. He claims (p. 113) that no trace of documentary evidence was found to support the notion that the plan was deliberate. Morris's argument is moot because the Palestinians did leave as a result of a plan which, *in effect* (the only thing historically important), caused their removal through force and fear. Morris says that Plan Dalet 'provided for the conquest and permanent occupation, or levelling, of Arab villages and towns' (p. 63).
24. The Stern Gang was a fascist terrorist group led by Abraham Stern that committed a number of atrocities against Palestinians, British and Jews. One of its leaders, Yitzhak Shamir, went on to become Prime Minister of Israel.
25. *Yediot Aharonot*, 4 April 1972.
26. Davis, op. cit., pp. 97–8.
27. Haganah Radio, clandestine, in Arabic, 12 April 1948, 1:00 p.m. E.S.T.; FBIS, 13 April 1948, p. II–5.
28. Benny Morris, 'The Causes and Character of the Arab Exodus from Palestine', *Middle Eastern Studies*, XXII, 1 January 1986, p. 102.
29. ibid., p. 117.
30. ibid., p. 206 and p. 345 note 23.
31. ibid., p. 229.
32. ibid., p. 230–31.
33. *Davar*, 6 September 1979.
34. In Benny Morris, 'Haifa's Arabs: Displacement and Concentration, July 1948', *Middle East Journal*, XLII, 2, Spring 1988, p. 252.
35. David Vital, *Origins of Zionism*, Oxford University Press, 1975, p. 85; in Walter Lehn in association with Uri Davis, *The Jewish National Fund*, Kegan Paul International, 1988.
36. Walter Laqueur, *A History of Zionism*, Weidenfeld and Nicolson, 1972, p. 231.
37. *Palestine Royal Commission Report* (Peel Commission), Cmnd 5479, His Majesty's Stationery Office, 1937, p. 391.
38. Shabtai Teveth, *Ben-Gurion and the Palestine Arabs*, Oxford University Press, 1985, p. 89; quoted in Benny Morris, *The Birth of the Palestinian Refugee Problem, 1947–1949*, Cambridge University Press, 1988, p. 25.
39. ibid., p. 26.

40. *Palestine* (a Zionist periodical), II, 9–10, November–December 1945, p. 16.
41. *Ha'aretz*, 26 May 1980.
42. James McDonald, *My Mission to Israel*, Simon and Schuster, 1952, p. 176.
43. Edgar O'Ballance, *The Arab–Israeli War, 1948*, Praeger, 1957, pp. 171–2.
44. UN Document A 1618, p. 14.

Recommended Reading

Erskine Childers, 'The Other Exodus', in Walter Laqueur and Barry Rubin, eds., *The Israel–Arab Reader: a Documentary History of the Middle East Conflict*, Penguin, 1984, pp. 143–51.

Childers, 'The Wordless Wish: from Citizens to Refugees', in Ibrahim Abu-Lughod, ed., *The Transformation of Palestine: Essays on the Origin and Development of the Arab–Israeli Conflict*, Northwestern University Press, 1971, pp. 165–202.

Steven Glazer, 'The Palestinian Exodus of 1948', *Journal of Palestine Studies*, 36, Summer 1980, pp. 96–118.

Sami Hadawi, *Palestinian Rights and Losses in 1948: A Comprehensive Study*, Saqi Books, 1988.

Walid Khalidi, 'Why Did the Palestinians Leave?', *Middle East Forum*, XXXV, 7, 1959, pp. 21–35.

Benny Morris, *The Birth of the Palestinian Refugee Problem, 1947–1949*, Cambridge University Press, 1988.

Morris, 'The Causes and Character of the Arab Exodus from Palestine: the Israel Defence Forces Intelligence Branch Analysis of June 1948', *Middle Eastern Studies*, XXII, 1, January 1986, pp. 5–19.

Nafez Nazzal, *The Palestinian Exodus from Galilee 1948*, Institute for Palestine Studies, 1978.

Michael Palumbo, *The Palestinian Catastrophe: the 1948 Expulsion of a People From Their Homeland*, Faber and Faber, 1988.

Edward W. Said and Christopher Hitchens, *Blaming the Victims: Spurious Scholarship and the Palestinian Question*, London: Verso, 1988.

Chapter 3

The Palestinian Refugees

Zionists claim that the number of Palestinian refugees in 1948 was quite small and therefore the problem of the Palestinians is really an insignificant one.

Zionists argue that the 1948 war actually created two refugee problems – one Arab and one Jewish. The Palestinian exodus, as a result of the conflict, has been balanced, they say, by a comparable exodus of Jewish refugees from the Arab world and that nothing worse than a 'population exchange' or a 'double exodus' had occurred.

What are the Facts?

There are three issues to be considered. First, what are the definitions often given for a 'refugee' and which one is appropriate?

Secondly, there is not one group of refugees, but three sets of refugees that exist. The first are those refugees from Palestine who fled the 1948 war prior to Israel's independence on 15 May 1948. Second are the refugees from Palestine who were made refugees by Zionist forces after 15 May until the end of the year; and, finally, there are those refugees forced out by the 1967 war on the West Bank. Many of the 1967 refugees were refugees twice over. The question of how many refugees there were refers to the number of Palestinians displaced by the 1948 conflict.

The third issue is the need to explain the discrepancy between the figure given by Zionists for the total number of refugees and that given by the Arabs and the Refugee Office of the United Nations Palestine Conciliation Committee.

There has arisen a confusion about the meaning of the term 'refugee' which needs to be clarified before any discussion can take place. Clearly, the term will have different meanings in different contexts. The most restricted meaning of a 'refugee' is a person who is in need of relief. For this, a refugee has to satisfy a rather narrowly drawn definition which the United Nations Relief Works Agency (UNRWA) had adopted for the administration of its relief services and which requires at least two years' residence before 1948 in the territory that became Israel, proof of current residence in one of the host countries (including the West Bank and Gaza), and proof of continuing need. So the three elements used by UNRWA to define refugees are that they lost their home, lost the means of livelihood and are in need.

The inadequacy of the UNRWA definition of refugee status directly affects the numerous population of the border villages whose homes were retained but whose farmland was taken by Israel and, who, therefore lost their means of livelihood. They were not considered refugees by UNRWA.

Another definition of 'refugee' is that category of person who is entitled to compensation, meaning those who possessed property in Palestine which they lost as a result of the conflict. This is also a limiting definition since many refugees were not property owners.

The broadest category of 'refugee' is that of those entitled to *repatriation*, meaning those who before 1948 were ordinarily resident (however the term is defined) in the territory that became Israel. When people speak of the 'Palestinian refugees' it must be understood in this sense.[1]

By adopting different definitions of a 'refugee' it is possible to arrive at quite different conclusions as to the total number of people involved. For example, by arbitrarily deciding that only those needing relief are 'refugees', hundreds of thousands of

Palestinians who are genuine refugees in the sense that they were uprooted from their homes, but who do not happen to be in need of UNRWA's help, are automatically excluded.

By picking and choosing statistics and definitions Zionists could argue that the Palestinian refugees are few in number. In order to avoid further confusion it might be best to think of the refugees as 'displaced persons'.

Zionists claim that the real number of 'refugees' in 1948 was only some 500,000.[2] The generally accepted estimate, however, is that made by the UN Economic Survey Missions' report in 1949, which put the number of refugees at 726,000. This was disputed as an underestimate by the Arab side and by the UN Palestine Conciliation Committee.

There are two problems with the Zionist figure for the number of refugees. In the first place, it is not possible to reconcile so small a number of refugees with the known distribution of the Arab population in Palestine before the fighting broke out at the end of 1947. Secondly, it is again not possible to reconcile retrospectively so small an original number of refugees in 1948 with the known size and location of the Palestinian population twenty years later after the second exodus resulting from the June 1967 war.

The Arab population of Palestine at the time of the exodus in 1948 was about 1,400,000.[3] This figure is a projection from the British Mandate government's estimate of 1946 (see appendix 2). According to an Israeli census taken in November 1948, there were about 120,000 Palestinians remaining in the new state of Israel.

If it were true that the number of refugees were only 500,000 this would mean that the Arab population belonging to the area which became Israel (constituting 77 percent of Mandate Palestine) had only been 620,000. This would mean that the remaining 780,000 people to be accounted for belonged in the remainder of Palestine which stayed in Arab hands (constituting 23 percent of Palestine, that is, the West Bank and Gaza) when the fighting ended. This is not accurate.

The British Mandate government published detailed population statistics of all villages and towns and from these it is possible to derive a figure for the resident population in 1948 in the areas under Arab control. The Mandate government's statistics show that the Arab population in the West Bank and Gaza was between 454,000 to 508,000 people. This means that the number of refugees must have been some 770,000 to 780,000.[4]

By June 1967 the total Palestinian population had risen by natural growth to about 2,700,000. Since the Palestinians are a young population (nearly half are under eighteen) they have a high birth rate and a low death rate. Jordanian, Israeli and UNRWA statistics all estimate the rate of natural increase in the Palestinian population to be about thirty-five per 1,000. Compounded over twenty years, this produces a figure of 2,700,000 on the basis of the 1948 population of 1,400,000.[5]

Israel's 1967 census of the Palestinian population in the territory they had recently occupied showed 597,000 in the West Bank (excluding the Jerusalem area later annexed by Israel), 66,000 in the Jerusalem area and 354,000 in Gaza – making a total of 1,017,000.[6] Of this total more than half, 540,000, were classified by UNRWA as refugees.[7] The remainder were residents of the West Bank and Gaza.

Israel's 1967 census also showed that there were 313,000 Palestinians within Israel. Therefore the total number of Palestinians counted by Israel was 1,330,000, of whom 790,000 were residents and 540,000 refugees.

But there are 1,370,000 Palestinians still unaccounted for. They had not vanished into thin air! Clearly, they were living as exiles, that is, as *refugees* outside the area controlled by Israel.

Thus the total Palestinian refugee population in 1967 was 1,910,000. Of this total, 540,000 still lived in their native land, although uprooted from their homes. The June 1967 war also created 400,000 more refugees (included in the total above), most of whom were refugees twice over. But of the 1,910,000 total number of refugees in 1967, 127,000 were newly displaced persons, being residents of the West Bank and Gaza who were not 1948 refugees.[8] Therefore the total number of people made refugees in 1948 *and* their descendants was about 1,783,000.

If this number is projected backwards to 1948 (using the rate of natural increase of thirty-five per 1,000), we arrive at a figure of over *900,000* for the original number of Palestinian refugees. In 1951 the Refugee Office of the UN Palestine Conciliation Commission adopted a figure of 900,000 for the total number of refugees based on an evaluation of abandoned Palestinian property in Israel.[9]

The Zionist estimate of Palestinian refugees is far too low. Therefore, how many Palestinian refugees were there? Certainly no less than 780,000 and probably many more.

Was the Palestinian refugee problem 'balanced' by the Jewish 'refugees'?

The 'double exodus' is a myth because the two movements of population are not comparable for the following reasons: first, the Palestinians are true refugees; their exodus was involuntary and enforced. Jews of the Arab world, Oriental Jews, came to Israel, in most cases, voluntarily. A small minority of them may have suffered in the countries of their birth, but the large majority moved to Israel of their own accord or in response to Zionist recruiting efforts in the Arab lands.

Secondly, the movement of Oriental Jews into Israel did not occur concurrently with, or immediately after, the Palestinian exodus. Only about 126,000 Oriental Jews (mostly from Iraq and Yemen) emigrated to Israel in the two or three years immediately following the Palestine conflict in 1948. The remainder who elected to move to Israel, particularly those from North Africa, did so much later. The whole emigration of Oriental Jews was thus spread over twenty years.

Israel regularly portrays the lot of Oriental Jews in Arab countries as one of misery, fear and anti-Semitism. But Jews of the Arab world had never experienced the 'race hatred' so common in European anti-Semitism. In general, Jews lived in harmony with their Muslim compatriots. When Jews did experience persecution during their 1,300 years under Muslim rule it was not *because* they were Jews – for many others also suffered under particular despotic rulers (see chapter 17).

Only after the Zionist threat to Palestine became real did hostility develop against Oriental Jews in some, but not all, Arab countries. There is also no denying that there are serious reactionary and fascist Arabs who, in the name of nationalism, persecute Jews and other minorities.

The emigration of Oriental Jews to Israel was not a result of force. For many, the motive to move was economic. For others, the majority, the chance to live in a Jewish state as Jews was greatly desirable and attractive. The chance to trade in their

31

minority status in their countries of origin for a majority status in the new Jewish state was very exciting for the Jews of the Arab lands.

For many others, direct covert pressure from Zionist *agents provocateurs*, in need of Jewish settlers, stimulated their emigration. Operations 'Magic Carpet' and 'Ali Baba' simply scooped up Yemeni Jews and flew them to Israel.

In Iraq, Zionist agents planted a series of bombs directed against the Iraqi Jewish community. As a result all but a few thousand left for Israel, believing that the bombs were the result of anti-Jewish sentiment. The facts were first revealed, in part, in 1966 when Yehuda Tagar, an official in the Israeli Foreign Ministry broke silence about his part in the business. Zionist terrorist activities against Jews in Iraq are well documented but not well known.[10]

If any individual Oriental Jew has a legitimate grievance against an Arab government this would in no way diminish the responsibility which the state of Israel has towards the Palestinians whom they uprooted.

One should remember that, according to Zionism, Jews who come to Israel do so as the culmination of millennial aspirations. Migration to Israel on the part of world Jewry is considered a duty. In Israel, an immigrant Jew is an *oleh*, someone who has 'ascended', who has fulfilled *aliyah*. Therefore, the situations of the Palestinians and Oriental Jews are thoroughly dissimilar and not parallel.

The Palestinian refugees were forced out against their will, have never relinquished their claims to their land and homes, and have consistently reaffirmed their wish to return. The Oriental Jews living in Israel emigrated by choice, gave up their citizenship in the Arab countries from which they came, and believe themselves to be fulfilling a duty to return to their 'ancestral' homeland.[11]

Notes to Chapter 3

1. This chapter concerns the refugees from 1948 and is based on the work of Walid Khalidi. The offspring of these refugees are also refugees.
2. See, for example, Terence Prittie and Bernard Dineen, *The Double Exodus: a Study of Arab and Jewish Refugees in the Middle East*, London: Goodhart Press, n.d.
3. This chapter's demography is based on the work of Janet Abu-Lughod, 'The Demographic Transformation of Palestine', in Ibrahim Abu-Lughod, ed., *The Transformation of Palestine: Essays on the Origin and Development of the Arab–Israeli Conflict*, Northwestern University Press, 1971, pp. 139–63.
4. Government of Palestine, Department of Statistics, 'General Monthly Bulletin of Current Statistics', XII, 1947.
5. Abu-Lughod, op. cit., pp. 161–2.
6. Fred J. Khoury, *The Arab–Israeli Dilemma*, Syracuse University Press, 1968, p. 379.
7. ibid.
8. ibid.
9. UN Document A/1985, p. 26.
10. *The Black Panther*, 9 November 1972 (Jerusalem), a magazine for Oriental Jews, tells much of the story. See also Yigal Allon, *The Making of Israel's Army*, Universe, 1970, pp. 133–5; *Ha'Olam Hazeh*, 29 May 1966, which first printed Yehuda Tagar's testimony; *HaModia*, 5 October 1950, the official organ of Agudath Israel, published an article on what happened to Iraqi Jews once they reached Israel; Rabbi Moshe Schonfeld, *Genocide in the Holy Land*, Neturei Karta, USA, 1980, re-publishes in English some of the story. The story of Iraqi Jews and Zionists' efforts there is also told in Abbas Shiblak, *The Lure of Zion: the Case of the Iraqi Jews*, Al Saqi Books, 1986.
11. For information on the intervention by Zionist *agents provocateurs* and the movement, generally, of Oriental Jews to Israel see Elie Kedourie, *The Chatham House Version and Other Middle Eastern Studies*, Weidenfeld and Nicolson, 1970, pp. 311–12; Alfred Lilienthal, *The Other Side of the Coin: an American Perspective of the Arab–Israeli Conflict*, Devin-Adair, 1965, pp. 37–8; *Hapantera Hashoura*, 9 November 1972; *Israleft News Service*, 6, 20 November 1972; Allon, op. cit., pp. 133–5 and Schonfeld, *Genocide in the Holy Land*, Neturei Karta, 1980.

Recommended Reading

Alfred Lilienthal, *What Price Israel*, Henry Regnery, 1953.
Amos Oz, *In the Land of Israel*, Harcourt, Brace, Jovanovich, 1983.
Moshe Schonfeld, *Genocide in the Holy Land*, Neturei Karta, 1980.
Tom Segev, *The First Israelis*, Free Press, 1986.
Abbas Shiblak, *The Lure of Zion: the Case of the Iraqi Jews*, Al Saqi
    Books, 1986.

Chapter 4

The Palestinian State and the 'Miracle of Israel'

Zionists claim that the Palestinians only became interested in their own state very recently, after they saw the purported 'successes' of Israel; after Zionists' 'made the desert bloom'.

Zionists belittle the struggle of the Palestinians before, and after, 1948 to secure their national aspirations. The Zionists claim that the Palestinians only began to think of themselves as Palestinians, that is, as a people distinct from the general mass of Arabs, after the establishment of Israel in 1948. They point out that between 1948 and 1967 when the West Bank and Gaza were ruled by Jordan, they did not press for a state with the vigor they do now and, therefore, their desire for a state need not be admitted.

What are the Facts?

The views of the Palestinians towards the nature of a future state have varied greatly over the past 100 years since the Arab–Israel conflict began. In the mid-nineteenth century most Palestinians held their loyalty to the Ottoman Turks who then ruled Palestine. By the early part of the twentieth century the Palestinians were motivated by the rise of Arab nationalism and demonstrated their patriotism in various ways. In fact, contrary to common Zionist belief, the Palestinians developed a consciousness *as* Palestinians and thought of Palestine as a separate and distinct entity.

> *Awake! It is your homeland. Do not let it be sold to strangers.*
>
> Muhammad Isaf al-Nashashibi, a Palestinian poet, 1910.
> 'Palestine and the New Colonization', in Khalid A. Sulaiman, *Palestine and Modern Arab Poetry*, Zed Press, 1984.

One of the most nationalist publications of the Palestinians in 1911 was the newspaper *Palestine*. Furthermore, the Palestinians were quite aware of the danger the Zionist movement posed. In 1913, for example, Arif al-Arif, later the mayor of Jerusalem, wrote that 'if this state of affairs continues . . . then the Zionists will gain mastery over our country, village by village, town by town; tomorrow the whole of Jerusalem will be sold and then Palestine in its entirety'. Tragically for the Palestinians, this is exactly what happened.[1]

It is clear that no matter how the Palestinians conceived of national self-determination, and no matter how their ideas may have changed as a result of outside political forces, they have been entirely consistent since the earliest days on one point: that Palestine should be independent of European colonialism, either as part of a larger Arab state or as a separate Palestinian Arab state.

The Zionist claim that the Palestinians did not desire a state until recently is incorrect. The Palestinians fully expected that, with the dissolution of the Ottoman Empire, their desire for independence could be sought and fully expressed.

As early as 1920, the Palestinians, at the Third Palestine Arab Congress held in Haifa, asked the British, who occupied Palestine 'to establish a native government responsible to a representative assembly whose members would be chosen from the populace which was Arabic-speaking and which had resided in Palestine before the war'.[2] A year later, with heightened fears of Zionist encroachment in their homeland, Palestinian leaders petitioned

Winston Churchill, then the Colonial Secretary, demanding that the British end the Zionist 'state within a state' and grant the establishment of a national Palestinian government.[3]

The Palestinians, not unreasonably, assumed that the Palestine Mandate would promise them eventual independence in conformity with Article 22 of the Covenant of the League of Nations (see appendix 6). It is now recognized that the Palestine Congress in Haifa was representative of such political opinion as existed in Palestine at that time, and there is no evidence that the Palestinians have since changed their minds about their desire for independence. If anything, their thirst for freedom grows stronger as their oppression and exile extends longer.

The Palestinian demand for independence was not just an isolated phenomenon of the 1920s but persisted through the founding of the Palestine Liberation Organization (PLO) in 1964 until today. In 1930 a Palestinian delegation met with the British prime minister to demand a national parliamentary government.[4]

Palestinian demands for independence and national self-determination have been consistent and constant from the early part of the century to the declaration of independence in 1988.

A well-known claim made by Zionists is that they 'made the desert bloom' and once they did the Palestinians became envious and wanted a state. Prime Minister Shimon Peres has written: 'The country was mostly an empty desert, with only a few islands of Arab settlement, and Israel's cultivable land today was indeed redeemed from swamp and wilderness.'[5] Another Prime Minister, Levi Eshkol, asserted that it was only after the Zionists 'made the desert bloom' that 'they [the Palestinians] became interested in taking it from us'.[6]

The country was mostly an empty desert, with only a few islands of Arab settlement.

Shimon Peres
David's Sling: the Arming of Israel, Weidenfeld and Nicolson, 1970, p. 249.

The Zionist claim to have transformed the land from a desert to a land of milk and honey is a wild exaggeration which vastly overstates the extent of Jewish achievements and grossly understates Arab cultivation and the natural fertility of Palestine.

Some elementary facts reveal the Zionist claim as nothing more than propaganda. First, only half of the area of Palestine has a true desert climate. This mainly consists of the Negev desert which stretches south from Beersheba to the Gulf of Aqaba. Second, the remaining half of Palestine has a Mediterranean climate with substantial rainfall. It is naturally fertile. The average annual rainfall at Tel Aviv, for example, totals 539 mm., 639 mm. at Nazareth and 486 at Jerusalem.

Thirdly, it was the Palestinians who expanded agricultural production and techniques during the eighteenth and nineteenth centuries before the arrival of European Jewish settlers. For example, the Jaffa orange which is closely identified with Israel, had already been developed by Palestinian expertise before the Zionist colonization of Palestine was under way. In 1886 the American consul in Jerusalem, Henry Gillman, called attention to the excellent quality and superior grafting techniques of Palestinian citrus farmers: 'I am particular in giving the details of this simple method of propagating this valuable fruit [the Jaffa orange] as I believe it might be adopted with advantage in Florida.'[7]

Fourthly, by about 1930 all the land capable of being cultivated by the indigenous Palestinians with the means available to them was already being cultivated.[8] In 1930 a comprehensive study of Palestine's agricultural potential was undertaken by Sir John Hope Simpson. Simpson reported that: 'It has emerged quite definitely that there is at the present time and with present methods of Arab cultivation no margin of land available for agricultural settlements by new immigrants.'[9]

Fifthly, by the end of the British Mandate the total land area under cultivation by Palestinian farmers (excluding citrus) was 5,484,700 dunams (a dunam equals about a quarter of an acre), and the area cultivated by Jewish farmers was 425,450 dunams.[10] As Walid Khalidi, the noted Palestinian scholar, pointed out, with regard to desert cultivation, in 1935 the Palestinians were farming 2,109,234 dunams in the Negev region, whereas total Jewish *landholdings* in the Negev, even by 1946, did not exceed 21,000 dunams. 'Thus it was the Palestinians who made the desert bloom!'[11]

Israel also claims that it has expanded the cultivated area since 1948. But the immense expansion of the cultivated area which Israel claims is grossly exaggerated since the figures have been 'doctored' by including, as reclaimed land, the huge areas of farmland left behind by the Palestinian refugees expelled by Israel in 1948. This was treated as 'abandoned property' by the Israelis and then 'reclaimed' when Jewish settlers took over production. It had, however, been under cultivation up to the time of the Palestinian exodus. No less than 80 percent of the 2,185,000 dunams that Israel claims to have 'brought into cultivation' since 1948 constituted farmland belonging to Palestinian refugees and previously cultivated by them.[12]

Zionists claim that the period 1948 to 1967, when the West Bank was under Jordanian rule, saw little Palestinian political activity demanding a state. They claim that this inactivity exemplifies the spuriousness of the Palestinian claim for an independent state.

The Zionist position is incorrect. It is quite wrong to imply that before 1967 the Palestinians were not in favour of an independent state. Every year a Palestinian delegation was given a hearing (against the sole dissenting vote of Israel) in the Special Political Committee at the United Nations and every year they reaffirmed their rights to their land and homes. And every year they were supported in this by all the governments of the Arab world.

The Zionists claim that when the Palestinians spoke of a state they never spoke in terms of a state confined to the West Bank and Gaza. This was true because there was no reason for them to do so.

In 1967 the United Nations (including the United States and all other major powers) maintained the position adopted in 1947 and reaffirmed two years later. This position called for a territorial settlement in accordance with the United Nations Partition Resolution of November 1947. At the time of its admission to the UN Israel had itself undertaken to respect that resolution. If the Palestinians had proposed the establishment of a Palestinian state on the West Bank and Gaza this would have been seized on by Israel as evidence that they were acquiescing to Israel's acquisition of the territory alloted to the Arab state, under the Partition Plan, which was captured and never returned during the 1948 war.

All this story about the danger of extermination [of Jews] has been blown up . . . to justify the annexation of new Arab territories.

Mordechai Bentov, Israeli Cabinet Minister
Al Hamishmar, 14 April 1972.

Map 2   'Eretz Israel' According to the World Zionist Organization—1916

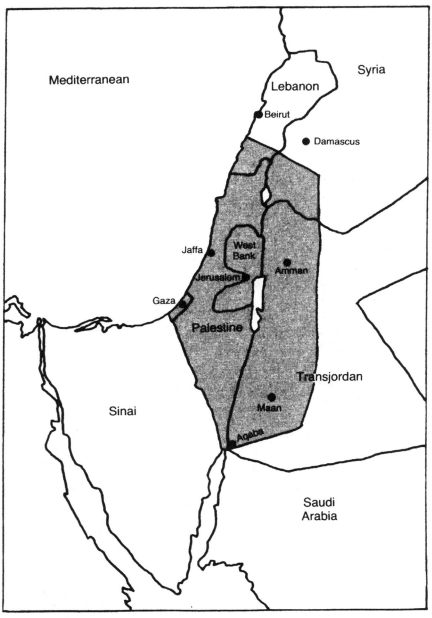

Shown with 1949 ceasefire boundaries.
Source: H. Sacher, ed., *Zionism and the Jewish Future: by Various Writers*, John Murray, 1916, pp. 212–13.

Map 3   'Eretz Israel' According to the World Zionist Organization Delegation to the 1919 Versailles Peace Conference

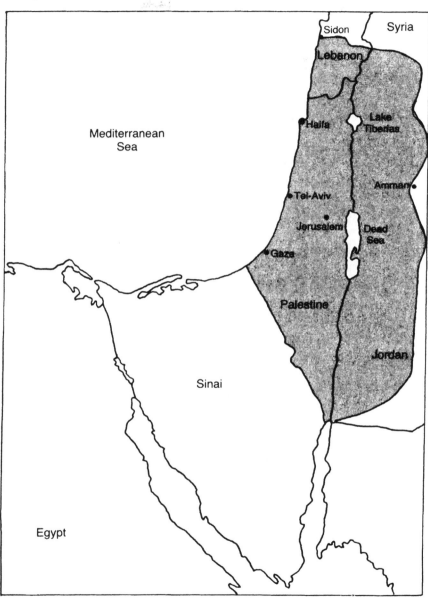

Shown with British Mandate boundaries.

Another reason for the general lack of activity by the Palestinians for a decade after the creation of Israel was a result of the dislocation they suffered arising from the 1948 war.

Nineteen forty-eight was not just a date marking an Arab–Israeli war, or a year that Hollywood celebrated in films glorifying Israel, such as *Exodus*, but was an unmitigated catastrophe for the Palestinians. It represented not only the dissolution of a political entity, but the destruction of hundreds of villages (see appendices 18 and 19), the expulsion of some 800,000 Palestinians and an attempted effacement of a distinct cultural heritage. The leading political figures were among the refugees. In these circumstances no state was possible.

With their country dismembered and their people scattered, the Palestinians were able to do nothing more than provide for their basic daily needs. But Palestinian misfortune did not mean, as Zionists often imply, that they were abandoning their rights of title to the land or to an independent nationhood whenever that might be realized.

Zionists claim that the Palestinians didn't press the Jordanian and Egyptian regimes for the establishment of a state when those two countries ruled the West Bank and Gaza respectively and, therefore, their claims against Israel are cynical at best and anti-Semitic at worst.

The volume of the 1880 harvest was 36 million oranges.

British report on Palestinian agriculture before the Zionists.
Parliamentary Papers, 1881/xc, Beyrout, 19.3.1881.

Zionists fail to mention that the arrangements made by Egypt for the administration of Gaza specifically recognized the provisional nature of their rule. Although Jordan annexed the West Bank, opposition to the Hashemite Kingdom on the part of the Palestinians had always been vigorous.

The situation of the Palestinians after 1967 was fundamentally changed. Israel had now overrun the whole of their native land.

Ironically, it was Israel's seizure of the whole of Palestine that gave a new impulse both to the assertion of Palestinian nationhood and the readiness of the international community to recognize it.

After the 1967 war the Palestinians were face to face with the Israeli occupying power, totally deprived of national, civil and human rights. Their very physical existence was threatened by expulsion. Clearly, the Palestinians felt, the time had come to take their national cause into their own hands and force world attention to it.

Lastly, the Zionist argument implies that because the Palestinians have shifted positions over the last four decades they cannot be believed or are irrational. On the contrary, what the change in positions has indicated is that the Palestinians are pragmatic in seeking a peaceful solution to the Arab–Israeli conflict and are not the inflexible fanatics portrayed by the Zionists.

Zionists also overlook the fact that the rise of nationalism is historically conditioned and not determined by the time it arises. The fact that nationalism might arise, for example, in one country in the early nineteenth century and not until the twentieth century in another does not in any way make one legitimate and the other illegitimate.

Notes to Chapter 4

1. Neville J. Mandel, *The Arabs and Zionism before World War I*, University of California Press, 1976, pp. 32–92, 128, 139–40; A. W. Kayyali, *Palestine: a Modern History*, Croom Helm, n.d.; George Antonius, *The Arab Awakening: the Story of the Arab National Movement*, Capricorn, 1965.
2. Text is in Matill E.T. Mogannam, *The Arab Woman and the Palestine Problem*, Herbert Joseph, 1937, pp. 125–7.
3. Cairo Conference, Cabinet Papers, 24/126 (Public Record Office), p. 150 cited in A. W. Kayyali, op. cit., p. 93.
4. Kayyali, op. cit., p. 157.
5. Shimon Peres, *David's Sling: the Arming of Israel*, Weidenfeld and Nicolson, 1970, p. 249.
6. Levi Eshkol, *Jerusalem Post*, 17 February 1969.
7. US Government, Documents of the Jerusalem Consulate (Gillman to Porter), 16 December 1886, in Walid Khalidi, *Before Their Diaspora: a Photographic History of the Palestinians 1876–1948*, Institute for Palestine Studies, 1984, p. 131. See also the photographs

and commentary by Khalidi on pp. 125–36 of his book.

8. Frances Newton, *Fifty Years in Palestine*, Coldharbor, 1940, p. 253.
9. *Palestine, Report on Immigration, Land Settlement and Development*, Sir John Hope Simpson, Cmnd 3686, His Majesty's Stationery Office, 1930.
10. *A Survey of Palestine: Prepared in December 1945 and January 1946 for the Information of the Anglo–American Committee of Inquiry* ([British] Government of Palestine), I, p. 323, in Khalidi, op. cit., p. 125.
11. *The Area of Cultivable Land in Palestine*, Jewish Agency, 1936, p. 13, in Walid Khalidi, op. cit., p. 125.
12. United Nations, General Assembly, *Progress Report of the United Nations Conciliation Commission for Palestine*, Suppl. 18, 11 December 1949–23 October 1950, pp. 5–6, 12–15. See also Peter Beaumont, Gerald Blake and J. Malcolm Wagstaff, *The Middle East: A Geographical Study*, John Wiley, 1976; Don Peretz, *Israel and the Palestine Arabs*, Middle East Institute, 1958; *Village Statistics, 1945*, Government of Palestine, 1945; John Ruedy, 'Dynamics of Land Alienation', in Ibrahim Abu-Lughod, ed., *The Transformation of Palestine: Essays on the Origin and Development of the Arab–Israeli Conflict*, Northwestern University Press, 1971, pp. 119–38; Alan George, '"Making the Desert Bloom": A Myth Examined', *Journal of Palestine Studies*, 30, Winter 1979, pp. 88–100.

Recommended Reading

George Antonius, *The Arab Awakening: the Story of the Arab National Movement*, Capricorn, 1965.

Alan George, '"Making the Desert Bloom": a Myth Examined', *Journal of Palestine Studies*, 30, Winter 1979, pp. 88–100.

A. W. Kayyali, *Palestine: a Modern History*, Croom Helm, n.d.

Neville J. Mandel, *The Arabs and Zionism before World War I*, University of California Press, 1976.

Muhammad Muslih, *The Origins of Palestinian Nationalism*, Columbia University Press and Institute of Palestine Studies, 1988.

Y. Porath, *The Emergence of the Palestinian–Arab National Movement 1918–1929*, Frank Cass, 1974.

Chapter 5

Terror: Israel and the PLO

Israel claims that the Palestine Liberation Organization (PLO) is a ruthless terrorist organization bent on destroying Israel. Israel furthermore denies that the PLO is the legitimate representative of the Palestinian people.

The Israeli government claims that the PLO has a notorious history of killing innocent civilians. Indeed, the Israeli Knesset passed a resolution in 1977 forbidding talks with the PLO on the grounds that it 'seeks . . . the destruction and annihilation of the State of Israel' and that 'the murder of women and children and acts of terror against civilians is part of the ideology of this organization'. In 1986 a new law was passed which forbade Israelis from meeting any person associated with the PLO in any capacity.

What are the Facts?

It is unfortunately true that in the United States the word 'terrorist' has become almost synonymous with 'Palestinian'. This close identification of terrorism with Palestinian Arabs has clouded all reasonable discussion of the Arab–Israeli conflict. Invariably the Palestinian guerilla is said to engage in terrorist acts while the Israeli soldier honorably fights with 'purity of arms'. Unlike wars which may or may not be justified, terrorism, it is implied, always carries pejorative connotations.

As with any political or historical problem terrorism also has a context. Since the early decades of this century thousands of Palestinians and Jews have died in the struggle over territory. This struggle has taken many forms. The occasional Palestinian resort to terrorism cannot be understood unless those acts are squarely placed in the context of the complex and bitter struggle over land. Understanding terrorism in the Middle East is a story formed by the transformation of Ottoman and British Palestine into the modern state of Israel, rather than in the context of anti-Semitism.

First, what is terrorism? Second, how is the word 'terrorism' used when the Middle East is at issue? Third, who has used terror in the Middle East? Finally, is the PLO a terrorist organization and is it a legitimate organization? The authoritative and definitive *Oxford English Dictionary* defines terrorism as: 'A policy intended to strike with terror those against whom it is adopted; the employment of methods of intimidation.' To determine whether or not the PLO is terrorist, or for that matter any other group or state, the actual behavior of any particular group or state must fit this definition. But since both Israel and the PLO have resorted to forms of terror the question really becomes – does the use of tactics that terrorize in and of itself make the user a terrorist?

Neither Jewish ethics nor Jewish tradition can disqualify terrorism as a means of combat.

Yitzhak Shamir, *Hehazit*, Summer 1943 (journal of the LEHI, the Stern Gang) translated from the Israeli daily *Al-Hamishmar*, 24 December 1987 in *Palestine Perspectives*, March/April 1988.

It is interesting to note that Israel and its supporters tend to define terrorism in such a way that acts describable as 'terror' are applied mostly to resistance groups and rarely to states. For instance, the raids conducted by the PLO are called terrorist raids whereas Israeli Air Force attacks are justified as preemptive or retaliatory regardless of the fact that the number of Arab civilian casualties has invariably far exceeded that of Israelis.

A second and related consideration is the fact that in the context of the Palestinian–Zionist struggle 'terrorism' has acquired a very specific meaning as well as usage.

In order for a word to have any descriptive meaning at all there must, logically, be cases that fall outside the proposed meaning. For example, under what conditions could the Palestinians resist the occupation of their homeland and not be called terrorists? According to Israel all acts of resistance by the Palestinians are forms of terrorism, including acts against Israeli military forces. In other words, Israel claims that any and all forms of Palestinian resistance are terrorism. This kind of ascription renders the term 'terrorism' meaningless.

The use of the word 'terrorism' in the Middle East context has been expropriated for an exclusive use by one of the parties to the conflict to describe the activities of the other. The term, therefore, has a politically charged connotation which goes beyond being merely descriptive.

In addition, 'terrorism' has become a pejorative term, a buzzword, reserved for the description of all acts committed against the state of Israel. By utilizing the term 'terrorism' uncritically important issues are usually overlooked. For example, it has been common, historically, for the superior power to label its weaker adversary as terrorist. This phenomenon has been exemplified by the Nazi's description of the French resistance in Occupied France during the Second World War as terrorist. In more recent times, the label 'terrorism' has been applied to South African blacks by white supremacist Afrikaaners, to the Afghan resistance by the Russians and to the Palestinian resistance by the Zionists. This is not to say that the Free French forces, black South Africans, Afghans or Palestinians have not resorted to terror in their struggles against their enemies but that the important point is missed if only the means of their resistance is the issue.

Generally, any occupying power has described resistance to its occupation as terrorism. To give meaning to the word 'terrorism' one must distinguish legitimate resistance to oppression, as approved in the United Nations Charter, from terrorism for terror's sake. In other words, one must distinguish terrorists from freedom fighters.

In the context of the Palestinian–Zionist struggle this distinction has become so blurred, the identification of terrorism with the

Palestinians so pervasive, that the Palestinian has become the quintessential terrorist, the archetype.

This perverse and somewhat sophistic employment of terms finds its counterpart in the systematic vindication of all acts of bloodshed at the hands of the Israeli state. For example, in May 1974 an attack on the Israeli settlement of Ma'alot resulted in the death of twenty members of the Israeli paramilitary youth group (Gadna). While the PLO attack was described as a terrorist attack the Israeli napalm bombing of Palestinian refugee camps in Lebanon, in the weeks before the Ma'alot incident, that led to over 200 civilian deaths was not so called. The Ma'alot attack was systematically taken out of the context of the camp bombing that had preceded it and could not for that reason be even described as an act of military retaliation.[1] It is somewhat ironic that the state of Israel, which has been described not as a nation but as an army with a state, a modern Sparta, mourns its casualties at the hands of the Palestinians as civilians while among the Palestinians the women and children camp-dwellers bombed at the hands of the Israelis die the deserved death of terrorists.

The definition of terrorism does not make a distinction between retaliation and terrorism; therefore, all acts that are intimidating and meant to strike terror are terrorism regardless of the motive and the actors behind the act.

Distinguishing levels of violence is also important because one kind of violence, 'terrorism', is quite low in intensity compared to general war. War is certainly more intense and destructive than 'terrorism' and is the highest form of terrorism per se. Yet we do not in everyday discourse think of war as terroristic. Is there a difference between a bomb that explodes on a crowded bus and a missile from a fighter plane hitting an apartment building? Why is Israel allowed to make war on the Palestinians without criticism and Palestinian reaction is labelled terrorism?

The whole question of terrorism, as prominent as it has been in the newspapers, has been neglected as a topic to be studied and understood. The various 'terrorism experts' interviewed after one incident or another tend to concentrate on the heinousness of the crime rather than the motivation or purpose of its perpetrators. It has usually been the case that these experts treat terrorism as a fad, at once bereft of political and historical context, without a cause, purpose or meaning, and yet widespread and threatening.

The question is almost never asked as to why any human being would wilfully inflict pain and terror on another. Terrorists are, by implication, pathological killers, a mere foreign version of the psychotic local specimens that stalk our cities. Are the Palestinians just born terrorists, pathological fiends out to destroy the world and themselves? Or is the resort to terror tactics a result of a desperate condition that threatens them with extermination as an historical and political people?

Who uses terror? The Arab–Israeli conflict is notable in part because of the high incidence of terrorist acts. Terror comes from both sides. One side has the advantage of using its air force and, the other, its suicide missions.

Has Israel, and Zionists generally, employed terrorism to further their goals? Terror, as a useful and purposeful policy, was first adopted in the modern Middle East by Zionism. The first airplane hijacking was committed by Israel. On 12 December 1954 a civilian Syrian airliner was hijacked by Israel shortly after take-off. The first car-bomb was an invention of the Zionists, as was the assassination of United Nations personnel.[2] A Zionist truck-bomb blew up the King David Hotel in Jerusalem killing 88 in 1946.

Zionist terror in the 1930s and 40s has been neglected in the discussion about terrorism in the Middle East. Both former prime ministers, Menachem Begin and Yitzhak Shamir, were terrorist commanders responsible for numerous atrocities, including acts against Jews.

The archives of the Haganah contain the names of forty Jews who were killed by Begin's and Shamir's groups.[3] Shmuel Lahis, the Secretary-General of the Jewish Agency until 1981, was a notorious terrorist who personally murdered several dozen Arab civilians during operations in October 1948. He was arrested but immediately received an amnesty which denied the punishment and the charge as well.[4]

The Zionist record of terror is long and bloody before the creation of Israel. In the single month of July 1938 the Irgun killed seventy-six Palestinians in terrorist attacks.[5] The official history of the Irgun describes in glowing terms the murder of twenty-seven Palestinians who were celebrating the British Mandate government's decision to limit Jewish immigration; it also describes the murder, in another incident, of fifty-two Palestinians when an Irgun member was arrested by the British.[6]

Many former terrorists are today honored in Israel. For example, the Israeli Cabinet issued a series of commemorative stamps for Shlomo Ben-Yosef, hanged by the British for crimes against Arabs; for the murderers of Lord Moyne in 1944 and for two men who planted terrorist bombs in Cairo in 1954.[7] One of the assassins of UN Mediator Count Folke Bernadotte was a close friend of David Ben-Gurion who never revealed this secret until it was discovered by his biographer.[8]

The personal diaries of former Prime Minister Moshe Sharett who was the head of the Jewish Agency's Political Department from 1933 to 1948, Israel's Foreign Minister from 1948 to 1956 and Prime Minister in 1954 and 1955 describes how a policy of terrorism was a deliberate attempt to create political instability in the Arab world.[9]

The use of terror by Zionists is not well known. Between 13 December 1947 and 10 February 1948 161 Palestinians were killed and 320 injured by Irgun, Stern and Haganah terrorist attacks on market-places and cafes. Bus attacks in the same period killed fifteen Palestinians. On 30 December 1947 the Palmach, the strike force of the Haganah, attacked and massacred sixty Palestinian villagers of Bald as-Shaikh.

On 14 April 1948 the Irgun and Stern gang attacked the village of Deir Yassin and massacred 254 men, women and children.

On 14 October 1953 Unit 101, under the command of Ariel Sharon, attacked the village of Qibya in Jordan; sixty-six men, women and children were murdered. The Israeli government denied responsibility at the time but admitted the atrocity two years later.

On 28 March 1954 the Israeli army launched a massive attack on the village of Nahlin, near Bethlehem, massacring several dozen villagers and demolishing homes.

One of the most notorious acts of terror, which caused a political crisis in Israel at the time, was the Lavon affair. In July 1954 an Israeli spy ring operating in Cairo under the orders of the head of Israeli military intelligence, Benjamin Gibli, planted bombs in British and American cultural and information centers, cinemas and Egyptian public buildings. Their instructions were to 'break the West's confidence in the existing [Egyptian] regime . . . to prevent economic and military aid from the West to Egypt'.[10]

When the terrorists were caught and put on trial Israel orchestrated a propaganda campaign against Egypt, claiming the charges were trumped up and basically a result of anti-Semitism. In Israel there was embarrassment, not for the acts of terror but that the terrorists were caught.

On 28 February 1955 the Israeli army attacked Gaza and killed thirty-nine civilians including children.

In July 1956 Israeli agents assassinated Egyptian Lt-General Mustafa Hafez and the Egyptian military attaché in Amman.[11]

On 29 October 1956 the Israeli army committed the massacre of Kafr Qasem, a Palestinian village in Israel. The Israeli officer on the scene, Lt Gavriel Dahan, who had been convicted of murdering forty-three Palestinians in one hour, was pardoned and appointed military officer responsible for Arab affairs in the Palestinian town of Ramleh after his release.[12]

In September 1972 the Israeli Air Force indiscriminately attacked the Syrian resort town of al-Hama, in suburban Damascus, killing more than 200 civilians. Survivors recounted how they were machine-gunned as they ran for cover.[13]

In July 1981 an Israeli bombing run hit the Fakhani district of Beirut, a Palestinian neighbourhood, and killed 300 people, all civilians.

In late 1987, during the Uprising on the West Bank and Gaza, the Israeli army, operating under a policy of beatings and use of live ammunition, killed more than sixty people, half of whom were children. More than twenty others died as a result of the use of extreme force, including six babies who died from tear gas inhalation.[14] One year later more than 300 had been killed.

These incidents are a few examples of Israeli terrorism.

The PLO also has used terrorism as an instrument of policy. PLO terrorism has been so well documented that Americans generally associate terrorism exclusively with that organization in the Middle East. It is a regrettable fact of the Palestinian–Zionist conflict that both sides have reverted to terror. But Israel's use of terror has been qualitatively and quantitatively much greater than that of the PLO. The number of people killed by terrorist actions by Israel both before the establishment of the state of Israel and after has far exceeded the number killed by the PLO. For example, in 1982 alone, the number of Israeli civilians killed by the PLO was less than ten. The number of Lebanese and Palestinian civilians killed by Israel was over 19,000.[15]

In the Cairo Declaration of 1981 the PLO renounced the use of terrorism and drew a clear distinction between legitimate armed struggle and terrorism. The international community recognized that the Palestinians have the right of armed resistance against military targets of the occupying power but that violence against civilians was wholly indefensible. Although the PLO renounced terrorism other Palestinian groups have not, for instance, the Abu Nidal group which operates under the name 'Fatah Revolutionary Council'. Since a major party in the PLO is 'Fatah', headed by Yasser Arafat who is also chairman of the PLO, many heinous acts are routinely attributed to Arafat in confusion. This is not to say that the PLO has not committed terrorist acts. It has and it is rightly condemned for them as should Israel for acts it commits against civilians.

Israel's attitude towards attacks upon civilians was best summed up by Prime Minister Menachem Begin in a debate in the Israeli Knesset on 12 August 1982. In response to the question of whether or not the Palestinian civilian population should be punished, Begin replied, 'And how! Not even for one moment did I have any doubts of this, that the civilian population deserves punishment.'[16]

Finally, is the PLO a terrorist organization? That is, given the definition of terrorism, is the PLO's sole purpose the employment of methods of intimidation as an end in itself? To answer this question we need to know what the PLO is and why it was created.

As a result of the war in Palestine in 1948 60 percent of the Palestinian population fled or was expelled. Palestinian leaders were discredited, dead or in exile themselves. The Palestinians were unorganized, leaderless and, most importantly, landless. Until the mid-1950s their existence was all but forgotten by the world which celebrated Israeli exploits. The Palestinians had not forgotten their homeland and slowly began the process of organizing themselves.

Israel was quite successful in portraying Palestinian hostility and frustration as irrational, fanatical, genocidal and incorrigible. Using

What is peculiar about the Palestine conflict is that the world has listened to the party that has committed the offense and has turned a deaf ear to the victims.

Arnold Toynbee
'Forward', in Ibrahim Abu-Lughod, ed., *The Transformation of Palestine: Essays on the Origin and Development of the Arab–Israeli Conflict*, Northwestern University Press, 1971, p. viii.

world sympathy for Jewry in general because of the revelations about the Nazi extermination program, Israel was able to avoid debating the real issue of the Arab–Israeli conflict, its denial of Palestinian rights.

For a long time Israel was able to portray Palestinian resistance as purely malevolent, as coming out of nowhere. The impression Zionist propagandists wished to convey was that the Palestinians were merely covetous and had no legitimate grievances which might have been cause for them to engage in their violent reaction against Zionist colonialism.

Since (and before) the dismemberment of Palestine the Palestinian people have (and had) attempted to form organizations which could function for the purpose of redressing their grievances. The latest national political organization to emerge from the wreckage of Palestinian life was the Palestine Liberation Organization.

In 1964 the first modern Palestine National Congress (PNC) was held which resolved to establish a Palestine Liberation Organization. The Arab governments had a strong hand in its establishment since they hoped it would control the numerous resistance groups that had arisen in the 1950s as a result of growing weariness among the Palestinians about their condition.

By 1969 the PLO was fully independent of the Arab states and began to develop what represents the infrastructure of an embryonic Palestinian state and government. In this sense it was truly an umbrella organization where virtually all shades of Palestinian political opinion from the far left to the far right were represented.

The constituency of the PLO is the Palestinian people. The PLO in turn has developed a civilian and military infrastructure, as would a state, to address the needs and aspirations of this community.

The highest policy-making body of the PLO is the Palestine National Council (PNC), commonly known as the Palestinians' parliament. It is composed of nearly 400 members who represent all sectors of the Palestinian people, geographically and culturally. Those seats alloted to Palestinians from Israeli-held territories remain vacant since Israel does not allow Palestinians it controls to attend. The membership of the PNC is drawn from three main categories: the resistance organizations, popular associations and independents.[17]

The PNC is the supreme authority for formulating policies and programs for the PLO. A Central Council of sixty members acts as an intermediary advisory organ between the PNC and the Executive Committee of the PLO which has fifteen members empowered to perform four major functions: to act as the official representative of the Palestinian people; to supervise the various institutions of the PLO; to issue directives, draw up programs and make policy decisions; and to execute the financial policy and budget of the PLO. The PNC is the forum that democratically elects the chairman of the PLO.

The most important constituent of the PNC is the resistance groups. These eight resistance organizations are, in fact, political parties representing a range of political opinion from left to right. Each of these resistance organizations has its own internal structure separate from the PLO as a whole. They each have armed forces separate from the Palestine Liberation Army which is a constituent part of the PLO. Yasser Arafat, chairman of the PLO, is also the head of one of these resistance groups, Fatah.

The second important category or pillar of the PLO is the trade and professional associations. There are now ten general unions representing constituencies ranging from students to engineers and doctors. The General Union of Palestinian Doctors, for example, is the second largest in the Arab world, after Egypt. This is a remarkable achievement when one considers that Egypt's population is ten times greater and that the Palestinians do not have a state in which to organize their professional, political and personal lives.

Another important component of the PLO is the Palestinian Red Crescent which provides medical and health care to the Palestinian people through 130 fully equipped clinics and hospitals (many of which were targeted by Israeli military forces during the 1982 war). The Palestinian Red Crescent has observer status in the International Red Cross.

Israel contends that the PLO is not a legitimate organization and does not have the backing of the Palestinians themselves. This contention is, for the most part, propaganda for American consumption. The evidence for PLO legitimacy is so overwhelming that Zionists hardly use this kind of propaganda in Europe where awareness of the Palestinians is so much higher. That the PLO commands wide support not only among Palestinians of the

Diaspora but also among Palestinians within Israel and the West Bank and Gaza is taken as self-evident nearly everywhere except in the United States. The West Bank municipal elections in 1976 showed overwhelming support for PLO supporters among the candidates. So overwhelming was the support that the Israeli occupation authorities banned elections. A *Time* magazine poll released in 1982 showed that 86 percent of the Palestinians on the West Bank wanted a state run solely by the PLO.[18] Zionists claim that support for the PLO, on the West Bank, is the result of intimidation and terror. But a poll sponsored in 1986 by *Newsday*, of Long Island, NY, the Australian Broadcasting Corporation and *Al-Fajr* of Jerusalem, showed that 93 percent of the West Bank Palestinians believe the PLO is their sole legitimate representative.[19] An Israeli study completed in 1986 shows that even Palestinian citizens of Israel have a high regard for the PLO.[20]

Although Israel claims that the PLO has no legitimacy, more nations recognize the PLO than they do Israel. More than 110 nations recognize the PLO as the sole representative of the Palestinian people and more than 70 recognize the state of Palestine. Only seventy countries maintain diplomatic relations with Israel.[21]

The Arab League, representing more than 130 million people, recognizes the PLO as the sole legitimate representative of the Palestinian people. The world community also recognizes the PLO as the sole legitimate representative of the Palestinian people. On 22 November 1974 the United Nations recognized its status as 'the representative of the Palestinian' people. The PLO was also granted observer status at the United Nations, the first liberation organization ever to receive this status. The PLO later became a full member of all United Nations sub-organizations.

Further recognition that the PLO is the sole legitimate representative of the Palestinians came in 1982 when Yasser Arafat met with Pope John Paul II at the Vatican's invitation. In 1988 the US recognized the PLO for the first time.

The PLO is not an organization in a strict sense. It is, in essence, the structure of a future Palestine state. The PLO is the general organizational framework within which all Palestinian organizations – resistance groups, trade unions, professional associations, as well as prominent national figures – meet to work for the achievement of Palestinian national goals.

Does the PLO seek the destruction of Israel? This question is ironic because it is Israel that has already destroyed Palestine and continues to harass Palestinians, wherever they are, in a very real way.

The crux of this question is the meaning placed on the word 'destruction'. The term is often used by those who ask the question above in an emotive way that conjures up images of genocide and devastation. The actual terms of the Palestine National Charter make clear that the aim is simply to replace a system that bases nationality on Jewishness to one based on democratic principles where Jew, Muslim and Christian would live as equals. To do this would require a fundamental change in the nature of Zionism. Such a change would mean the end of the kind of Zionism which promotes exclusive Jewish communities. It is in this sense that the PLO speaks of the elimination of Zionism.

In his speech before the United Nations General Assembly in 1974 the chairman of the PLO Yasser Arafat was emphatic that the PLO's program does not call for the elimination or expulsion of the Israelis:

> I proclaim before you that when we speak of our common hopes for the Palestine of tomorrow we include in our perspective all Jews now living in Palestine who choose to live with us there in peace and without discrimination.[22]

Arafat spoke again to the General Assembly in December 1988 and offered the olive branch to the Israeli people and their leaders:

> Come let us make peace. Cast away fear and intimidation. Leave behind the spectre of the wars that have raged continuously for the past 40 years.[23]

It is incorrect to dismiss the PLO as a terrorist organization. To describe any people who violently resist a foreign invader or a native oppressor as terrorist is to render the word meaningless.

The Palestinians did not invent terrorism. They found it already institutionalized, a policy employed against *them*. The important question is whether the violence employed by the oppressed tends toward the end of terror or toward its self-perpetuation. The goal of the PLO is not terror but the establishment of a state for the Palestinian people.

56

Notes to Chapter 5

1. Edward W. Said, *The Question of Palestine*, Times Books, 1979, pp. 172, 249.
2. For a full list of Zionist 'firsts' see Walid Khalidi, 'Towards an Adjustment of Political Perception in Arab Society', in Margaret Pennar, ed., *The Middle East: Five Perspectives*, Information Paper 7, AAUG, October 1973, p. 14.
3. Nahum Barnea and Danny Rubenstein, *Davar*, 19 March 1982.
4. *Al Hamishmar*, 3 March 1978. Lt-Col. Dov Yirmiah exposed the story of Lahis. See Noam Chomsky, *The Fateful Triangle: the United States, Israel and the Palestinians*, South End, 1983, pp. 165, 237.
5. Noam Chomsky, op. cit., p. 165. See also Simha Flapan, *Zionism and the Palestinians*, St Martin's Press, 1977, ch. 2.
6. See Israel Shahak, *Begin and Co.: as They Really are*, Jerusalem, 1977.
7. *Jerusalem Post*, 15 February 1982.
8. Michael Bar-Zohar, *Ben-Gurion: a Biography*, trans. Peretz Kidron, Delacorte Press, 1977, pp. 180–81. Concerning the assassination of Count Bernadotte see Cary David Stanger, 'A Haunting Legacy: the Assassination of Count Bernadotte', *Middle East Journal*, XLII, Spring 1988, pp. 260–272, especially the endnotes.
9. Livia Rokach, *Israel's Sacred Terrorism: a Study Based on Moshe Sharett's Personal Diary and Other Documents*, AAUG, 1980.
10. The text is reproduced from the Acts of the Olshan-Dori Inquiry Commission of the 'Affair', annexed to Sharett's *Personal Diary*, pp. 659, 664, in Rokach, op. cit., p. 38.
11. Ehud Ya'ari, *Mitsraim Ve'Ha Fedayeen*, Givat Haviva, 1975, in Rokach, op. cit., p. 64.
12. Sabri Jiryis, *The Arabs of Israel*, Monthly Review, 1976, p. 111.
13. *L'Orient Le Jour*, 10 September 1972; *Daily Star*, Beirut, 10 September 1972.
14. *Middle East International*, London, 20 February 1988, p. 9.
15. The exact number of those killed ranges between 18,000 and 30,000. Most Zionist publications either do not mention the number of casualties, claim that those killed were all terrorists or deflate the number killed. The most accurate figures are those of the Lebanese National Police which counted those who died in, or were taken to, hospitals. The International Red Cross and the International Commission to Enquire into Reported Violations of International Law confirm a figure near 19,000 killed. See *Israel in Lebanon: the Report of the International Commission to Enquire into Reported Violations of International Law by Israel during its Invasion of the Lebanon*, Ithaca Press, 1983.
16. ibid., p. 57.

17. The resistance organizations are Fatah, Popular Front for the Liberation of Palestine, Democratic Front for the Liberation of Palestine, Saiqa, Arab Liberation Front, Popular Front for the Liberation of Palestine-General Command, Palestine Liberation Front, Palestinian Popular Struggle Front, Palestine Communist Party.

     The popular associations are General Union of Palestinian Writers and Journalists. General Union of Palestinian Workers, General Union of Palestinian Women, General Union of Palestinian Students, General Union of Palestinian Teachers, General Union of Palestinian Engineers, General Union of Palestinian Lawyers, General Union of Palestinian Doctors, General Union of Palestinian Painters and Artists, General Union of Palestinian Peasants.

     Independents are persons not affiliated with the resistance organizations and include persons from Palestinian communities outside Palestine.
18. *Time*, 25 May 1982.
19. The poll had a 3–5 percent error factor. The polling methods and questions were reprinted in *Al-Fair*, Jerusalem, English ed., 12 September 1986.
20. The study was conducted by Ra'anan Cohen, the Labor Party's advisor on Arabs at Tel Aviv University; Sheli Gabbai, *Ma'ariv*, 5 March 1986.
21. Abdallah Frangi, *The PLO and Palestine*, trans. Paul Knight, Zed Press, 1982, p. 144.
22. Address to the UN General Assembly in Walter Laqueur and Barry Rubin, eds., *The Israeli–Arab Reader: a Documentary History of the Middle East Conflict*, Penguin, 1984, p. 517.
23. *New York Times*, 14 December, 1988.

Recommended Reading

Helena Cobban, *The Palestinian Liberation Organization: People, Power and Politics*, Cambridge University Press, 1984.

Noam Chomsky, *Pirates and Emperors: International Terrorism in the Real World*, Claremont Research, 1986.

Facing the PLO Question, Foundation for Middle East Peace, 1985.

Alain Gresh, *The PLO: the Struggle within, towards an Independent Palestinian State*, Zed Press, 1983.

Abu Iyad with Eric Rouleau, *My Home, My Land: a Narrative of the Palestinian Struggle*, Times Books, 1981.

Alan Hart, *Arafat: Terrorist or Peacemaker?*, Sidgwick and Jackson, 1984.

Rashid Khalidi, *Under Siege: P.L.O. Decisionmaking during the 1982 War*, Columbia University Press, 1986.

William B. Quandt, Fuad Jabber, Ann Mosely Lesch, *The Politics of Palestinian Nationalism*, University of California Press, 1973.

Chapter 6

Israel and Democracy

Israel has described itself as a bastion of Western democracy and as the only democratic state in the Middle East. To demonstrate that theirs is a democratic country Israel points out that Palestinians in Israel have the right to vote, that there are Palestinians in the Knesset (Israeli Parliament), that they have a higher standard of living than Arabs in other lands, that Arabic is an official language of Israel and that the only distinction Israel makes between Jews and Arabs is that Arabs are not required to serve in the armed forces.

What are the Facts?

The question as to the democratic character of the Israeli state may be broken down into three components: to what extent can Israel lay claim to democracy when it understands itself as a Jewish state? The idea of a Jewish state was put most succinctly by David Ben-Gurion in 1947. 'When we say . . . "Jewish State" we mean Jewish country, Jewish soil, we mean Jewish labor, we mean

Jewish economy, Jewish agriculture, Jewish industry, Jewish sea.'[1] In other words, how is one to reconcile the democratic spirit with an exclusionary definition of state as a Jewish state rather than a state for the Israelis? Given that the majority of Jews are not Israeli and that a substantial number of Israelis are not Jewish the question becomes crucial.

These distinctions are important: the United States, for example, does not define itself as the state of all English speakers, and no specific criteria are stipulated to determine who is, in principle, a potential American. If America is the American state, why is it not the case that Israel is simply the Israeli state? The self-definition as Jewish refers not to the religion of the majority of the inhabitants, nor the state religion, but to the character of the state and to the qualifications of its actual and potential nationals.

The second component naturally involves the practical rather than the theoretical implications of a Jewish democracy: are the rights then of non-Jews equal to those of Jews in a Jewish state? To be declared a democracy the answer to this question must be affirmative (also see chapters 7 and 8).

The third and final component deals with Israel's unique relationship to non-Israeli Jews. This significant component highlights the problematic aspects of Israeli democracy in that it involves a measure of extra-territoriality and establishes between the state and non-Israeli Jews a legal bond that surpasses the state's relationship with its own resident non-Jewish population.

Israel was declared a *Jewish* state rather than the state of the Jews because the Zionists of Israel were only a small part of the Jewish people world wide.

It is in the formation of . . . public opinion that we find the principal task of Zionism.

Dr S. Berstein
'Fundamentals of the Judenstaat: Herzl's Conception of the Jewish State' in Meyer W. Weisgal, ed., *Theodor Herzl: a Memorial*, New Palestine–Zionist Organization of America, 1929, p. 88.

To comprehend the significance of a *Jewish* state we can look at three fundamental laws of the state of Israel. One of these laws is known as the *Law of Return of 1950* which declared that all Jews, whatever their nationality, wherever they were born, wherever they lived, had the inalienable right to immigrate to Israel and become Jewish nationals automatically.

> *Land is to be acquired as Jewish property and . . . shall be held as the inalienable property of the Jewish people.*

Israeli Law
Basic Laws of Israel, Article 3 (d) of the constitution of the Jewish Agency incorporated into the 'Basic Laws' by an act of the Knesset in the World Zionist Organization/Jewish Agency (Status) Law.

The Law of Return codifies the fundamental principle of Zionism which states that Israel is the sovereign state of the Jewish people. Its sovereignty is not limited to the Jewish citizens of the existing state of Israel, but to all Jewish persons wherever they live or were born. In theory there is no Israeli nationality defined by the geographic boundaries of the state. But this geographic expansion of nationality is simultaneously limited to Jews. It represents, in other words, the practical legal side of the Zionist claim that Zionism is the only true Judaism of the modern era.

Israeli law stipulates that there is an extra-territorial Jewish nationality which is accorded to all who are said to be Jews. A Jew, in Israel, is a person who has descended, matrilinearly, from the descendants of Abraham through Isaac, or who has been converted according to the Halacha (Jewish law). Since conversion is allowed in Jewish law many assume that genetics plays no role in determining who is a Jew. This is not the case. The religious faction which is dominant in Israel is not at all concerned with the religious belief of a Jew but with that person's lineage, a euphemism for genetic make-up.

Further evidence concerning the role blood plays in determining who is a Jew, for the Jewish community, is the phenomenon of 'self-hatred' in Jewish culture. According to some Jews a self-hating Jew is a person who denies his or her Jewishness. A Jew who converts to Christianity, for example, is still considered a Jew by the Jewish community, albeit a self-hating one. A Christian who decides to become a Buddhist, let's say, would never be vilified as a self-hater by his or her community, although conversion may be lamented. Since a Jew always remains a Jew, according to

Jewish law and custom, even if he or she converts, then the criteria for who is a Jew are not religious but more to do with lineage, that is, genetics.

Only those who qualify as Jews can take advantage of the Law of Return. Palestinians, therefore, who are not Jews, cannot take advantage of the consequences of the Law of Return. Arabs possess 'Arab nationality' in Israel but cannot, of course, possess 'Jewish nationality'. Since Israel is a Jewish state Jewish nationals are able to accrue special rights which non-Jews cannot do. Logically, an Arab national has no place in a 'Jewish' state. The way in which Israel describes the difference between 'Arab nationality' and 'Jewish nationality' in a Jewish state shows that, in practice, the two nationalities reduce to the distinction between 'citizenship' and 'nationality'. Arabs have 'citizenship' in Israel but they are not citizens 'by return', as stipulated by the Law of Return, and therefore can never be 'nationals', nor take advantage of rights accorded to Jews by virtue of their being Jews in a Jewish state.

The phrase 'by return' is a peculiar and unique concept in the modern world. It means that a Jew who may never have laid eyes on the Holy Land and whose ancestors may very well have converted has the right to live there and be accorded all the rights associated with a Jewish state. This means that Arabs do not possess Jewish nationality in Israel, for 'the Jewish' nationality is the only nationality status recognized by the state and only to the 'Jewish people' can several fundamental laws of Israel apply. Zionists argue that Arabs are able to have 'Arab' listed under the category 'nationality' on their identification papers and therefore are accorded nationality. This argument is meaningless, though, because Israel is a Jewish state not a multinational or binational state.

I have asked employment offices not to hurry to fill vacant jobs with Arabs but to look for Jewish workers.

Moshe Katzav, Israeli Labor Minister, 1984
Toronto Star, 10 December 1984.

It is difficult for us to understand how special privileges might accompany Jewish nationality since in no other country in the world is there a distinction between 'citizenship' and 'nationality'.

This distinction is not evident in the actual terms of Israeli law but becomes evident when consideration is given to the meaning of 'Jewish state' for non-Jewish citizens of that state. There is no 'Israeli nationality' in Israel (see chapter 8).

The Israeli Population Registry Law is revealing in this regard. The Population Registry issues identity cards to all residents, but there is no provision for registering an 'Israeli' nationality. Although there is an entry for 'nationality' an 'Israeli' designation is not offered as an option for either Jews or non-Jews. Jews must indicate their nationality as 'Jew'. Arabs must indicate 'Arab'. But under the entry 'citizenship' Jews and non-Jews alike may specify 'Israeli', confirming the separation in Israel of nationality and citizenship. In a landmark case in 1972 the Israeli Supreme Court affirmed the absence of 'Israeli' nationality.[2]

It is necessary to declare it openly: Israel is a single-nationality Jewish state. The fact that an Arab minority lives within the country does not make it a multinational state.

Yigal Allon
A Curtain of Sand, Hakibbutz Hameuchad, 1959, p. 337 (in Hebrew).

A second fundamental law, the *Nationality Law of 1952*, bestows upon all persons who are accorded 'Jewish nationality' in the Law of Return the right to claim 'Israeli citizenship by return', automatically, without any formal procedures.

The importance of this distinction between nationality and citizenship becomes clearer when examining the consequences of the third fundamental law, the *World Zionist Organization/Jewish Agency (Status) Law of 1952 (WZO/JA Law)*. These two organizations, along with the Jewish National Fund (JNF), were the principal pre-state quasi-governmental political entities which functioned as a state within a state under the British Mandate.

Once the state of Israel was established the WZO/JA Law regularized the legal status of the two organizations and the JNF and recognized these organizations as equals to the state of Israel and incorporated their constitutions into the Basic Laws of Israel.

This 'fundamental law' is important because article 3 of the constitution of the Jewish Agency, which was incorporated into the Basic Laws of Israel, states:

> Land is to be acquired as Jewish property and . . . the title to the lands acquired is to be taken in the name of the Jewish National Fund, to the end that the same shall be held as the inalienable property of the Jewish people.

The JNF is precluded from selling or leasing any part of this land to Arabs or even allowing Arabs to work on it.

The WZO/JA Law codifies, in practice, the benefits accorded to Jews over non-Jews. According to the law, 'The State of Israel regards itself as the creation of the entire Jewish people.' It states that 'gathering the exiles is the central task of the State of Israel and the Zionist Movement'.

On the face of it these laws appear to serve an humanitarian purpose for persecuted Jews. Their significance, however, reaches far beyond humanitarian interests. First, since Israel does not have a written constitution these fundamental laws form a substitute constitution. Second, the language, in English translation, of the WZO/JA Law, in particular, is misleading because it gives the impression that the motivation is to provide refuge for homeless Jews. Actually the Zionist objective is much more significant; it is, as they state, to 'ingather' all Jews.

Another phenomenon which confuses the issue is the distinction between 'national' institutions and 'government' institutions. The institutions that officially, conceptually and practically operate for the exclusive benefit of Jews are identified as 'national'. They include the World Zionist Organization, the Jewish Agency and the Jewish National Fund.

Government institutions, such as the various ministries, officially, theoretically and practically serve the citizens of Israel.

When the Jewish National Fund, for example, openly discriminates against Arabs by, say, refusing to sell them land Zionists claim that the Fund is a philanthropic Jewish institution and not a democratic Israeli government institution. But it is the WZO/JA Law which contradicts this claim. This law legitimizes an arrangement between the government and the WZO and JA which makes the government a full and equal partner in activities which provide advantages to Jews which are legally denied to other citizens, namely, Arabs.

The powers and resources of these agencies are vast. The Jewish Agency, for example, through the Jewish National Fund, controls 92 percent of the land in Israel, much of which was expropriated from the Arabs. These lands, once acquired, are transferred by the government of Israel to the Jewish Agency in a process called 'redeeming the land'. Arabs are deprived of their use by the provisions of the Jewish National Fund Charter which grants 'redeemed' land only to 'the Jewish people'.

Arabs, and all non-Jews, are not only unable, by law, to own the land, but they cannot either lease it or work upon it.[3]

These three fundamental laws, along with a number of others, legalize discrimination against non-Jewish citizens of Israel. The Law of Return establishes exclusive nationality rights for Jews; non-Jews do not and cannot have Jewish nationality in Israel, the Jewish state. The Law of Nationality establishes a class of citizenship for Arabs that leaves them permanently disadvantaged.

The Arab does not possess the attributes necessary to be a full member of the community which defines Israel's essence and existence and therefore is disallowed from participating in the full political, social and economic life of the Jewish state. The extent to which the non-Jew is a participant in the life of Israel is relegated to the electoral realm and thereby allows access to the Knesset.

The WZO/JA Law facilitates legal, economic, political and social discrimination against Arabs by delegating a wide range of services to Zionist institutions serving only Jews and by openly identifying these agencies with the state of Israel. For example, since Israel is a *Jewish* state many services for Jews are provided through the philanthropic Jewish agencies which are legal appendages to the government (WZO/JA Law). The funds made available to these Jewish agencies by the government are not available to Arabs.

Many basic services are not available to the Arabs because of a Catch-22 situation. The government claims that those basic services are provided by the philanthropic agencies. But since the 'philanthropic' agencies are exclusively Jewish they do not provide services to the Arab population. Services such as child care, neighborhood programs or housing for the elderly are not available to the Arab population because they are not Jewish.

*There is an Israeli law [Penal Revision Law (State Security) of Israel] that
authorizes the police and the security services to pick up and detain for
questioning any Israeli citizen who is in contact with a foreigner without
official permission.*

US Central Intelligence Agency
Israel: Foreign Intelligence and Security Services, Secret Document, CIA,
March 1979, p. 23, reprinted in *Counterspy*, May–June 1982, p. 47.

In conclusion, any state whose ideology forces it to categorize
its citizenry into separate segments and provides preferential
treatment for one segment cannot be called democratic. Israel's
appearance as a democracy is an illusion because it is a democracy
for Jews.

No state that specifies its existence on race, religion or ethnic
purity can be considered a democracy. The 'American', 'English'
and 'French' states do not specify who can or cannot be a national
of the state based on race or religion. So, today, there are black
Englishmen and Muslim Frenchmen who exist as nationals, with
no qualifications, co-equal with descendants of Anglo-Saxon and
Frankish tribes, respectively. No such situation obtains in Israel
and therefore Israel cannot be described as a democracy.

The various 'rights' that non-Jews do have in the Jewish state,
such as the right to vote, or the right to have their language listed
as an official language, or serve in the Knesset are seen to pale
when compared to the more fundamental rights, that is, human
rights, that are denied to them because they are not Jews.[4]

Therefore, to the extent that Israel is a *Jewish* state it cannot
be a democratic state.

Notes to Chapter 6

1. Jewish Agency, *The Jewish Case: before the Anglo-American
   Committee of Inquiry on Palestine as Presented by the Jewish Agency
   for Palestine*, Jerusalem, 1947, p. 66.

2. George Raphael, *Tamarin vs. State of Israel*, 1972, C.A. 630/70.
3. Theoretically, this is what the law stipulates. Practically speaking, most Jewish Israelis are so unwilling to do lowly jobs that many Arabs are employed to do work such as janitorial or heavy labor.
4. For a fuller discussion on the importance of military service in Israel for its citizens see chapter 8.

Recommended Reading

Uri Davis and Walter Lehn, 'And the Fund Still Lives: the Role of the Jewish National Fund in the Determination of Israel's Land Policies', *Journal of Palestine Studies*, 28, Summer 1978.

Abdelwahab M. Elmessiri, *The Land of Promise: a Critique of Political Zionism*, North American, 1977.

R. Garaudy, *The Case of Israel: a Study of Political Zionism*, Shorouk International, 1983.

Walter Lehn, in association with Uri Davis, *The Jewish National Fund*, Kegan Paul International, 1988.

Akiva Orr, *The UnJewish State: the Politics of Jewish Identity in Israel*, Ithaca, 1983.

Israel Shahak, ed., *The Non-Jew in the Jewish State: a Collection of Documents*, 2 Bartenura St, Jerusalem, 1975.

Chapter 7

Zionism, Racism and Anti-Semitism

Israel and its supporters claim that anti-Zionism is just a cover, a new guise, for anti-Semitism. After the United Nations General Assembly passed a resolution in 1975 declaring Zionism a form of racism and racial discrimination Zionists, in turn, called the resolution anti-Semitic.

Zionists say that Israel is not a racist state and cite an anti-racism law passed in 1986 which declares that it is against the law to discriminate against a person on the basis of race, color or ethnic background.

What are the Facts?

Zionism arose in the late nineteenth century in Europe as a result of, specifically, anti-Semitic events in Russia. The early Zionists believed that the Jewish predicament would only be solved by the establishment of a Jewish state. They believed that the struggle against a rising tide of European anti-Semitism was hopeless, that the Jews would never be accepted into the societies in which they lived, and therefore would find the solution to their situation not by assimilating but by establishing a 'national home' and living separately.

Zionism was, and is, a political ideology to establish a Jewish state and to 'ingather' all Jews into this state. At the first Zionist Congress convened in Basle the World Zionist Organization was established in order to secure, by public law, a Jewish national home in Palestine. Although some early Zionists considered Uganda as well as Argentina and the Sinai as possibilities, for the majority of Zionists Palestine remained the only alternative.

The plan for the 'ingathering' of all Jews in a national home to be established in Palestine not only sought to blur the distinction between Judaism and Zionism; it sought to forge a political identity out of a historico-religious ethnicity of which Zionism would be the only legitimate expression. The Zionist rejection of assimilation of the Jew into his European environment had its counterpart in the concept of collective assimilation of the Jews as a political group in the international arena. And before long it had become commonplace to argue that anti-Zionism, by virtue of the fact that it is directed against the only legitimate collective Jewish self-expression in the modern era, constitutes anti-Semitism.

The charge of anti-Semitism is a powerful and destructive claim which must be put in its proper context, otherwise mere questioning of the behavior of Israel may be labeled anti-Semitic, as indeed it has frequently been.

This issue is significant and relevant mostly as a result of two phenomena: 1) the actual practice of the state of Israel vis-a-vis Jews and non-Jews; and 2) the United Nations General Assembly Resolution declaring Zionism to be a form of racism and racial discrimination (see appendix 13).

Although the UN Resolution caused an outcry leading Daniel Moynihan, then US Ambassador to the United Nations, to declare it to be anti-Semitic, none of its critics has actually addressed the issues behind the arguments considered for the passage of the resolution.

The only relevant question is simple: do the ideology of Zionism and the laws of Israel sanction discrimination against non-Jewish citizens of Israel? If they do, does this discrimination rest upon race, religion or origin?

A national Jewish Palestine must necessarily mean a state founded on a peculiar race, a tribal religion, and a mystic belief in a peculiar soil.

Morris R. Cohen, Professor of Philosophy, Harvard University
New Republic, 1919.

Before arriving at an answer three preliminary questions must be explored. First, what is racism and racial discrimination? What are the differences between scientific and popular concepts of race? Second, why is there a distinction between 'nationality' and 'citizenship' in Israel? Finally, who is a Jew?

The word 'race' is, strictly speaking, a biological term. Terms such as 'English race' or 'French race' are, therefore, incorrect usages. The concept of race, popular in the nineteenth century, has been discarded by modern anthropologists.

The mixture of popular concepts of 'race' with biological concepts led to the misuse of race classifications and the massacre of millions of people in Europe under the Nazi regime.

The Nazi model stands as the best example of racism. From that model three major components can be identified to characterize a racist system: 1) a declaration that the majority or ruling population is racially distinct from other segments of the population; 2) a rationalization for discrimination based on groups of racial superiority and inferiority; and 3) a prohibition of intermarriage to prevent 'contamination' of the racial purity of the allegedly superior group.

The major problem with using this model for identification purposes rests on the fact that the Nazi regime and racial concepts per se are now so odious that more subtle and sophisticated means are utilized to justify racial superiority and laws based thereon. The South African government, for example, justifies its racial policies by arguing that separation of the races contributes to the better development of both. Racism, today, is often cloaked behind claims of benevolent concern. For example, South Africa does not maintain or declare officially that Blacks are inferior.

The domination of Jewish agriculture by Arab workers is a cancer in our body.

A. Uzan, Israeli Minister of Agriculture
Ha'aretz, 13 December 1974.

71

Can Zionism be described as racist? Since Israel was proclaimed a Jewish state when it was created, what is the status of non-Jews in a Jewish state? Are non-Jews in Israel legally discriminated against because they are not Jews?

Zionists argue that they are not racist and point to the fact that non-Jews have the right to vote and be elected to the Knesset. Zionists also cite the 'anti-racist' law passed in the Knesset in 1986 which prohibits discrimination on the basis of race, color or ethnic heritage.

The 'anti-racist' law in Israel is unique in that, although it stipulates that there shall be no discrimination on the basis of race, there can be discrimination on the basis of religion. 'Religion' was purposely left out of the law and therefore religious discrimination in Israel is not illegal. The practical result is that non-Jews are discriminated against in Israel but that this discrimination is not considered racist.

Those who deny that Zionism is a form of racism by relying on a biological definition of the term, as discrimination by one race against another, and argue that since Jews are not a race they cannot be racist, ignore two points: first, they ignore that the charge is against Zionism not Judaism and, second, they ignore the definition adopted by the United Nations which is also common usage.

If anti-Semitic practices are racist, despite the absence of race differences between Jews and their persecutors, it follows that practices against non-Jews are also racist. A government need not emulate the Nazis, openly proclaiming racial superiority, to be judged a racist state.

It is true that Arabs in Israel have the right to vote and hold Israeli citizenship. But unlike anywhere else in the world, citizenship in Israel is distinguished from nationality. Mere citizenship does not bestow upon the individual equal rights. (The distinction between citizenship and nationality and its importance in understanding the question of equal rights in Israel is discussed in chapters 6 and 8.)

Finally, why is the question 'Who is a Jew?' so important in understanding whether Zionism is racism or anti-Zionism a form of anti-Semitism?

The question is important because Israel was declared a state like no other. Israel was declared a state of the Jewish people.

Not just Jews who happen to have Israeli passports, but a state for all Jews wherever they live. This phenomenon is quite different from a state religion. For instance, the state religion of Great Britain is Anglican Protestantism; the state religion of Jordan is Islam – but not any Anglican or Muslim may go to those respective countries and automatically become a national by mere virtue of shared religion. Naturally, the question of who was a Jew became very important.

Interestingly, the definition of a Jew is one of the most controversial of all political issues in Israel. Some argue that anyone who identifies with Jewish culture and ethnicity and believes themselves to be a Jew, is a Jew. In Israel, and therefore 'officially', only the Orthodox rabbinate is followed and recognized.

The Orthodox insist that Jewish nationality (or ethnicity) and Jewish religion are inseparable, and that the only acceptable definition of a Jew is derived from the Halacha, or Jewish law. This definition declares that a Jew is one born of a Jewish mother or converted to Judaism in a conversion authenticated by the Orthodox rabbinate. The state of Israel in practice does not accept conversions done by the other two schools of Jewish thought, Reform and Conservative. The Orthodox rabbinate is not concerned with a Jew's religious beliefs or lack thereof, but only his or her biological status as a Jew. Because the rabbinate considers even non-Orthodox or, for that matter, Communists who are born of a Jewish mother, to be Jews, they have overlooked religious faith and go straight to the question of biology; that is, is the mother Jewish? They believe that only by a strict interpretation of religious rules can Jewish nationality be determined. In this manner the Orthodox have created an equation between religion and race.[1]

There can be only one national home in Palestine, and that a Jewish one, and no equality in the partnership between Jews and Arabs.

Montague David Eder, President of the Zionist Federation of Great Britain, 1931
in Doreen Ingrams, comp., *Palestine Papers 1917–1922: Seeds of Conflict*, George Braziller, 1973, p. 135.

Many secular Zionists are uncomfortable with the application of Jewish law to the regulation of a Jewish state because it is impossible to maintain that the state is a secular democracy. A secular definition of a Jew cannot be insisted upon, though, since one of Israel's claims to legitimacy, that the land is God given, is based on the precept that Zionism and Judaism are inseparable.

Until 1970 no legal definition of a Jew existed in Israel. Because of several practical legal issues raised by immigrants to Israel – one a man having been born to a Jewish mother, converted to Christianity – the Knesset, as a result of pressure from the religious faction, enacted legislation defining a Jew in conformity with religious law. The law now states that ' "Jew" means a person who was born of a Jewish mother or has become converted to Judaism and who is not a member of another religion.' Now, Israeli secularists no longer have legal grounds for objecting to a religious requirement for nationality. If religion were to be rejected as a basis for nationality, then Israel would become, according to its own logic of equating Judaism with Zionism, a non-Zionist state. Some liberal Zionists, however, believe that Zionism could tolerate a secular 'ethnic' definition in principle.

Much of modern Israel is quite paradoxical. Leaders such as former Prime Ministers Menachem Begin and Golda Meir were not religious and often made cryptic statements about the Jews. Golda Meir said that 'a long invisible thread ties Jews from generation to generation . . .' and that 'there are mixed marriages in numbers that scare me'.[2]

The concern about intermixture between Jews and non-Jews led to the Law of Marriage and Divorce which prevents Jews from marrying non-Jews. There is no civil marriage in Israel.[3]

The question of who is and who is not a Jew, that is, the question of Jewish purity, is extremely sensitive in Israel. It should be unthinkable that Israelis would make claims about the genetic distinctiveness of Jews and non-Jews, especially since authoritative studies demonstrate substantial non-Jewish admixture in Jewish populations and, more importantly for Jews, it was just this kind of thinking which caused the Nazi genocide against them.

Nevertheless, geneticists in Israel are working to show that Jews are, in the words of Dr Bonné-Tamir, Professor of Human Genetics at the Sackler School of Medicine of Tel Aviv University, 'genetically distinctive'. As any scientist knows, this is in effect saying that the Jews are a race.[4]

Bonné-Tamir does not advocate biological superiority for Jews, but there is a danger that others will. After all, the seemingly benign race theories of H. S. Chamberlin later became the underpinnings of Nazi racial policies. The danger is magnified when genetic research is used for political purposes. At a Presbyterian conference held in New Mexico in 1985 a Zionist representative did just this by citing these Israeli genetic studies as proving that today's Jews are the 'seed of Abraham', thus legitimizing policies detrimental to non-Jews in Israel.[5]

But as objective research shows, there is abundant historical evidence that the genetics of Jewish populations were considerably modified through the centuries by proselytism, intermarriages and extramarital sexual relationships, both violent and voluntary. The Jews, much of this research shows, are not a relatively inbred group that has genetic distinctiveness. Certainly, there are examples of small Jewish communities which have displayed unusual distinctive characteristics, such as the high incidence of tuberculosis among the Jews of Prague in the nineteenth century. But these anomalies have no greater meaning, just as the fact that inbreeding among Appalachian hillbillies has no greater meaning for the American population at large.

The very nature of a state which specifies its citizens and codifies the differences in law, so that advantages accrue to one segment of the population and not the other, can be considered racist. A nation which discriminates against a portion of its population on the basis of race, religion, color, ethnic heritage or creed can be judged 'racist' in the common usage of the term.

'Racism' is correctly applicable to systematic discrimination of one population against another, notwithstanding the racial composition of either population.

The UN Resolution in 1975 declaring Zionism to be a form of racial discrimination is a valid declaration. Being critical of Zionism is not being anti-Jewish and therefore is not anti-Semitic.

Notes to Chapter 7

1. A curiosity has arisen because of the possibility of conversion, according to Jewish law, authenticated by the Orthodox rabbinate. A female convert's children will be Jewish even though this is biologically impossible.
2. Avika Orr, *The UnJewish State: The Politics of Jewish Identity in Israel*, Ithaca Press, 1982, pp. 74–5, 176.
3. Claude Klein, *Le Caractère Juif de l'Etat d'Israel*, Paris: Editions Cujas, 1977, pp. 123–4.
4. The statement is in N. Meyers, 'Genetic Links for Scattered Jews', *Nature*, 314, 21 March 1985, p. 208. Other 'race' research by Israelis is found in the *American Journal of Human Genetics*, XXXI, 3, May 1979, pp. 341–65; R. M. Goodman and A. G. Motulsky, *Genetic Diseases*, Raven, 1979; B. Bonné-Tamir, 'A New Look at Jewish Genetics', *Mada*, XXIV, 4–5, 1980, trans. from the Hebrew by Norton Mezvinsky.
5. Roselle Tekiner, *Jewish Nationality Status as the Basis for Institutionalized Racism in Israel*, Paper 40, EAFORD, 1985, p. 24. This chapter draws extensively from Ms Tekiner.

Recommended Reading

EAFORD and AJAZ, *Judaism and Zionism? What Difference for the Middle East?*, Zed Press, 1986. (EAFORD = International Organization for the Elimination of All Forms of Racial Discrimination; AJAZ = American Jews against Zionism.)

International Organization for the Elimination of All Forms of Racial Discrimination, *Zionism & Racism* (proceedings of an international symposium), North American, 1979.

Abdeen Jabara, *Zionism and Racism*, Arab World Issues, Occasional Papers 3, AAUG, 1976.

O. Kraines, *The Impossible Dilemma: Who is a Jew in the State of Israel?*, Bloch, 1976.

Abram Leon, *The Jewish Question: a Marxist Interpretation*, Pathfinder, 1970.

Akiva Orr, *The UnJewish State: The Politics of Jewish Identity in Israel*, Ithaca, 1982.

Tabitha Petran, *Zionism: a Political Critique*, New England Free Press, n.d.

Maxime Rodinson, *Cult, Ghetto and State: the Persistence of the Jewish Question*, Al Saqi, 1983.

Fayez Sayegh, *Zionism: 'A Form of Racism and Racial Discrimination': Four Statements Made at the U.N. General Assembly*, Office of the Permanent Observer of the Palestine Liberation Organization to the United Nations, 1976.

Roselle Tekiner, *Jewish Nationality Status as the Basis for Institutionalized Racism in Israel*, Paper 40, EAFORD, 1985.

Chapter 8

Do Palestinians in Israel have Equal Rights?

Israel claims that its Palestinian citizens have full and equal rights; that they are co-equal with Jews in the state of Israel. They claim that there is no discrimination in Israel and that Palestinians have equal opportunity under the law. Zionists often point out that the Palestinians have the right to vote, serve in the Knesset and that they have higher standards of living than some Arab states (see chapters 6 and 7).

What are the Facts?

First, it is important to remember the distinction mentioned in chapter 6 between citizenship and nationality when discussing the rights of the Palestinians in Israel. There is only one officially recognized nationality group in Israel which benefits from *all the fundamental laws of Israel*, namely, the Jews. Although the Palestinians can be citizens of Israel they cannot be nationals.

It is a fundamental Zionist principle, embodied in the Basic Laws of Israel and expressed in the Declaration of the Establishment of the State of Israel, that the Palestinians *cannot* constitute a 'national minority'. Although all Israeli citizens are classified by what the translation from Hebrew calls 'nationality' for example, Jew, Arab, Druze, and by religion (Jew, Muslim, Christian), in practice the other 'nationalities' cannot, logically, have equal rights in a state where one of the 'nationalities', namely Jews, are in a superior position by virtue of the fact that Israel was declared a 'Jewish state' and not, as Zionists imply in public, a state of Jews, Arabs and other minority nationalities. Therefore, in Israel, the Palestinians are officially known as the Arabs of the Land of Israel (Arvei Eretz Israel). 'While their Jewishness is not sought after, their Palestinianness is denied.'[1]

The Palestinians of Israel comprise about 17 percent of the population of the Jewish state. They live in three main areas. The majority, some 50 percent, are in the Galilee, in northern Israel. Thirty percent live in 'the Triangle' in central Israel and the rest in the Negev. Seventy percent of the Israeli Palestinians are Muslim, 20 percent are Christian and 10 percent are Druze (see appendix 16).

Those Palestinians who remained in what became Israel did not automatically become Israeli citizens.[2] A non-Jew can never be a national of Israel although they can be a citizen. A non-Jew is considered a citizen only if 1) they were registered under the Registration of Inhabitants Ordinance on 1 March 1952; *and* 2) they were living in Israel on 1 April 1952; *and* 3) they were living in Israel or in an area which subsequently became Israeli territory from the date of the state's establishment until 1 April 1952.

Many of the Palestinian residents of Israel never registered during the first years of the state's existence because of difficulties created by Israeli military authorities. First, those Palestinian civilians who had been expelled or who fled from the war zone were not allowed to return to their homes when hostilities ceased. Second, the main legal framework for the suppression of the civil and political rights of the Palestinians, the British Defence (Emergency) Regulations of 1945, was applied.[3]

The Defence (Emergency) Regulations of 1945 were draconian laws inherited from the British and applied almost exclusively to the Palestinian citizens of Israel (some Jews have been subjected to them, for example, Jewish women married to Arab men). These laws were so odious that the future Israeli Minister of Justice, Yaacov Shapira, said in 1946 that

> even in Nazi Germany there were no such laws . . . Only in an occupied country do you find such a system resembling ours . . . It is our duty to tell the whole world that the defense regulations destroy . . . the very foundations of justice in this land.[4]

> *I hope that the Jewish frontiers of Palestine will be as great as Jewish energy for getting Palestine.*
>
> Chaim Weizmann
> *Chaim Weizmann: Excerpts from His Historic Statements, Writings and Addresses*, Jewish Agency for Palestine, 1952, p. 48.

In January 1950 the military government was formally and legally established, based on the Defence (Emergency) Regulations of 1945, to deal with the Arabs who still remained in Israel. Article 125 was the most notorious. It granted the military governor the power to proclaim any area a forbidden area. Thus, each Arab village was separated from the other and declared a closed area from which no one could leave or enter. Even Emile Habibi, a one-time Palestinian member of the Israeli Knesset, was for two years forbidden to leave his town except with a special permit to attend sessions of the Knesset.[5]

These oppressive laws were not applied to the Jewish citizens of Israel. An Israeli government report stated that 'Jews are not expected to have such permits and, in general, criminal actions are not brought against Jews when they offend against the provisions of Article 125.'[6]

The Palestinian citizens of Israel lived under this internal Israeli military occupation until 1966. Afterwards the Office of the Advisor to the Prime Minister on Arab Affairs emerged as the agency most directly responsible for the government's Arab policies.

Harassment of the Palestinian citizens of Israel continues. Many Palestinians are, under the Emergency Regulation of 1948, not allowed to travel freely. In August 1986 the Rector of Christ Evangelical Anglican Church in Nazareth, Canon Riah Abu al-

Assal, was forbidden to travel outside Israel for fear of what he might tell about life in Israel.[7]

For both the military authorities and the Arab Advisor's office, Arab economic underdevelopment made blackmail a very effective technique for keeping individual Arabs or Arab villages dependent on the authorities. Blacklisting has also been used, primarily by the Advisor's office in connection with the employment of young Palestinian intellectuals.

The Information Center-Arab Branch acts as the Advisor's liaison with the security services and maintains lists of high-school students who express Palestinian nationalist sympathies or who exhibit leadership qualities.[8]

Although Israel claims that the military government was abolished in 1966, in fact there was a mere transfer of authority to the 'Special Duties Branch' of the Israeli police.[9]

Another method used by Israel to enforce the dependence of Palestinians on the Jewish authorities is the issuing or refusal of building permits. The Palestinians are very vulnerable to this type of manipulation because of overcrowding in Arab villages from the constant expropriation of their lands. Building permits are granted or demolition orders rescinded only when the Palestinian citizen surrenders all claims to his land.[10]

All the land and buildings belonging to Palestinian refugees was formally seized through the Abandoned Areas Ordinance of 1948. It was followed by the Cultivation of Waste Lands Regulation which was not only applied to all land owned by the refugees but also lands owned by Palestinians who were (and are) citizens of the state.

Those Palestinians fortunate enough not to have been expelled suffered from another set of laws. The Absentee Property Law of 1950 extended the definition of absentee to include those Palestinians who left their place of residence temporarily (for example, to go to work in another town or to escape bombardment). The Land Acquisition Law of 1953 completed the Palestinian dispossession of 1948.

The Law for the Requistioning of Property in Times of Emergency of 1949 (which remained in force until 1958) allowed the government to 'requisition' Arab lands under the pretext of security and national defense. The land seized under the pretext of these laws was then transferred to irrevocable state ownership under the Land Acquisition (Validation of Acts and Compensation) Law of 1953. This law meant that the land could never be resold to Arabs.

The land question is important because the UN Partition Resolution of 1947 which was used, on the one hand, by the Zionists to justify the creation of Israel (see Chapter 11), is ignored when it expropriates Palestinian land.

Article 8 of chapter II of the Partition Resolution states that there shall be 'no expropriation of land owned by an Arab in the Jewish State', except for public purposes. Israel has, in fact, expropriated thousands of acres by using the Defence (Emergency) Regulations and other confiscatory measures, as mentioned above, in overt violation of the Partition Resolution.

Of the 370 new Jewish settlements established between 1948 and 1954, more than one third of Israel's Jewish population lives on expropriated Palestinian property and nearly a third (250,000) of new Jewish immigrants are settled in urban housing belonging to refugee Palestinians.[11] Former Israeli Defense Minister Moshe Dayan said that

> there is not a single Jewish village in this country that has not been built on the site of an Arab village [see appendices 18, 19 and 20].[12]

Hebrew University Professor Israel Shahak, chairman of the Israeli League for Human and Civil Rights, stated that:

> The truth about Arab settlements which used to exist in the area of the 'state' of Israel before 1948 is one of the most guarded secrets of Israeli life. No publication, book or pamphlet gives either their number or their location. This is done on purpose, so that the accepted official myth of an 'empty country' can be taught and accepted in the Israeli schools and told to visitors . . . The destroyed villages in almost all cases were destroyed completely, with their houses, garden walls and even cemeteries and tombstones, so that literally a stone does not remain standing, and visitors are passing and being told that 'it was all a desert'.[13]

The ability of the remaining Palestinians to function in an

economically viable situation was severely curtailed through the passage of the World Zionist Organization/Jewish Agency (Status) Law of 1952 which incorporated the constitution of the Jewish Agency into the Basic Laws of Israel (see chapter 6). Article 3 section (e) of the Jewish Agency constitution stated that the Agency shall promote colonization 'based on Jewish labor, and in all works and undertakings carried out or furthered by the Agency, it shall be deemed to be a matter of principle that Jewish labor be employed'.

It should be clear that there is no room for both peoples to live in this country . . . up to this point, Zionists have been content to 'buy land', but this is no way to establish a country for the Jews. A nation is created in one move . . . and in that case, there is no alternative to moving the Arabs to the neighboring countries . . .

Joseph Weitz, Jewish National Fund director responsible for Zionist colonization, 1940
My Diary and Letters to the Children, Massada, 1965, II, p. 181 (in Hebrew).

In Israel, the question of the presence of the Palestinians is called the 'Arab problem' or, euphemistically, the 'demographic problem'. The problem is most acute for the Zionists in the Galilee, in northern Israel. The military occupation of the Galilee was not altogether successful for the Israelis in 1948.

The Galilee was originally intended in the UN Partition Plan to be a part of the Arab state that was to have come into being. After the 1948 war Israel was unable to expel enough Palestinians to make them an insignificant minority in the Galilee. Even today they comprise, in certain sub-districts, a large majority.

Israelis have been worried that this large Arab population might dilute the Jewish purity of Israel. Since the goal of Zionism was to transform Palestine into a Jewish land, depopulating the land of Arabs quickly became a top priority. The Galilee region of Israel had always, and still does, demographically defy the Jewish character of Israel.

The plan to solve the 'demographic problem' was made most explicit by Joseph Nahmani, head of the Jewish National Fund from 1935–65, in a 1953 memo to then Minister of Defense, David

Ben-Gurion; this was entitled 'Project for the Judaization of the Galilee'. Nahmani wrote:

> Though Western Galilee has not been occupied it still has not been freed of its Arab population, as happened in other parts of this country. There are still fifty-one villages and the city of Nazareth whose inhabitants have not left.

His statements were made about *minority citizens of Israel* and not about some faraway enemy.

The strategy for the 'Judaization of the Galilee' was explained in an October 1975 Israeli Ministry of Agriculture publication:

> . . . the special problem of the Galilee region is that the Jewish population is out-numbered by the non-Jewish population . . .
>
> It is necessary to change the existing situation regarding the demographic ratio between the Jewish population and the non-Jewish . . .[14]

This concept of Judaizing is quite frightening to the non-Jewish population of Israel just as a policy of Christianizing New York would be to New Yorkers.

The pattern of Arab and Jewish apartness in Israel is most clear in the military sphere. The military constitutes the single largest and most important organization in the Israeli government and, in fact, in Israeli life. Forty percent of the country's budget is allocated for the military. All Jewish citizens, with few exceptions, are required to serve in the military and afterwards annually in the reserves. Participation in the military is the most salient and conspicuous feature of life in Israel.

Palestinian Arabs, though, except for the Druze, are not conscripted into the military. This de facto prohibition has enormous impact on the Arabs. The possession of veteran status is a prerequisite to a wide variety of jobs and public-assistance programs. For example, children whose parents served in the military are eligible for 40 percent more allowances from the National Insurance Institute. Arab children are not eligible. Since they are excluded from the ranks of the military Arabs are thus cut off and apart from the major dynamic processes of social integration and mobility which exist in Israel.[15]

Apartness has also been seen in the economic sphere itself as a result of the dominant force in the Israeli economy, the Histradrut, Israel's national labor union, which controls approximately 21 percent of Israel's industry. The Histradrut is more than a union; it is a welfare organization that was notorious in the 1930s for violently demonstrating against Jewish firms that employed Arabs. Arabs were not admitted until 1959.

The Histradrut has not, though, made a contribution to Jewish–Arab integration. Until very recently, in thousands of Histradrut-owned firms and factories, not one was located in an Arab village. Nor are there any Arabs among the more than 600 managers of industries owned by the Histradrut.[16]

Other examples of discrimination against the Palestinian citizens of Israel are exemplified in the fact that they are not allowed to become members of a kibbutz. There are no Palestinian airline pilots flying for El Al, the national airline. There are no Palestinian musicians in the Israeli Philharmonic. Only 4 percent of university students are Palestinians, although they make up 17 percent of the population.

Discrimination also takes other more obvious forms. For example, of the 1,860 officials listed in Israeli government ministries there were only twenty-six Arabs, all of whom worked for the offices responsible for their own religious or municipal affairs.[17] Arab citizens are not served by the Ministries of Housing, Education, Labor or the Interior but by special 'Arab Departments' for Arabs only.[18]

Government aid to Arab municipalities is nowhere near the level it is to Jewish municipalities. In 1976 only one of 104 Arab villages had a sewer system.[19]

Arab affairs are governed by the Office of the Advisor to the Prime Minister on Arab Affairs. Thus government institutions relate to the Jewish and Arab sectors in a highly segregated fashion. Arab clerks by and large do not work in offices which serve the Jewish population.

Israeli attitudes towards its Arab minority have been expressed in official pronouncements. For example, Uri Lubrani, Advisor to the Prime Minister on Arab Affairs from 1960–63, declared that the Israeli Palestinians were the 'sworn and everlasting enemies' of Israel.[20]

In 1976 the District Commissioner of the Galilee of the Ministry of the Interior, Israel Koenig, wrote a confidential memorandum entitled 'Handling the Arabs of Israel'. The report recommended the creation of a new political force in the Arab sector which the government would 'control' by means of a 'covert presence'. He also advocated the intensification of economic discrimination against Arabs.[21] In 1987 a secret document came to light in the Israeli press which outlined ways of tightening control over the Palestinian people in Israel.[22]

Israel's supporters, when discussing the Palestinians who are Israeli citizens, often stress the high standards of living they have achieved in comparison to other Arab countries. It is true that their standard of living is higher now than in 1948 and that it is higher than a few Arab states. It is also true that the achievements of the Arab sector are overwhelmingly due to the earnings of Arab workers in Jewish industries and agriculture.

But when this, as Israel calls it, 'prosperity' is measured in terms of the establishment of Arab businesses, the formation of financial institutions, or the diversification of agriculture, one can see that no Arab economic development has taken place. This was due primarily to discrimination in favor of the Jewish sector with respect to development projects of all kinds.

The argument comparing the economic situation of the Palestinians in Israel with the economic situation of other Arab states is absurd. It is like comparing the situation of Chinese-Americans with the situation of Chinese in China; it is not relevant nor germane to the issue, which is the situation of the Palestinians within Israel compared to others within Israel.

The Palestinians within Israel have been threatened with past policies of expulsion and intimations of future expulsion, rendering the claim that they are better off than their Arab neighbors spurious.

Although the Palestinians comprise 17 percent of Israel's population they are not, generally, privileged to share in the life of the country. For example, in 1962 they received only 1 percent of the government's housing allocation.[23] Twenty years later the figure was only slightly higher. Certain Arab areas of the country are not included under the development zones stipulated in the Law for the Encouragement of Capital Investments.[24]

The Palestinian position within Israel has not changed for the better. In fact, the mere presence and even existence of the Palestinians has long presented Zionism with a dilemma. It is apparent that, traditionally, the great majority of Zionists, as represented by the Arab policies of both the Labor Party and the Likud, have attempted to solve this dilemma through de-Arabization or, as Israel unabashedly terms it, Judaization. In conclusion, it is evident that the status of the Palestinians is that of an underclass and is likely to remain so.

Notes to Chapter 8

1. Khalil Nakhleh, *The Two Galilees*, Arab World Issues, Occasional Papers 7, AAUG, 1982, p. 12.
2. A Palestinian can never become a 'national' of Israel. On the citizenship–nationality distinction and its importance see chapter 6.
3. Israel supplemented this law, a holdover from the British Mandate government, with their own Emergency (Security Zones) Regulation 5709.
4. *Hapraklit*, February 1946, pp. 58–64, in Sabri Jiryis, *The Arabs of Israel*, trans. Inea Bushnaq, Monthly Review Press, 1976, p. 12.
5. Eric Rouleau, *Le Monde*, 11 March 1966.
6. 'Report of the State Controller on the Ministry of Defense for the Financial Year 1957–59', 9, 2 February 1959, p. 56, in Muhammad Farah, *Legal Status of Israel and the Occupied Territories*, Information Papers 15, AAUG, 1975, p. 16.
7. Cablegram, Palestine Human Rights Campaign, Chicago, IL., 1 August 1986.
8. *New Outlook*, XIV, 2, March 1971, pp. 10–24; Eli Rekhess, *A Survey of Israeli–Arab Graduates from Institutions of Higher Learning in Israel (1961–1971)*, Shiloah Institute for Middle Eastern Studies and African Studies Series, American Jewish Committee, 1974, pp. 30–31.
9. Sabri Jiryis, *Democratic Freedoms in Israel*, Institute for Palestine Studies, 1972, p. 44.

10. Ian Lustick, *Arabs in the Jewish State: Israel's Control of a National Minority*, University of Texas, 1980, p. 195.
11. Don Peretz, *Israel and the Palestine Arabs*, Middle East Institute, 1958, p. 144.
12. *Guardian*, Manchester, 14 November 1973.
13. ibid.
14. Saliba Chamis, 'The Battle over the Land', *Zuhaderech*, 17 March 1986, trans. in *Israleft*, 1 April 1976 and cited in 'The Land Question in Israel', *MERIP Reports*, 47, August 1977, p. 4.
15. Ian Lustick, op. cit., p. 94.
16. ibid, pp. 96–7.
17. *Israeli Government Yearbook 1976*.
18. Lustick, op. cit., p. 91.
19. ibid., p. 191.
20. Zeev Schiff, 'If I were an Arab', *Ha'aretz*, 4 April 1961, in Lustick, op. cit., p. 68.
21. Lustick, op. cit., pp. 68, 69.
22. The report was written by Moshe Arens and his Arab Affairs Advisor, Reserve General Amos Galbo'a, and reported in *Ha'aretz* and *Ma'ariv*, *Al Fajr*, Jerusalem, 1 November 1987.
23. *Israeli Government Yearbook 1962/1963*, p. 256.
24. Lustick, op. cit., p. 186.

Recommended Reading

Fouzi al-Asmar, *To be an Arab in Israel*, Institute for Palestine Studies, 1975.

Sabri Jiryis, *The Arabs in Israel*, Monthly Review Press, 1976.

Ian Lustick, *Arabs in the Jewish State: Israel's Control of a National Minority*, University of Texas Press, 1980.

Khalil Nakhleh, *The Two Galilees*, Arab World Issues, Occasional Papers 7, AAUG, 1982.

Basheer K. Nijim, *Toward the De-Arabization of Palestine/Israel 1945–1977*, Kendall/Hunt and the Jerusalem Fund for Education and Community Development, 1984.

Don Peretz, *Israel and the Palestine Arabs*, Middle East Institute, 1958.

Israel Shahak, ed., *The Non-Jew in the Jewish State: a Collection of Documents*, Israeli League for Human Rights, 1975.

Elia Zureik, *Palestinians in Israel: a Study in Internal Colonialism*, Routledge and Kegan Paul, 1979.

Chapter 9

The West Bank and Gaza

Israel has declared that its objective in the West Bank and Gaza is to abide by the principles of international law. Israel maintains that the West Bank and Gaza, which it captured in 1967, were 'liberated' and therefore the Fourth Geneva Convention does not apply to its occupation army nor to its settlements policy.

Israel has claimed that it is not confiscating land from the Palestinians on the West Bank and Gaza. Israel claims, in defense of its land acquisition policy, that the process is being carried out in accordance with the law in force in the West Bank.

Israel claims that its occupation is benign.

What are the Facts?

The West Bank, East Jerusalem and Gaza, along with the Sinai and the Golan Heights, were captured by Israeli forces in the June 1967 war.

The primary reason for Israel's retention of the West Bank and Gaza in the face of a hostile native Palestinian population rests on the principal motive embodied in the philosophy of Zionism itself: that this land is part of historic Eretz Israel (Land of Israel) and belongs to the Jews in the same sense that the rest of Palestine belongs to the Jews.

According to Zionism, the West Bank and Gaza are part of the Land of Israel to which the Jews have an historic right (see chapter 16). Zionists have been quite consistent in insisting that the West Bank and Gaza belongs to, in fact is the heart of, Israel (see maps 4 and 5).

When Israel came in control of the West Bank and Gaza in 1967 it was populated by more than one million Palestinians. The problem faced by successive Israeli governments has been to increase the Jewish, and decrease the Palestinian, population and weaken the Palestinian capacity for organization and resistance. Settlement building supported by the military has characterized the Judaization of the West Bank and Gaza. On the other hand the Palestinian population has been reduced through destruction of political leadership, prevention of economic development, physical separation of the Palestinian population from one another by road building, oppressive military occupation and outright expulsion.

The most important requirement for Judaizing the West Bank and Gaza is the possession of land.[1] From 1967 until 1979 the most frequently used method for acquiring land was 'requisition for military purposes'. After 1979 the most prevalent method was by declaring areas to be 'state' land. Since the 'state' is a Jewish state, lands that are seized are immediately turned over to Jewish individuals or corporations in a process Israel calls 'redeeming the land', so that it cannot then be resold to Arabs

According to Israeli Military Orders (amending Jordanian law) which are applied to the land but not to the non-Jewish inhabitants of the West Bank, 'redeemed' land is the inalienable property of the 'Jewish people' and can never be resold to an Arab. The most recent figures for West Bank land already acquired by Israel range from 27 to 64 percent of the total area of the West Bank.[2]

Israel, in order to accomplish its goals on the West Bank and Gaza, pursues a number of different avenues which all have the practical effect of securing land for Jewish settlements.

Israel uses regional schemes and road planning, devised to serve Israeli interests and to cut off Palestinians from one another and prevent them from developing their land. Two other methods of land acquisition include declaring property to be 'abandoned', or 'closed' for military purposes.

Israel confers on the Palestinians in the West Bank and Gaza a legal status equivalent to that of alien residents with none of the rights, privileges and guarantees normally enjoyed by nationals or permanent residents. Those Palestinians who were outside their homes in the West Bank and Gaza when they were captured in 1967 do not have any status.

Israel subjects the Palestinian population in the Occupied Territories to repressive laws created by the military authorities without Palestinian participation or consultation.

Israel pursues policies of harrassment and intimidation of the population and denial of its basic human rights, including the right to self-determination.

Although Israel claims it is not a belligerent occupier both the United Nations and the United States consider Israel to be a belligerent occupant of the West Bank and Gaza and hold the position that the Fourth Geneva Convention applies to Israel's occupation of the territories captured by force in the June 1967 war.

According to the laws of belligerent occupation, the occupying state must preserve the laws which were previously in force in the area occupied. Article 23 (g) of the Hague Regulations forbids the occupying power 'to destroy or seize enemy property, unless such destruction or seizure be imperatively demanded by the necessities of war'. Article 49 of the Fourth Geneva Convention declares that 'the occupying power shall not depart or transfer parts of its civilian population into the territory it occupies'. Israel violates both these laws.

Israel claims that it is doing nothing wrong. But the declared objective of the World Zionist Organization is

> to disperse maximally large Jewish populations in areas of high settlement priority, using small national inputs and in a relatively short period by using the settlement potential of the West Bank and to achieve the incorporation [of the West Bank] into the [Israeli] national system.[3]

The priorities this master plan sets are meant to interconnect existing and future settlements and to restrict Palestinian growth. The plan bears the official stamp of the Israeli government and, according to Meron Benvenisti, former deputy mayor of Jerusalem, 'it cannot be viewed as other than the official land use plan for the West Bank'.[4]

In order to accomplish these plans it has been necessary for Israel to install different laws than those which were in force when the territory was captured from Jordan. Israel did this with Military Order 418 which effectively abolished the Jordanian Planning Law of 1966 which required local participation in development and planning operations. Now, as a result of the Israeli military order, all land-use planning in the West Bank is in the hands of military officers appointed by the military occupation army. The master plan shows that it is meant neither to benefit the Palestinian population nor to ensure the security of the army. Therefore, according to international law, what Israel is doing in the West Bank and Gaza with regard to the takeover of the land and the settlement of Jews is illegal.[5]

The legal effect of Israel's occupation of the West Bank and Gaza is unique. Israel does not recognize the native Palestinians as Israeli citizens. West Bank Palestinians generally hold Jordanian passports and are recognized as Jordanian nationals by Israel. Yet Israel does not recognize the land upon which they exist as part of Jordanian territory and therefore does not believe international law applies to occupation of these territories. But at the same time Israel appeals to international law when it claims that it holds these territories in order to protect its security.

As with any military occupation of a country, Israel severely restricts the Palestinians who are unable to enter a sizeable portion of their own country. There are special restrictions which limit the Palestinians' freedom of movement.[6] For example, the use of general curfews applies only to Palestinians; Jews are not affected.

Israel's policies towards the economies of the West Bank and Gaza have a profound effect on the lives of Palestinians. These policies exploit for economic gain and suppress Palestinian nationalism. In addition to the large amount of land seized from Palestinians other economic benefits accrue to Israel, for example, from water use. Palestinians are allotted only a quarter of the region's water while the rest is piped to Israel. Israel also enjoys open markets to the Occupied Territories. The West Bank and

Gaza are the second largest export market for Israel after the United States; there are no trade barriers to restrict the selling of Israeli goods to Palestinian markets. But Israeli laws prohibit Palestinian goods, competitive with Israeli products, from being sold in Israel. Israel also restricts Palestinian access to money loans for development by not allowing non-Israeli banks to operate in the Occupied Territories. The two that do operate with permission have limited access to credit.[7]

Barring forcible mass expulsion of the Palestinians, Israel does not expect to have enough Jewish settlers in the West Bank to annex it de jure for several years or maybe decades. Therefore, it is creating a legal relationship with the West Bank to be employed in the interim. The problems faced by Israel in its attempt to expand its borders are 1) how to apply Israeli law to the Jewish settlements while the West Bank is not under Israeli sovereignty; 2) how to avoid applying Israeli law to the Palestinians in the West Bank; and 3) how to reconcile this unusual legal situation with international law.

To solve the first problem, Israel extended its laws extra-territorially thereby giving Jewish settlements a different legal status. Extra-territoriality was established through regular laws passed by the Knesset and by Military Orders. Military Orders established a separate administration for the settlements, in the form of local councils.

These Jewish local councils on the West Bank enjoy, under the law, a far greater measure of autonomy than the Palestinian village councils. The Jewish councils are permitted to elect their own leaders while the mayors of Palestinian villages are appointed by the Israeli military commander. These 'mayors' of Palestinian villages are usually Israeli military reserve officers or carefully selected quislings.

Jewish councils have also been empowered to exercise wider functions and have greater latitude to impose taxes than is the case in Palestinian villages.

The most significant restriction, which applies solely to Palestinian villages, is the need to request permission from the military authorities to borrow money and accept gifts. Jewish settlements have no such restriction.

Jewish councils also receive state services. The budgetary allocations for these exclusive services is included in the budgets of the Israeli ministries.

Israel claims that it ended the military administration of the Occupied Territories in 1981 through Military Order 947 and established a civilian administration. In truth, Military Order 947 established the civilian administration and its head is chosen by the military commander. All the powers of the head of the civilian administration are delegated to him by the military. The entire civilian administration is, therefore, subsidiary to the military area commander and accountable to him. The so-called 'civilian' administration is situated within the military base at Beit El and entrance to it is restricted.

The means by which Israel avoids applying Israeli law to the Palestinians yet still retains judicial control over the West Bank is through a three-tiered judicial system. The first system of justice is the existing local courts. These courts have had most of the jurisdiction stripped away and, furthermore, are in need of improvements concerning court services, inspections and other areas of modernization. Israel has no interest in improving their efficiency.

The second system of justice is the military courts and tribunals. This system is highly efficient. The Palestinian offenders before military courts have no absolute right of legal representation. Israel claims that they do have such a right, but the relevant order, Military Order 29, says that the right to legal representation is subject to the discretion of the Israeli prison commander. Furthermore, Palestinian offenders are presented with judgments based on confessions or statements written in Hebrew, a language few can understand. Judgments by the military courts are not subject to appeal outside the military judicial system.

The third system of justice is the Israeli civilian courts in the West Bank. These courts may try Israeli settlers in criminal matters.

Even before the Palestinian Uprising in late 1987 and 1988 which saw massive and severe Israeli oppression of civilians, resulting in more than 300 deaths and thousands of severe beatings, there was considerable evidence to refute Israel's claim that its occupation is 'benign'.

During the two-year period between March 1977 and January 1979 the American Consulate General in Jerusalem sent over forty reports to the US State Department documenting Israeli torture of Palestinian prisoners. All five American officers of the consular section participated in the research and authorization of these reports.[8] Alexandra Johnson, one of the consular officers, was removed by the US State Department after pressure from Israel's supporters in Washington.

In 1977 the renowned London *Sunday Times* 'Insight' Team, using an exhaustive series of investigative techniques, revealed that torture of Palestinians is a regular, methodical and officially sanctioned device by Israel in the West Bank and Gaza. Since Israel's supporters describe all negative reports about Israel as anti-Semitic, this fear kept all American newspapers from reporting the findings except the *Boston Globe*.[9]

Another report included a study of human rights' violations commissioned by the World Council of Churches which produced numerous affidavits documenting systematic brutality against the Palestinian population.[10]

The International Commission of Jurists also produced a report documenting systematic abridgments of academic freedom on the West Bank. The extensive censorship by Israeli military occupation authorities even banned William Shakespeare's *The Merchant of Venice*, among a thousand other books.

Israel banned *all* books dealing with Palestinian–Arab nationalist feelings and national heritage.[11] The depiction in any form of the following has been banned: the Palestinian flag, calligraphy including the word 'Palestine' and guns, grenades or rifles.

Israeli laws against Palestinian freedom of the press are severe. In August 1986 Na'ama Al Hilu of the Women's Work Committee in Jabaliya Refugee Camp in Gaza went on trial for 'possession of forbidden literature'. The 'forbidden literature' consisted of material on women, peace and equality and a magazine that appears on International Women's Day.[12]

Amnesty International reported in 1984:

Palestinians from the Occupied Territories arrested for security reasons and interrogated by the Shin Beth (Israeli internal secret police) . . . in a number of different detention centers have been hooded, handcuffed and forced to stand without moving for many hours at a time for several days, and have been exposed while naked to cold showers or cold air ventilators for long periods of time. Detainees have also been deprived of food, sleep and toilet and medical facilities and have been subjected to abuse, insults and threats against themselves and the female members of their families. [13]

Every imaginable form of harassment has been devised by the Israelis to encourage emigration. Nothing escapes the Israeli authorities' obsession with the expression of Palestinian culture. For example, Fathi Ismail Ghabin, an artist from Gaza, was sentenced to one year in prison in 1984 for a painting found objectionable by the authorities.

Although Zionists still claim, but not as vigorously as before, that the occupation is 'benign', the images the man on the street can see every evening on television of Palestinian children throwing rocks at heavily armed Israeli troops who shoot them down has dissolved this propaganda line. The degree of harshness to the occupation sharpened in 1988 so that a youth throwing a stone can be slapped with a twenty-year prison sentence. [14] Besides, the phrase 'benign occupation' is a contradiction in terms. The main reason for Israel's oppressive policies on the West Bank is the desire to fully annex the West Bank to Israel without the problem of a native population.

Any notion that Israel's occupation is benign was finally laid to rest as a result of the Uprising in 1988. After five months of demonstrations there were more Palestinians in Israeli custody without charge than there were blacks in South Africa, proportional to the population. Since 1967 more than 300,000 Palestinian men, women and children have been imprisoned in Israeli jails at one time or another. [15] This represents one fifth of the population and is a phenomenon unmatched even in Nazi-occupied Europe. After eight months of demonstrations against Israeli occupation more than 200 Palestinians had been killed. Israeli response to the Uprising changed periodically, depending on the situation. In April 1988 Prime Minister Yitzhak Shamir promised that the Palestinians would be crushed 'like grasshoppers'. [16] The Israeli Justice Minister called for the demolition of dozens of Palestinian homes and the expulsion of the Palestinians. The Israeli Religion Minister called for smashing 'the skull of the viper of death'. [17]

Yitzhak Rabin, the Defense Minister, gave Israeli armed civilians in the West Bank the right to shoot freely any Palestinians if they were suspected of holding firebombs.[18]

Zionists recognize that for Israel to remain a Jewish state it cannot be put in a position whereby it affords rights to 1.3 million Palestinians as citizens on top of the 700,000 who already receive these. The only solution is either to withdraw from the territories or to expel the Palestinian population. The first choice has been rejected ever since the West Bank was captured.

Israeli policy since 1967 has been the continuous establishment of Jewish settlements that prohibit Palestinians from living there. This policy has manifested itself in the establishment of over 100 exclusively Jewish settlements by successive Israeli governments and by the Israeli declaration that the West Bank and Gaza not only belong to Israel but are, in fact, the heart of Israel.

Some people talk of expelling 700,000 to 800,000 Arabs in the event of a new war, and instruments have been prepared.

Aharon Yariv, former chief of Israeli military intelligence, 1980
Inquiry, 8 December 1980.

All Zionists, whether they believe that Israel should or should not retain the West Bank and Gaza, also believe, if they are logically consistent, that if the Zionist claim and right to pre-1967 Israel is legitimate, based on historical and Biblical grounds, then its claim to the West Bank and Gaza is equally legitimate.

Those Israelis who argue against retaining the Occupied Territories make the argument from practical political considerations. They are a small minority in Israel. The vast majority of Israelis do not wish to relinquish the Occupied Territories.

Notes to Chapter 9

1. For more on the Israeli concept of 'Judaizing' see chapter 8.

2. The former Israeli deputy mayor of Jerusalem, Meron Benvenisti, estimates 40 percent of the land has been acquired; *The West Bank Data Project: a Survey of Israel's Policies*, American Enterprise Institute, 1984, p. 19. Another study says that 70 percent of the West Bank could be made available to Jews by various means of acquisition open to Israeli authorities; see Don Peretz, *The West Bank*, Westview, 1986, pp. 59, 66.
3. Benvenisti, *West Bank Data Project*. See appendices 9 and 10 on the covenant between the government of Israel and the World Zionist Organization and Jewish Agency.
4. Quoted in Raja Shehadeh, *Occupier's Law: Israel and the West Bank*, prepared for Law in the Service of Man, the West Bank Affiliate of the International Commission of Jurists, Institute for Palestine Studies, 1985, p. 51. For more on the Israeli concept of 'Judaizing' see ch. 8.
5. Two plans already published by the military Planning Department are known as Plan 1/82 and Road Plan no. 50.
6. Military Order 5 and Military Order 378, Article 90.
7. Dan Sisken, 'Economics under Occupation: the West Bank and Gaza', *The Washington Report on Middle East Affairs*, May 1988, p. 13.
8. 'Israel and Torture', *Journal of Palestine Studies*, 34, Winter 1980, pp. 79–117.
9. London, *Sunday Times*, 19 June 1977.
10. *Human Rights Violations in the West Bank: in Their Own Words*, affidavits collected by Law in the Service of Man, World Council of Churches, 1983.
11. Adam Roberts, Boel Joergensen and Frank Newman, *Academic Freedom under Israeli Military Occupation: Report of WUS/ICJ Mission of Enquiry into Higher Education in the West Bank and Gaza*, World University Service (UK) and International Commission of Jurists, 1984.
12. Cablegram, Palestine Human Rights Campaign, Chicago, IL., 1 August 1986.
13, *Torture in the Eighties*, Amnesty International, 1984, pp. 223–4.
14. Military Order No. 1108. See Raija-Leena Punamaki, 'Experiences of Torture, Means of Coping, and Level of Symptoms among Palestinian Political Prisoners', *Journal of Palestine Studies*, 68, Summer 1988, pp. 81–96.
15. George Katsiaficas, *Boston Globe*, 5 June 1988.
16. *New York Times*, 7 April 1988.
17. *New York Times*, 9 April 1988.
18. *New York Times*, 14 June 1988.

Recommended Reading

American Friends Service Committee, *The Compassionate Peace*, Hill and Wang, 1982.

Naseer Aruri, ed., *Occupation: Israel over Palestine*, AAUG, 1983.

Israeli Settler Violence in the Occupied Territories: 1980–1984, Palestine Human Rights Campaign, 1985.

'Israel's Strategy of Occupation', *MERIP Reports*, 116, July–August 1983.

Felicia Langer, *With My Own Eyes: Israel and the Occupied Territories 1967–1973*, Ithaca Press, 1975.

Ann Lesch, *Political Perceptions of the Palestinians in the West Bank and the Gaza Strip*, Middle East Institute, 1980.

Sally V. and W. Thomas Mallison, *Settlements and the Law: a Juridical Analysis of the Israeli Settlements in the Occupied Territories*, American Education Trust, 1982.

Raja Shehadeh, *Occupier's Law: Israel and the West Bank*, prepared for Law in the Service of Man, the West Bank Affiliate of the International Commission of Jurists, Institute for Palestine Studies, 1985, p. 51.

Torture in the 1980s, Amnesty International, 1984.

Chapter 10

Israel and Peace

Peace in the Middle East will, at a minimum, involve trading lands held by Israel for recognition withheld by the Arab states. Peace will require the establishment of a Palestinian state and guarantees for Israel's security.

What are Israel's positions on this possibility? First, is Israel willing to trade land for peace? Second, has Israel accepted United Nations (UN) Resolution 242 which stipulates that it should withdraw from the territories it invaded in 1967 and that the Arabs states should recognize Israel? Finally, how will the settlements constructed by Israel in the Occupied Territories affect chances for peace?

As for the first question, Israel claims that everything is negotiable and it would withdraw from the Arab territories pending a peace agreement recognizing its security requirements.

Concerning the second question, Israel claims that it has accepted UN Resolution 242 (see appendix 12), but that the resolution does not *require* Israel to withdraw from all the territories it captured in 1967.

On the third question, Israel has insisted that it must retain large parts, if not all, of captured Arab territories, because the 1967 armistice lines provide more security than do the 1948 lines and because its settlements there need security.

If I was an Arab leader I would never make [peace] with Israel. That is natural: we have taken their country.

David Ben-Gurion
in Nahum Goldmann, *The Jewish Paradox*, Weidenfeld and Nicolson,
1978, p. 99.

What are the Facts?

Is Israel willing to trade land for peace? Official Israeli statements usually refer to Israel's willingness to do so, at the same time as Israeli leaders say they will never return to the 1967 borders. These are contradictory claims, so what does Israel mean?

First, 'Israel', the state, is unique in being geographically different from 'Israel', the land. When the state of Israel was established its international boundaries were intentionally left undeclared and undefined. In the minds of its Zionist founders, the 'Israel' of 1948 was a truncated state that did not fill out the actual territorial expanse of 'Israel' the land, that is, the Land of Israel (Eretz Israel). Zionist leaders, at that time, wished to leave open the possibility that Israel could expand its borders to conform fully with the boundaries of what they considered to be 'historic' Israel.

When the West Bank, Gaza and East Jerusalem were captured from the Arabs in 1967, Israel claimed, and maintains today, that these lands were not captured, but were 'liberated', since they are, for the Zionists, the heart of 'historic' Israel.

To this day Israel has not declared its borders. Official maps, though, indicate what Israel believes its borders should be. Maps 4 and 5 represent the most important elements of official Zionist thinking in Israel as to 'Eretz Israel'. All the land that has come under control of the Israeli army since 1967 and which it still controls is considered part of 'Eretz Israel'.[1]

These occupied lands, the Lebanon south of the Litani River, the West Bank, East Jerusalem, Gaza and the Golan Heights, the only lands described by UN Resolution 242 (except for the Litani), are considered part of Israel and therefore show that Israel is not willing to trade land.

Map 4   'Israel' According to the Labor Party

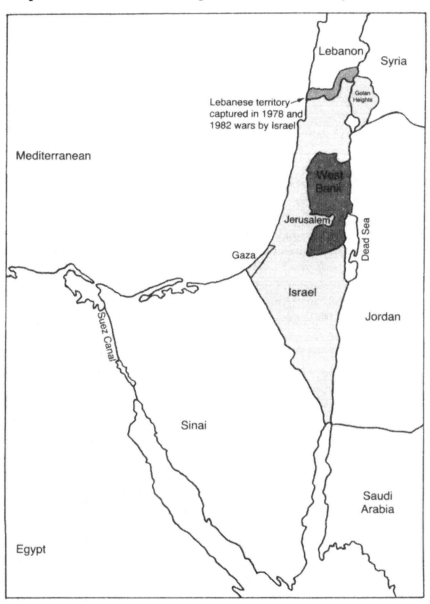

Shown with 1967 ceasefire boundaries.

■ Proposed Israeli territory with local Palestinian autonomy.

▨ 'Israeli security zone'.

Map 5   *'Eretz Israel' According to the Likud Party*

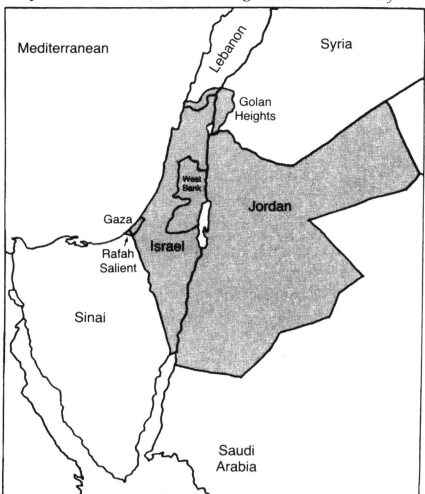

To lay the matter to rest, Prime Minister Yitzhak Shamir said, of the occupied West Bank and Gaza, that 'Israelis will continue to reside in those areas'. As far as UN Resolution 242's call to withdraw to the 1948 armistice lines, Shamir said, 'Israel will not entertain any notion of a return to those lines or anything approximating them. On this point there is, in Israel, virtually universal agreement.'[2]

Has Israel accepted UN Resolution 242 and how does it interpret the Resolution? The Resolution calls upon Israel to withdraw from the territories occupied in the 1967 war. The Resolution was passed after months of negotiations which sought clarification of the key areas of disagreement between Israel and the Arab states.

The Arab states insisted upon full Israeli withdrawal prior to the end of belligerency. Israel, on the other hand, held out for direction negotiations and a 'package settlement' in which withdrawal would occur after the conclusion of a peace agreement.[3]

Israel says that it has accepted UN Resolution 242 in principle; but its actions are to the contrary. First, Israel considers the territories occupied to be a part of the Land of Israel and shows no intention of withdrawing. Secondly, since 1967 successive Israeli governments, under both the Labor Party and the Likud, have established more than 100 colonial settlements on Arab land, settling about 50,000 Jews. These settlements are in deliberate defiance of other UN Resolutions and of international law which prohibits such settlements on captured land. Thirdly, Israel has already annexed two portions of the captured land, East Jerusalem and the Golan Heights, thereby annulling its professed willingness to withdraw from the captured territories.

Israeli officials often cite Israel's withdrawal from the Sinai as an example of its good faith in negotiating 'land for peace'. They fail to mention that 1) the Sinai is not part of Eretz Israel;[4] 2) that a *tactical* withdrawal served a *strategic* purpose, namely, neutralizing Egypt and Israel's southern front in order to solve its Palestinian problem in the West Bank and eliminate the Palestine Liberation Organization in Lebanon; and 3) that the United States provided what amounts to a $3 billion bribe ($1,000 for every Jewish national of Israel) to secure the diplomatic victory of the Egyptian–Israeli agreement at Camp David. The United States also built two new air bases for Israel for free.

Israel argues that the key phrase in UN Resolution 242 calling for Israeli withdrawal from the Occupied Territories does not mean that it must withdraw from *all* the territories. The resolution calls for 'withdrawal of Israeli armed forces from territories occupied in the recent conflict', i.e., the June 1967 war. Israel points to the omission of the definite article 'the' in the phrase 'from territories occupied', to support their claim that they are *not* required to withdraw from all the Occupied Territories, but only to the extent necessitated by the establishment of 'secure and recognized boundaries' (to which reference is made subsequently in the Resolution). Hence, Israel argues that it is entitled, within the terms of the Resolution, to retain East Jerusalem, the West Bank and Gaza.

The Israeli argument is invalid because it ignores the fact that the references in the Resolution to 'withdrawal' and to 'secure and recognized boundaries' are subject to the general principle of the 'inadmissibility of the acquisition of territory by war' which is stated in the preamble to the Resolution and which governs all that follows.

The significance of the missing 'the' is that the Resolution was drafted so as not to exclude minor modifications of the existing (pre-1967) borders which might be mutually agreeable *provided* that such modifications did not materially offend against the general principle of the inadmissibility of the acquisition of territory by war. The classic statement of this interpretation of the Resolution was furnished by US Secretary of State, William Rogers, in 1969:

> 'We believe that while recognized political boundaries must be established, and agreed upon by the parties, any changes in the existing lines should not reflect the weight of conquest and should be confined to insubstantial alterations required for mutual security. We do not support expansionism. We believe troops must be withdrawn as the Resolution provides.[5]

This statement stands on the record as the official position of the US government twenty years later.

The Israelis reject this interpretation. Zionists also argue that, under President Ronald Reagan, this interpretation had been rejected and that Reagan supports Israeli settlement and retention of the West Bank. While it is true that Reagan made such public statements he has also said that the Palestinians should return to their homes![6] As most observers know, President Reagan often made mutually exclusive comments, or 'misspoke', and therefore one needs to look at the clarifications by the US State Department for the American position on any issue. The official position remains the same as when it was stated by Secretary Rogers.

The undeniable fact is that the French (and Russian) texts of Resolution 242, which are equally authentic as UN records, do not omit the definite article 'the' from the phrase 'from occupied territories'. As argued above the English text does not specifically exclude the possibility of total withdrawal; it merely leaves the door open to something less. It does not speak of withdrawal from 'some' or 'parts' of the Occupied Territories. It specifies generally 'withdrawal from territories occupied'.

The 'creation of facts', that is, settlements on the West Bank and Gaza, are the clearest indices, along with statements by a variety of Israeli leaders, that Israel does not accept UN Resolution 242.

In the light of Israeli rejection of UN Resolution 242 US insistence that bilateral negotiation between Israel and the PLO be conditional upon the latter's recognition of the same Resolution appears cynical as well as confusing. Even though the Resolution does not even mention the Palestinians the PLO has said that it accepts 242.[7]

A third argument Israel uses to justify retaining the territories occupied in 1967 rests upon its security needs and the fact that there are now more than 100 settlements on the West Bank alone that cannot be abandoned. Israel argues that the territories occupied in 1967 provide more defensible lines and greater warning in the event of attack. Some Israeli commentators point to the October 1973 war to justify how necessary it is for them to retain the lands captured from the Arabs in 1967. Otherwise, they argue, they would have had to fight the war on their 'borders' or inside 1967 Israel. This argument stands logic on its head: it was after all Israel's own refusal to give up the Occupied Territories that led to the 1973 war. Secondly, the more settlements established on conquered territory, the more land is needed to provide 'security'. There then can never be, under this logic, any withdrawal or trading of land for peace.

We should there [in Palestine] form a portion of the rampart of Europe against Asia, an outpost of civilization as opposed to barbarism.

Theodor Herzl
The Jewish State, London, 1896, p. 29.

For their part the Arabs are convinced that Israel's concern with 'security' is a camouflage for the expansion of its borders. Zionist intentions regarding territory have a long and well-documented history that dates to 1897, the year when Theodor Herzl convened the first Zionist Congress. Since then subsequent Zionist Congresses have consistently laid claim to lands far beyond what Israel controls today. Theodor Herzl's diaries described a Jewish state, the frontiers of which were 'in the north the mountains facing Cappadocia [in Turkey], in the south, the Suez Canal and in the east, the Euphrates [see map 6].[8]

Map 6 'Eretz Israel' as Envisioned by Theodor Herzl – 1904

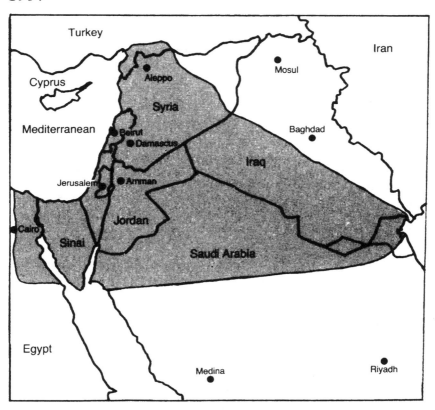

Shown with 1967 ceasefire boundaries.
Source: Theodor Herzl, *The Complete Diaries*, II, p. 711.

The abundance of war-like statements made by Israeli leaders confirms its bellicose intentions. In the opinion of most Arabs the image that Israel enjoys in the United States appears fanciful.

Zionists are fond of evoking the image of a David and Goliath in describing their confrontation with their Arab neighbors. The statements of their leaders belie such a description. David Ben-Gurion described the strategic aims of Israel in 1948 as follows:

> . . . we should prepare to go over to the offensive with the aim of smashing Lebanon, Transjordan and Syria . . . When we smash the [Arab] Legion's strength and bomb Amman, we will eliminate Transjordan too, and then Syria will fall. If Egypt still dares to fight on, we shall bomb Port Said, Alexandria, and Cairo.[9]

Menachem Begin said in the Knesset on 12 October 1955:

> I deeply believe in launching preventive war against the Arab States without further hesitation. By doing so we will achieve two targets: firstly, the annihilation of Arab power; and secondly, the expansion of our territory.

Defense Minister Moshe Dayan said:

> During the last 100 years our people have been in a process of building up the country and the nation, of expansion, of getting additional Jews and additional settlements in order to expand the borders here. Let no Jew say that the process has ended. Let no Jew say that we are near the end of the road.[10]

Is Israel's strategic argument for the retention of occupied territory valid? Many of these arguments have been outdated by the evolution of military technology.

Real security for Israel would be more likely found in recognizing the Palestinians' right to exist and by accepting the various peaceful resolutions offered by the Arabs

The first genuine Arab peace offer came directly after the establishment of Israel from King Abdullah of Transjordan.[11] Other offers also came, for instance, in 1970 when Egyptian President Gamal Nasser declared his country's willingness to institute a durable peace with Israel.[12] There was no response from Israel.

In February 1971 Nasser's successor, Anwar Sadat, offered a

full peace treaty to Israel, which it rejected, although international consensus supported the Sadat offer which conformed to the US position.[13]

In 1975, Syrian President, Hafiz al-Assad, in an interview with Arnaud de Borchgrave of *Newsweek* magazine said his fundamental position was to make a peace treaty with Israel. Israel ignored the offer and claimed that it was a propaganda statement directed at the United States.[14]

In 1982 the Fez Plan of the Arab League called for guarantees of peace for all states in the region. This declaration was scoffed at by Israel.

The PLO has also on numerous occasions stated its willingness to recognize Israel through mutual simultaneous recognition. On 21 October 1987 Yasser Arafat, the chairman of the PLO, said that he was ready to meet any Israeli to discuss peace. This significant gesture towards peace was ignored by the Israelis and barely covered by the Western news media.[15] In an interview on 10 March 1988 with two *New York Times* correspondents Mr Arafat, when asked if he was prepared to make peace with the Israeli government, responded, 'Yes, definitely.'[16]

At the Arab summit meeting held in June 1988 the press spokesman for PLO chairman Yasser Arafat, Bassam Abu Sharif, circulated a statement that called for direct negotiations between Israel and the Palestinians. Israel did not respond directly to this offer but described it as propaganda.

In November and December 1988 the PLO launched a major peace initiative that renounced all forms of terrorism, recognized UN Resolution 242, and recognized the existence of Israel. Arafat spoke directly to the Israelis, 'let us make peace'. Israel described the peace offering as 'double talk'.[17]

The typical Israeli response to Palestinian peace offers was expressed by former Prime Minister, Yitzhak Rabin, when he said that 'the only place the Israelis could meet the Palestinian guerillas was on the field of battle'.[18]

Peace occurs when enemies agree to stop fighting. They can agree to stop fighting once they agree to talk to one another. The Arab–Israeli conflict is the conflict between Zionists and Palestinians. The legitimate representative of the Zionists is the state or government of Israel. The legitimate representative of the Palestinians is the Palestine Liberation Organization. The PLO has said that it will talk to Israel and Israel has said that it will never talk to the PLO.

Notes to Chapter 10

1. The territory that Israel has either returned to the Arabs, for example, the Sinai, or withdrawn from, for example, Lebanon north of the Litani, are not considered to be a part of Eretz Israel by Zionism.
2. Yitzhak Shamir, 'Israel's Role in a Changing Middle East', *Foreign Affairs*, LX, 4, Spring 1982, pp. 792, 793.
3. William B. Quandt, *Decade of Decisions: American Policy toward the Arab–Israeli Conflict, 1967–1976*, University of California Press, 1977, pp. 64–5.
4. Only in the most extreme version of 'Israel' considered by Theodor Herzl does one find the Sinai as part of Eretz Israel. See map 2.
5. *New York Times*, 11 December 1969.
6. ibid., 5 February 1983.
7. For Palestinian acceptance of Resolution 242, see appendix 22 and excerpts from Yasser Arafat's speech to the UN General Assembly in *New York Times*, 14 December 1988.
8. Theodor Herzl, *The Complete Diaries*, II, p. 711.
9. Quoted in Noam Chomsky, *The Fateful Triangle: The United States, Israel and the Palestinians*, South End, 1983, pp. 162–3.
10. *Ma'ariv*, 7 July 1968.
11. See Avi Shlaim, *Collusion across the Jordan: King Abdullah, the Zionist Movement, and the Partition of Palestine*, Clarendon Press, 1988.
12. *Le Monde*, 19 February 1970.
13. John Kimche, *There Could Have been Peace*, Dial, 1973, p. 286.
14. In Moshe Ma'oz, *Asad: the Sphinx of Damascus, a Political Biography*, Weidenfeld and Nicolson, 1988, pp. 98–101.
15. A one-column-inch update appeared on p. 23 of the *Boston Globe*, 22 October 1987.
16. *New York Times*, 12 March 1988.
17. *New York Times*, 22 June 1988, and 14 December 1988 for Arafat's speech. Also see appendix 22.
18. ibid., 21 March 1977.

Recommended Reading

A Compassionate Peace: a Future for the Middle East, a report prepared for the American Friends Service Committee, Hill and Wang, 1982.

Noam Chomsky, *The Fateful Triangle: The United States, Israel and the Palestinians*, South End, 1983.

Lawrence Davidson, 'Israeli Reactions to Peace in the Middle East', *Journal for Palestine Studies*, 28, Summer 1978, pp. 34–47.

Avi Shlaim, *Collusion across the Jordan: King Abdullah, the Zionist Movement, and the Partition of Palestine*, Clarendon Press, 1988.

Chapter 11

Did the United Nations Create Israel?

Sometimes Israel and its supporters claim that the United Nations Partition Plan of 1947 created Israel. The claim refers to the creation of the state of Israel as an international fact, as a legitimate state recognized by the international community. The Treaty of Lausanne, signed between Turkey and the allies in 1923, had stipulated that Turkey renounce, among other things, suzerainty over Ottoman Palestine which had already been put under British Mandate by the League of Nations. Since the United Nations was the successor to the League it therefore, so goes the argument, had the legal right to partition the country.

Zionists still invoke the UN Partition Plan as an item of obligatory stature that the Arabs had, contrary to international adjudication, willfully 'disobeyed', they also say that this rejection was tantamount to Arab forfeiture of any future claim to Palestine. It is also implied that the Zionists respected the partition resolution and other UN resolutions concerning Palestine (see maps 9 and 10).

What are the Facts?

What is the historical background to the Partition Plan? Britain, unable and unwilling to continue its governance of Palestine, asked the United Nations to resolve the issue behind the civil strife between Palestinians and Zionists. In 1947 the United Nations General Assembly created a commission of inquiry, the United Nations Special Committee on Palestine (UNSCOP), to propose a solution to the conflict in Palestine. The committee was composed of eleven states: India, Iran, Canada, Australia, Uruguay, Guatemala, Peru, the Netherlands, Sweden, Czechoslovakia and Yugoslavia. This committee, which had no Arab or African members, recommended to the General Assembly that Palestine be divided into a Jewish and an Arab state. On 29 November 1947 the UN General Assembly resolved, by a two thirds majority, to endorse the plan. This was the alleged 'creation' of Israel.

To understand the meaning and importance of the Zionist claim five questions need to be answered:

First, was the UN General Assembly competent to 'create' Israel?

Palestine's detachment from Ottoman Turkey and the recognition of its independent status by Article 22 of the Covenant of the League of Nations made it a separate state, although not an independent one (see appendix 6). Although Palestine, in 1947, was still subject de facto to a mandate that had legally terminated as a result of the dissolution of the League of Nations, it did not affect its statehood or the sovereignty of its people, so the question of its future government was a matter that fell exclusively within its domestic jurisdiction and could not become subject to adjudication by the United Nations.

As with the League of Nations mandate to the British, the United Nations was not competent under international law to partition or otherwise dispose of the territory of Palestine against the wishes of the clear majority of its inhabitants.[1]

The United Nations did not possess any sovereignty nor had any other right over Palestine. It therefore had no power to partition Palestine or to assign any part of its territory to a religious minority of alien immigrants in order that they might establish a state of their own. Who gave the UN the right to partition Palestine?

Second, what was the legal validity of the Partition Plan, i.e., what force did it have?

The United Nations Partition Plan resolution was adopted by the General Assembly, not the Security Council. Resolutions of the General Assembly have the force of recommendations to member states of the United Nations but do not (unlike those of the Security Council) have any mandatory force. Therefore, the United Nations General Assembly vote to accept the recommendations of UNSCOP to partition Palestine into an Arab and a Jewish state did not mean that one or another state was being created over the objections of one of the parties. The Arabs rejected the plan, in part, because it was not fair. The UN General Assembly vote was not an override of the Arab rejection.

Third, on the question of fairness: was the Partition Plan fair?

The Partition Plan granted 55 percent of Palestine to the Jews, who were 30 percent of the population and owned 6 percent of the land. Within this Jewish state were to have been 407,000 Arabs. The Arab state was to comprise the remaining 45 percent of the land.

The major reason the Arabs rejected the partition resolution was on the grounds of fairness. It proposed to give the minority an exclusive right to the majority of the land. In 1946, the total population of Palestine amounted to 1,972,000 inhabitants, comprising 1,203,000 Muslims, 145,000 Christians, 608,000 Jews and 16,000 others.[2] Only one tenth of the Jewish population were part of the original inhabitants and belonged to the country[3] (see maps 7 and 8).

The Jewish population was composed of foreign immigrants, originating mostly from Poland, Russia and Central Europe.[4] Only one third of these immigrants had acquired Palestinian citizenship.[5]

Zionism is the most stupendous fallacy in Jewish history . . . I speak as a Jew.

Henry J. Morgenthau
All in a Life Time, Heinemann, 1923.

The partition also violated the principle of self-determination of peoples recognized by Article 1 of the United Nations Charter.

The carving out of 55 percent of Palestine for the creation of a *Jewish* state and the subjection of part of the original inhabitants (who were not Jewish) to its dominion was a violation of this principle.

The Western powers, who dominated the UN at the time, were so determined to create a Jewish state that when the Arab states recommended that the question of United Nations jurisdiction, which was in question, be referred to the International Court of Justice, they voted down the recommendation.

In terms of land ownership, it appears from the government of Palestine's *Village Statistics* that the Jews then owned 1,491 square kilometers (exclusive of urban property) out of a total of 26,323 square kilometers in Palestine.[6] Thus, Jewish land ownership amounted to 5.6 percent of the total area of the country. In contrast, the Palestinians owned the rest of Palestine, including all the areas which were public domain.

So what did the Partition Plan propose that the Arabs found unfair? It proposed to give to one third of the population of Palestine, largely foreigners, 55 percent of the country (see map 9). The territory allocated to the Jewish state included the coastal plain extending from Acre to Ashdod and other fertile lands, while the Palestinians were left mainly with mountainous and poor regions.

Zionists are eager to describe their acceptance of the Partition Plan as a compromise.[7] But their acceptance could not possibly have been a compromise because compromise implies mutual concession. What were the Zionists conceding? In fact they had nothing to concede and everything to gain at the expense of the Palestinians.

To what extent did Zionist pressure tactics facilitate what was, for them, the favorable Partition Plan?

Abba Eban, the former Israeli Foreign Minister, described the intense pressure put on US President Harry Truman.[8] On the opening day of the United Nations session on Palestine in November 1947, the delegate from the Philippines declared:

> The issue is whether the United Nations should accept responsibility for the enforcement of a policy which is clearly repugnant to the valid nationalist aspirations of the people of Palestine. The

Map 7 Land Ownership in Palestine – 1945

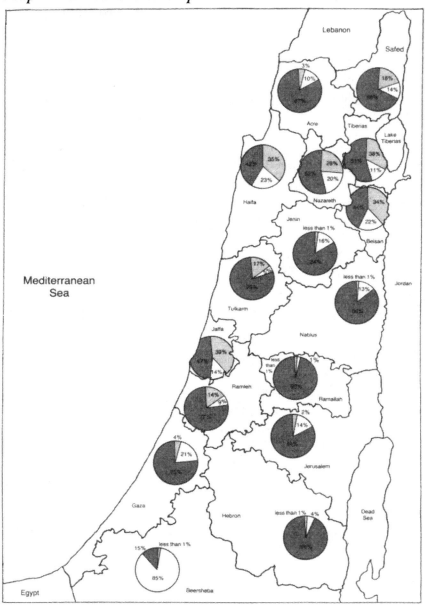

Palestinian   Zionist   Public and other

Source: Adapted from Walid Khalidi, *Before the Diaspora: a Photographic History of the Palestinians 1876–1948*, Institute for Palestine Studies, 1984, p. 237.

Map 8   *Distribution of Population in Palestine – 1946*

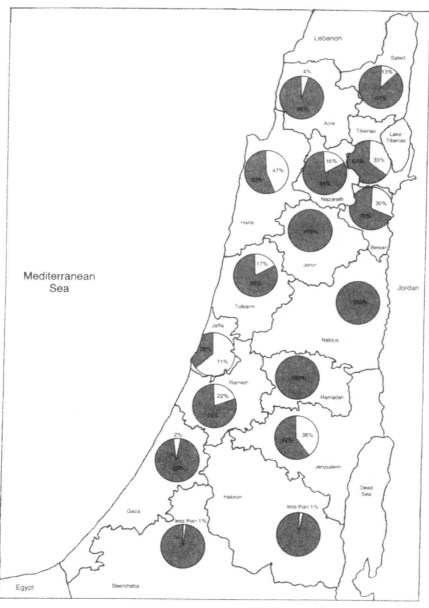

◀ Palestinian

◁ Jewish

Source: Adapted from Walid Khalidi, op. cit., p. 239.

> Philippines Government holds that the United Nations has the right
> not to accept such responsibility.

Two days later the Philippine delegate was recalled from his post. A phone call from Washington, DC, to President Roxas of the Philippines had reversed the Philippine position on Palestine. Congressman Sol Bloom, a Zionist and chairman of the US House Foreign Affairs Committee, helped out in applying pressure on the Philippine delegate.[9]

As the former US Central Intelligence Agency official Kermit Roosevelt wrote:

> The Zionists took the fight into their own hands. Rallying a group
> of influential Americans and selecting their targets with care, they
> exerted all possible influence . . . Six countries which had indicated
> their intention of voting against partition were chosen targets.

The delegates of these six countries, Haiti, Liberia, the Philippines, China, Ethiopia and Greece and their home governments were swamped with letters, telegrams and visits, not from their own nationals but from US Congressmen and others who invoked the name and prestige of the US government. An ex-governor, a prominent Democrat with White House connections, personally telephoned Haiti to change its vote. A well-known economist, also close to the White House and acting as a liaison with the World Zionist Organization, persuaded the Liberians to change their vote.[10]

Zionist pressure was so organized and effective that the columnist Drew Pearson reported that 'President Truman cracked down harder on his State Department than ever before to swing the United Nations' vote for the partition of Palestine.'[11] Truman's belief that Israel would serve American interests in the region explains the spectacular success of the Zionist lobbying efforts.

Not only the Western powers but the Soviet Union supported the Zionists. Soviet policy was not just confined to political support. The most important Soviet contribution to the establishment of the Jewish state came in the form of a massive supply of heavy arms, tanks and airplanes through Czechoslovakia. It was this arms deal to the Zionists in 1948 that tipped the military balance against the Arabs. The immediate Soviet objective was to oust Britain from the Middle East.[12]

Finally, what has Israel's attitude been to countless other UN resolutions concerning the Palestine question? Generally, Israel has ignored or violated nearly every other UN resolution pertaining to Palestine, the Palestinians or captured Arab territory. The first violation was of the partition resolution itself. As maps 10 and 11 show (pp. 124 and 126), the areas seized by the Israeli army in 1948 and 1949 were areas alloted to the Arab state. Israel refused to abandon these Arab territories and they were then annexed to the Jewish state.

Zionist apologists claim that since the Arabs rejected the partition resolution it has therefore lapsed. But their argument has no basis in law. The Arab refusal to accept partition in no way confers upon Israel the right to aggravate a wrong. In other words, the Arab–Israeli war of 1948 could not take away the rights of the Palestinians nor enlarge the rights of the Jews. The United Nations itself affirmed this view when Israel was admitted to the UN by recalling its resolutions which provided for the rights of the Arabs.

Appendix 14 lists some of the many UN resolutions that Israel has ignored or violated since 1948.

Notes to Chapter 11

1. Henry Cattan, *Palestine, the Arabs and Israel*, Longman, 1969, pp. 242–75.
2. UN Document A/AC 14/32, 11 November 1947, p. 304. See also appendix 2 for slightly different population counts.
3. The original non-European Jewish community did not favour partition or the establishment of a Jewish state. See Ronald Storrs, *Orientations*, Weidenfeld and Nicolson, 1945, p. 340 and Lord Islington, address to the House of Lords, *Hansard*, 21 June 1922, p. 1002.
4. Government of Palestine, *Statistical Abstract, 1944–1945*, p. 42.
5. ibid., pp. 36, 46.

6. Appendix VI, to the Report of Sub-Committee 2, UN Document A/AC 14/32, 11 November 1947, p. 270. The figure of land in Jewish possession on 30 June 1947 was given by Sub-Committee No. 1 of the Ad Hoc Committee on the Palestine Question as being 1,802 square kilometers. This figure, however, represents land in Jewish possession rather than in Jewish ownership and includes 200 square kilometers of public lands leased by the government of Palestine to the Jews in the Haifa area. Even if one takes as a basis land in Jewish possession instead of ownership, the percentage of total Jewish land holding is 6.8 percent of the area of Palestine.

7. Leonard J. Davis, *Myths and Facts 1985: a Concise Record of the Arab–Israeli Conflict*, Near East Report, 1984, p. 19. This book is published by the American–Israel Public Affairs Committee, the official lobby of Israel in the US.

8. Abba Eban, 'Tragedy and Triumph', in Meyer W. Weisgal and Joel Carmichael, eds., *Chaim Weizmann: a Biography of Several Hands*, Weidenfeld and Nicolson, 1962, pp. 301–3.

9. Alfred Lilienthal, *There Goes the Middle East*, Devin-Adair, 1957, p. 6; Carlos P. Romulo, *I Walked with Heros*, Holt, Rinehart and Winston, 1961, pp. 285–9.

10. Kermit Roosevelt, 'The Partition of Palestine: a Lesson in Pressure Politics', *Middle East Journal*, II, 1, 1948, pp. 13–16.

11. *Chicago Daily Tribune*, 9 February 1948.

12. Walid Khalidi, 'Introduction', in Walid Khalidi, ed., *From Haven to Conquest*, p. lxxiii; Arnold Kramer, 'Arms for Independence; When the Soviet Bloc Supported Israel', *The Wiener Library Bulletin*, xxii, 3, n.s. 12, 1968, pp. 19–23.

Recommended Reading

W. F. Abboushi, *The Unmaking of Palestine*, Middle East and North African Studies Press, 1985.

Henry Cattan, *Palestine and International Law: the Legal Aspects of the Arab–Israeli Conflict*, 2nd edn, Longman, 1976.

Walid Khalidi, *From Haven to Conquest: Readings in Zionism and the Palestine Problem until 1948*, Institute for Palestine Studies, 1971, especially pp. 645–754.

Chapter 12

Have the Arabs Started All the Wars?

Since the establishment of Israel there have been five major wars between the Arabs and the Israelis. These wars occured in 1948, 1956, 1967, 1973 and 1982. Israel claims that the Arabs started all the wars.

Although there has been low-intensity conflict in the intervening years and major conflagrations during the War of Attrition in 1969–70 and the 1978 invasion of Lebanon, and massive civil disobedience during the Uprising of 1988, it is these five wars Israel refers to when it makes its claims.

What are the Facts?

The 1948 War

The roots of the 1948 war go as far back as the first recognition on the part of the Palestinians that the Zionists wished to establish a Jewish state on their land. In late 1947 the United Nations proposed that Palestine be divided into a Palestinian Arab state and a Jewish state. The UN Partition Plan recommended that 55 percent of Palestine, and the most fertile region, be given to the Jewish settlers who comprised 30 percent of the population. The remaining 45 percent of Palestine was to comprise a home for the other 70 percent of the population who were Palestinians. The Palestinians rejected the plan because it was unfair (see chapter 11).

Zionists claim that the Arabs first attacked in January 1948 and then invaded Israel in May 1948. The truth is that by May 1948 Zionist forces had already invaded and occupied large parts of the country which had been allocated to the Palestinians by the United Nations Partition Plan. In January 1948 Israel did not yet exist! (See maps 9 and 10.)

The evidence that Israel started the 1948 war comes from Zionist sources. The *History of the Palmach* which was released in portions in the 1950s (and in full in 1972) details the efforts made to attack the Arabs and secure more territory than alloted to Israel by the UN Partition Plan.[1] Prime Minister David Ben-Gurion confirms this:

> Until the British left, no Jewish settlement, however remote, was entered or seized by the Arabs, while the Haganah, under severe and frequent attack, captured many Arab positions and liberated Tiberias and Haifa, Jaffa and Safad.[2]

Prime Minister Menachem Begin adds:

> In the months preceding the Arab invasion, and while the five Arab states were conducting preparations, we continued to make sallies into Arab territory. The conquest of Jaffa stands out as an event of first-rate importance in the struggle for Hebrew independence early in May, on the eve [that is, before the alleged Arab invasion] of the invasion by the five Arab states.[3]

Another Israeli Prime Minister, Yitzhak Rabin, also provided details of the Zionists' war plans, including plans to expel the Palestinian population. Rabin's memoirs were so explosive that

Map 9   United Nations Partition Plan – 1947

Compare this map with land ownership in Maps 7 and 15.

☐   Proposed Jewish state

■   Proposed Palestinian state

▨   Proposed International Zone

Map 10 *Palestinian Territories Seized by Israel in 1948 and 1949 in Violation of the UN Partition Plan*

Compare this map with Map 9.

 Palestinian territories seized by Israel.

the Israeli censors excised various damaging passages, although they were finally published by the *New York Times*.[4]

The most recent evidence that refutes the claim that the Arabs started the 1948 war is the evidence uncovered by Benny Morris, an Israeli researcher working in Zionist archives, and Simha Flapan, a leader of the Mapam Party. The Israeli Defense Force report Morris uncovered shows a deliberate Israeli policy to attack the Arabs should they resist and expel the Palestinians[5] (see chapter 2).

It is not true that the Arabs 'invaded Israel' in 1948. First, Israel did not exist at the time of the alleged invasion as an established state with recognized boundaries. When the Zionist leaders established Israel on 15 May 1948 they purposely declined to declare the boundaries of the new state in order to allow for future expansion.

What the French could do in Tunisia, I said, the Jews would be able to do in Palestine with Jewish will, Jewish money, Jewish power and Jewish enthusiasm.

Chaim Weizmann
Trial and Error, Harper, 1949, p. 244.

Secondly, the only territory to which the new state of Israel had even a remote 'legal' claim was that alloted to the Jewish state by the UN Partition Plan. But the Zionists had already captured areas that were alloted to the Arab state. (See chapter 11 concerning the claim that the UN created Israel and see map 10.)

Thirdly, those areas which the Arab states purportedly 'invaded' were, in fact, exclusively areas alloted to the *Arab* state proposed by the UN Partition Plan (see map 9). The so-called Arab invasion was a defensive attempt to hold on to the areas alloted by the Partition Plan for the Palestinian state.

Finally, the commander of the most effective Arab army, namely Jordan's Arab Legion, was under orders not to enter the areas alloted to the Jewish state.[6]

The 1956 War
Israel blames the 1956 Sinai war on Egypt's aggressive behavior.

The facts concerning the Sinai war once again come from Israeli sources.

A decisive and authoritative contribution exploding the myth of Israel's accusations are the revelations from former Prime Minister Moshe Sharett's *Personal Diary*.[7] The very frank Sharett diaries

Map 11   Zionist Military Operations inside UN Proposed Palestinian State before the Creation of Israel

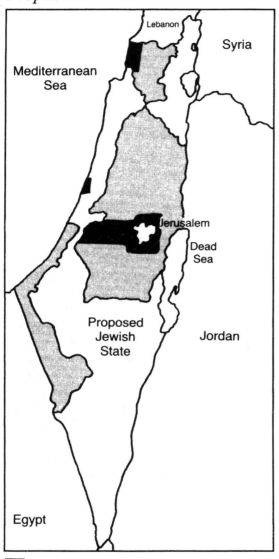

Proposed Palestinian state

Zionist military operations inside proposed Palestinian state.

Source: Walid Khalidi, *From Haven to Conquest: Readings in Zionism and the Palestine Problem until 1948*, Institute for Palestine Studies, 1987, p. 759.

demonstrate that, from the establishment of Israel onwards, the politico-military establishment never seriously believed in an Arab threat to the existence of Israel and devised tactics aimed at pushing the Arabs into unwinnable military confrontations. Many of the tactics employed involved, according to Sharett, large and small-scale military operations aimed at civilian populations across the armistice lines, especially in the Palestinian territories of the West Bank and Gaza. The purpose of these operations was to terrorize the Arab population, thereby creating permanent destabilization between the civilian populations and their respective governments.

Sharett shows that operations against Arab military installations in border areas were meant to undermine the morale of the armies and intensify the regimes' destabilization from inside their military structures.

Covert terrorist operations inside the Arab world were the Israeli policy used for purposes of espionage and in order to create fear, tension and instability.

Israel's strategy, Sharett reveals, was to be realized by new territorial conquests through war as well as political and military efforts towards the liquidation of all Arab and Palestinian claims to Palestine through the dispersion of the Palestinian refugees. The strategy also involved subversive operations designed to dismember the Arab world, defeat the Arab national movement and create puppet regimes.

The main reason often given for the origin of the 1956 war was Egypt's closing of the Suez Canal. But Sharett reveals that the Israeli leadership was planning the territorial conquest of the Sinai and Gaza as early as the fall of 1953. The Israeli attack on Gaza in February 1955 was undertaken as a conscious preliminary act of war.

The hawkish David Ben-Gurion became Prime Minister and Israel soon became very aggressive. On 28 February 1955 Israeli troops invaded Gaza killing thirty-seven Egyptians and wounding thirty-one. The attack came out of the blue. Egyptian President Gamal Nasser said it 'was revenge for nothing. Everything was quiet there.'[8] The Chief of Staff of the United Nations Truce Supervision Organization, Swedish General Carl von Horn, confirmed Nasser's claim: there had been 'comparative tranquillity along the armistice demarcation lines during the greater part of the period November 1954 to February 1955'.[9]

In the 1950s few people believed that Nasser had aggressive intentions towards Israel. Richard Crossman, a British Zionist, wrote in 1955 that

> not only Egypt, but the whole Middle East must pray that Nasser survives the assassin's bullet. I am certain that he is a man who means what he says, and that so long as he is in power directing his middle-class revolution, Egypt will remain a factor for peace and social development.[10]

The Gaza raid changed everything. Arab public opinion was outraged and demanded action, as it was intended to. Nasser needed arms to equip his army which was hopelessly outgunned by Israel. At first he sought American help. His request for arms was so small it led US President Dwight D. Eisenhower to exclaim 'Why, this is peanuts!'[11]

Western intelligence was convinced that Egypt had no intention of attacking Israel. The Americans rebuffed Nasser in any case and Egypt turned to the Russians who orchestrated the famous Czech arms deal which was used by Israel for feigned outrage.[12]

Nasser did not realize that he was being set up for the Israeli invasion, although he did recognize that the situation was heating up. In October 1955, a year before the war, Israeli Prime Minister David Ben-Gurion ordered his Chief of Staff, General Moshe Dayan, to prepare invasion plans. Ben-Gurion was determined, accordng to Dayan, 'not to miss any politically favorable opportunity to strike at Egypt'.[13] In fact, Ben-Gurion wanted to start the war with Egypt in 1955. The *Paratrooper's Book*, the semi-official history of the Israeli Airborne Corps, stated, 'It is today admitted that if it had been up to David Ben-Gurion, the Sinai war would have taken place a year earlier [than it did].'[14] Dayan expressed the hopes of the Israeli leadership when he said in December 1955, 'One of these days a situation will be created which makes military action possible.'[15]

Israel was supported by the Western powers: the United States, Britain and France. Frustrated with the decline of colonialism and the benefits lost to them, and with the resurgence of Islam, the Western powers found a scapegoat in Nasser.

The opportunity to make war against Egypt came in July 1956 when Nasser nationalized the Suez Canal, an act within the legal right of the Egyptian state. The Suez Canal was controlled by foreigners in 1956 and represented an important vestige of colonialism affronting the Arab people. Nasser's action was extremely popular although, in hindsight, politically cataclysmic. France and Great Britain, in one of the last spasms of European imperialism, colluded in a secret alliance with Israel to invade the Sinai and destroy Nasser.

On 29 October 1956 Israel attacked Egypt and captured the entire Sinai. French war equipment poured into Israel and French and British warships bombarded the coast. French and British troops landed and helped the Israelis. Eisenhower, who had been in the dark about the invasion plans and the secret alliance, demanded that the Israelis withdraw from Egyptian territory. Israel refused, leading Eisenhower to exclaim,

> Should a nation which attacks and occupies foreign territory in the face of U.N. disapproval be allowed to impose conditions on its own withdrawal? If we agree that armed attack can properly achieve the purpose of the assailant, then I fear we will have turned back the clock of international order. . . .[16]

The 1967 War

Israel claims that its attack against Egypt was a defensive measure to prevent Nasser from attacking.

The facts are that Israel began planning the re-conquest of the Sinai as soon as they had been forced to withdraw in 1956. As in 1956, Israel waited for favorable circumstances to put the plan into action. In 1967, though, they understood better the need for a sophisticated propaganda campaign to convince Western opinion that their offensive was an act of self-defense. The propaganda campaign was two-pronged: that the Arabs attacked Israel and that Israel was in danger of annihilation.

Both accusations were false. In the early hours of 5 June 1967 Israel announced to a believing Western world that the Egyptian Air Force was attacking. In fact the Israelis attacked the Egyptians and destroyed nearly their entire air force *on the ground*.

129

> *The thesis that the danger of genocide was hanging over us in June 1967*
> *and that Israel was fighting for its physical existence is only bluff, which*
> *was born and developed after the war.*[17]
>
> Israeli General Matityahu Peled
> *Ha'aretz*, 19 March 1972.

General Matityahu Peled, one of the architects of the Israeli victory, committed what the Israeli public considered blasphemy when he admitted the true thinking of the Israeli leadership.

Israeli Air Force General Ezer Weizmann declared bluntly that 'there was never any danger of extermination'.[18] Mordechai Bentov, a former Israeli cabinet minister, dismissed the myth of annihilation: 'All this story about the danger of extermination has been a complete invention and has been blown up *a posteriori* to justify the annexation of new Arab territories.'[19]

After the war Israel claimed it invaded because of imminent Arab attack. It claimed that Nasser's closing of the Straits of Tiran was an act of war. It also cited Syrian shelling on the demilitarized zone (DMZ) of the Syrian–Israeli border and bellicose Arab propaganda.

Admittedly the Arab countries engaged in what can only be described as provocative and foolish bombast that simply played into the hands of Israel. But the claim that the Arabs were going to invade was ludicrous. One third of Egypt's army was in Yemen and therefore quite unlikely to start a war. On the Syrian front, Israel was engaging in threats and provocations similar to the Gaza raid of 1955.

The demilitarized zone on the Syrian–Israeli border was established by agreement on 20 July 1949. But Israeli provocations were incessant as they extended their sovereignty, by encroachment, over the entire Arab area. According to one UN Chief of Staff Arab villagers were evicted and their homes destroyed.[20] Another Chief of Staff described how the Israelis ploughed up Arab land and 'advanced the "frontier" to their own advantage'.[21]

The armistice agreement stipulated that sovereignty for both sides would be suspended and that civilian lives would continue normally. But Israel attempted to evict the Arabs and annex the DMZ. When the Syrians responded, Israel claimed that 'peaceful' Israeli farmers were being shelled by the Syrians. Unmentioned was the fact that the 'farmers' were armed and using tractors and farm equipment to encroach on the DMZ.[22] This was part of a 'premeditated Israeli policy . . . to get all the Arabs out of the way by fair means or foul'.[23]

Shortly after the Syrian response on 7 April 1967 the Israeli Air Force attacked Syria, shooting down six planes, hitting thirty fortified positions and killing about 100 people.[24] It was unlikely that any Syrian guns would have gone into action had it not been for Israeli provocation.

Israel's need for water also played a role in its attack in 1967. The invasion completed Israel's encirclement of the headwaters of the Upper Jordan River. Its capture of the West Bank and the two aquifers arising there now supply all the groundwater for northern and central Israel.

The Israelis followed up their massive retaliation with stern warnings. On 11 May General Yitzhak Rabin said on Israeli radio: 'The moment is coming when we will march on Damascus to overthrow the Syrian Government.'[25] Syria sought Egypt's assistance under their Mutual Defense Pact of November 1966. Nasser could not afford to stand idly by. He ordered the removal of the small UN force stationed in Sinai and closed the Straits of Tiran. This action was the *casus belli* used by Israel.

Three separate intelligence groups had looked carefully into this matter and it was our best judgement that an [Egyptian] attack was not imminent.

Robert McNamara, US Secretary of State
in Lyndon Baines Johnson, *The Vantage Point*, Holt, Rinehart and Winston, 1971, p. 292.

Nasser's move was a gesture of solidarity with Syria and no threat to Israel's economy nor to its security. The closure of the Straits did not force Israel into war. Claims of economic strangulation were absurd since only 5 percent of Israel's trade went through the Straits of Tiran. No Israeli merchant vessel had passed through the Straits during the previous two years.[26]

The threat to Israel's security was non-existent. According to the respected British newspaper, the *Observer*, Nasser's purpose was clearly 'to deter Israel rather than provoke it to a fight'.[27] *New York Times* columnist James Reston reported that 'Egypt does not want war . . . certainly is not ready for war.'[28]

The Israelis themselves were perfectly aware of this as a result of their sophisticated military intelligence. Later, in the first days of the war, they were so concerned that their plans for attacking Syria would be discovered that they deliberately attacked the USS *Liberty*, killing thirty-three American sailors, in an attempt to prevent it from monitoring war preparations.

A few months after the war Yitzhak Rabin remarked: 'I do not think Nasser wanted war. The two divisions he sent to the Sinai on May 14 would not have been sufficient to launch an offensive against Israel. He knew it and we knew it.'[29]

General Peled put it more honestly:

> To pretend that the Egyptian forces massed on our frontiers were in a position to threaten the existence of Israel constitutes an insult not only to the intelligence of anyone capable of analysing this sort of situation, but above all an insult to the Zahal [Israeli army].[30]

Finally, in 1982, the Israelis admitted that they had started the war (although official Zionist propaganda in America does not!). Prime Minister Menachem Begin in a speech at the Israeli National Defense College said, 'The Egyptian army concentrations in the Sinai approaches do not prove that Nasser was really about to attack us. We must be honest with ourselves. We decided to attack him.'[31]

The 1973 War

The devastating Arab defeat of 1967 left Israel in control of the West Bank, Gaza, East Jerusalem, the Golan Heights and the Sinai. Israel rapidly moved to incorporate these captured Arab territories into its domain. Israel annexed East Jerusalem and began establishing settlements in all the Occupied Territories.

It was clear that the Arabs would not go on indefinitely watching the Israelis pump out Egyptians, Syrians and Palestinians and pump in Jewish settlers. By 1973 nearly 100 settlements had been established and hundreds of thousands of Palestinians had been displaced, expelled, imprisoned or deported.

On 6 October 1973 the Egyptian and Syrian armies attacked Israeli positions in the Sinai and on the Golan Heights in an attempt to liberate their territory captured by Israel.

The Secretary-General of the Arab League explained the Arab action:

> In a final analysis, Arab action is justifiable, moral and valid under Article 51 of the Charter of the United Nations. There is no aggression, no attempt to acquire new territories. But to restore and liberate all the occupied territories is a duty for all able self-respecting peoples.[32]

The 1982 War

Israel claimed that it attacked, not Lebanon, but the Palestine Liberation Organization (PLO) in Lebanon in order to put the Galilee region of Israel out of the range of enemy artillery.

The facts are that Israel invaded Lebanon on 6 June 1982 in order to totally destroy the PLO, not only its insignificant military capability but also all its civilian functions. The other basic war aim was described by Israeli Minister of Defense Ariel Sharon: 'The bigger the blow and the more we damage the PLO infrastructure, the more the Arabs in Judea and Samaria [the Biblical name for the West Bank used by Israel] and Gaza will be ready to negotiate with us'.[33]

Israel had hoped that with the destruction of the PLO Lebanon could be ripped from its Arab moorings in order to create an Israeli puppet regime of pro-Western Maronite Christian Lebanese, a minority of the population.

As early as 1954 David Ben-Gurion had urged that one of the 'central duties' of Israel's foreign policy should be to push the Maronite Christians to 'proclaim a Christian state'. Moshe Dayan had said the 'Israeli army will enter Lebanon, will occupy the necessary territory, and will create a Christian regime which will ally itself with Israel'.[34]

The Israeli claim that it invaded Lebanon in self-defense is not true. Between August 1981 and May 1982 the PLO maintained a truce, sponsored by the United States and Saudi Arabia, on Israel's northern border. Israel on the other hand violated the truce 2,777 times.[35]

The true reason for Israel's invasion was fear over the PLO's rising international legitimacy. Once again Israel only needed an excuse to make war. This time the *casus belli* was the assassination attempt on the Israeli ambassador to London, an act found out by Scotland Yard to have been conducted by the anti-PLO rogue Abu Nidal. In any case their excuse was so flimsy that, for the first time in the Arab–Israeli conflict, Israeli propaganda was not believed.

At first the Israelis operated under the pretense that they were only securing their borders and did not intend to go beyond a twenty-five-mile limit. But the truth was very different as described by the former chief of Israeli military intelligence, Aharon Yariv: 'I know in fact that going to Beirut was included in the original military plan.'[36]

The major targets during the invasion were the Palestinian refugee camps, many of which were destroyed. The Lebanese national police estimated that 19,085 people were killed by the Israelis. The Israelis claimed 340 were killed.[37] These estimates given by Israel were so ridiculed by reporters and relief workers that within Israel itself many began to worry about Israel's credibility. Thousands of Israeli troops were eyewitnesses to the carnage and, unlike in previous wars, they began speaking out against it.

The international press also related a viciousness known well by Palestinians, but generally unknown in the West. David Shipler of the *New York Times* dscribed how, after several Palestinian refugee camps in Lebanon were captured by the Israelis, the conquerors destroyed all remnants. An Israeli officer, 'when asked why bulldozers were knocking down houses in which women and children were living', responded by saying 'they are all terrorists'.[38]

The *Economist*'s correspondent, G. H. Jansen, described Israel's war tactics as surrounding cities and towns 'so swiftly that civilian inhabitants were trapped inside, and then to pound them from land, sea and air'. As for Israeli declarations of 'cease-fires' Jansen notes: 'For the Israelis the ceasefire is not a step towards a truce or an armistice, it is simply . . . an attempt to gain the spoils of war without fighting.'[39]

This was the first war Israel fought in which Israeli propaganda and Israeli public opinion were out of synchronization. To a large degree the Israeli public was worried about the true facts of the war and what it might mean for Israel's 'reputation'. After the war many Israelis ridiculed the official name for the 1982 war: 'Operation "Peace for the Galilee"'.

As soon as it became clear that the war was not the 'surgical' strike the Israeli public were accustomed to, and with casualties rising, they demonstrated in huge numbers against the war.

Israel claimed that it attacked only PLO targets. But since more than 90 percent of the PLO infrastructure is civilian the war amounted to an attack against civilians (see appendix 21).

The International Red Cross, World Vision International, UNICEF, among many other aid agencies all reported a deliberate policy to attack civilian targets, especially hospitals. The Acre and Gaza hospitals in Beirut were deliberately bombed.[40]

Newsweek magazine of 16 August 1982 has an extensive account of the massive devastation of the civilian sectors of Beirut.

Israeli Colonel Dov Yirmiah relates how the military authorities blocked shipments of food and medicine to civilians.[41] As Paulette Pierson-Mathay, a Belgian professor and eyewitness, testified, the 'weapons most used were fragmentation bombs and phosphorous bombs and shells, as well as booby-trapped toys; one explosive doll had caused the death of several children and horribly wounded some others'.[42]

The doctrine of attacking defenseless civilians has antecedents in David Ben-Gurion who wrote in his diary in the 1940s: 'What is necessary is cruel and strong reactions. We need precision in time, place and casualties. If we know the family – strike mercilessly, women and children included'.[43] Forty years later another Israeli leader, Defense Minister Yitzhak Rabin, declared a policy of 'force, might, beatings' against civilians who demonstrated against Israeli occupation.[44] The commander of Israeli troops on the West Bank, General Avram Mitzna, said that Israel would 'grab whom we can and some of them will be beaten'.[45]

Extreme hatred of Arabs is now on the rise in Israel. A recent poll of Israeli high-school students shows that 42 percent agree with statements supporting extreme race hatred of Arabs.[46]

Ze'ev Schiff, the noted Israeli military analyst, wrote in 1978 that 'In South Lebanon we struck the civilian population consciously, because they deserved it.'[47]

Israel describes its attacks against the Palestinians in Lebanon as reprisals for terrorism. One might well ask what the Palestinians were doing in Lebanon in the first place?

In September 1983, after the withdrawal of the PLO, the Israelis facilitated the massacre of more than 1,000 Palestinian men, women and children at the Sabra-Shatila refugee camp in Beirut. The Israeli army surrounded the refugee camps and sent in troops of the Lebanese Christian fascist party known as the Phalange. For thirty-six hours, as the Israelis watched, the killing continued.[48]

In conclusion, the real reason for the Israeli invasion of Lebanon and its ferocity was to make war against the Palestinians. It was a war not just against their representative at this particular point in history, the Palestine Liberation Organization, but against the Palestinian people themselves. As the linguist and social critic, Noam Chomsky, said, 'As long as any trace of an organized Palestinian presence remains anywhere nearby, the legitimacy of the Israeli national rebirth may somehow appear to be in question'.[49]

Notes to Chapter 12

1. Kibbutz Menchad Archive, Palmach Archive, Efal, Israel.
2. David Ben-Gurion, *Rebirth and Destiny of Israel*, Philosophical Library, 1954, p. 530. Although Ben-Gurion speaks of 'liberating' Jaffa it was alloted to the Palestinians by the UN Partition Plan. The Haganah was the mainstream Jewish terrorist organization, out of which grew the Israeli army.
3. Menachem Begin, *The Revolt*, Nash, 1972, p. 348.
4. Yitzhak Rabin, *Pinkas Shemit*, Ma'ariv, 1979, in Hebrew. The censored passages were published in the *New York Times* in October 1979.
5. Benny Morris, 'The Causes and Character of the Arab Exodus from Palestine: the Israel Defense Forces Intelligence Branch Analysis of June 1948', *Middle Eastern Studies*, XXII, 1, January 1986, pp. 5–19. Simha Flapan, *The Birth of Israel: Myths and Realities*, Pantheon, 1987.
6. Sir John Bagot Glubb, 'The Battle for Jerusalem', *Middle East International*, May 1973.
7. Moshe Sharett, *Yoman Ishi*, Ma'ariv, 1979, in Hebrew with portions

trans. in Livia Rokach, *Israel's Sacred Terrorism: a Study Based on Moshe Sharett's Personal Diary and Other Documents*, AAUG, 1980. Rokach is the daughter of Israel Rokach, the Minister of Interior in Sharett's government.

8. Kennett Love, *Suez: the Twice Fought War*, McGraw-Hill, 1969, p. 83.
9. Report to the Security Council, UN Document S 3373, 17 March 1955.
10. Richard Crossman, *New Statesman and Nation*, 22 January 1955.
11. Love, op. cit., p. 88.
12. The Russians had also used the Czechs to supply arms to Israel in 1948.
13. Major-General Moshe Dayan, *Diary of the Sinai Campaign*, Weidenfeld and Nicolson, 1966, p. 37.
14. *Paratrooper's Book* (in Hebrew) in Arie Bober, ed., *The Other Israel*, Doubleday, 1972, p. 70.
15. Love, op. cit., p. 106.
16. Address to the nation, 20 February 1957.
17. *Ha'aretz*, 19 March 1972.
18. *Ma'ariv*, 19 April 1972.
19. *Al Hamishmar*, 14 April, 1972.
20. Lt-General E.L.M. Burns, *Between Arab and Israeli*, Ivan Obolensky, 1962, pp. 113–14.
21. General Carl von Horn, *Soldiering for Peace*, Cassell, 1966, p. 79.
22. David Hirst, *The Gun and the Olive Branch: the Roots of Violence in the Middle East*, Faber and Faber, 1984, pp. 213–15.
23. von Horn, op. cit., p. 117.
24. Hirst, op. cit., p. 214.
25. Godfrey Jansen, 'New Light on the 1967 War', *Daily Star*, London, 15, 22, 26 November 1973.
26. Michael Howard and Robert Hunter, *Israel and the Arab World: the Crisis of 1967*, Adelphi Papers 41, Institute for Strategic Studies, 1967, p. 24.
27. The *Observer*, London, 4 June 1967.
28. *New York Times*, 4 and 5 June 1967.
29. *Le Monde*, 29 February 1968.
30. *Ha'aretz*, 19 March 1972.
31. *Jerusalem Post*, 20 August 1982.
32. *Sunday Times*, London, 14 October 1973.
33. *The Times*, London, 5 August 1982.
34. Rokach, op. cit., pp. 24–30.
35. United Nations records cited by Robin Wright, 'Israeli "provocations" in Southern Lebanon Fail to Goad PLO – So Far', *Christian Science Monitor*, 18 March 1982; Alexander Cockburn and James Ridgeway, *Village Voice*, 22 June 1982.
36. *Jerusalem Post*, 24 September 1982.
37. John Yemma, *Christian Science Monitor*, 21 December 1982 quotes the Lebanese national police. The Israeli figures are cited in George

Ball, *Error and Betrayal in Lebanon: an Analysis of Israel's Invasion of Lebanon and the Implications for U.S.–Israeli Relations*, Foundation for Middle East Peace, 1984, p. 47. The Israelis did not support their propaganda effort as vigorously as in the past because Western reporters were quite numerous in Lebanon and regularly reported the carnage Israel rained upon the Arabs. American television coverage of Israeli attacks against the civilian population of Beirut was also quite graphic.

38. *New York Times*, 3 July 1982.
39. G. H. Jansen, 'Terror Tactics', *Middle East International*, 2 July 1982.
40. William Branagan, 'Israeli Bombing of Hospitals', *Washington Post* (Manchester Guardian Weekly), 27 June 1982; Hal Piper, *Baltimore Sun*, 21 June 1982; Richard Ben Cramer, *Philadelphia Inquirer*, 24 June 1982; William E. Farrell, *New York Times*, 27 June 1982. See also Christopher Walker, *The Times* (London), 18 June 1982; *New York Times*, 12 August 1982; T. Elaine Carey, *Christian Science Monitor*, 13 August 1982; *Boston Globe*, 19 August 1982.
41. Dov Yirmiah, *My War Diary*, South End, 1984; *Hotam*, 16 July 1982; *Al Hamishmar*, 5 August 1982.
42. Franklin P. Lamb, ed., *Reason Not the Need: Eyewitness Chronicles of Israel's War*, Bertrand Russell Peace Foundation, 1984, p. 382.
43. *Yediot Aharonot*, 17 April 1983.
44. *New York Times*, 23 January 1988.
45. ibid., 22 January 1988.
46. The Van Leer Institute poll appears in *Yediot Ahronot*, 28 June 1985 reprinted in *Journal of Palestine Studies*, 57, Autumn 1985, pp. 163–5.
47. *Ha'aretz*, 10 May 1978.
48. Much has been written on the massacre; for two excellent sources see *The Beirut Massacre*, Claremont Research, 1982, a collection of newspaper and magazine articles, and Amnon Kapeliouk, *Sabra and Shatila*, AAUG, 1983.
49. Noam Chomsky, *The Fateful Triangle: the United States, Israel and the Palestinians*, South End, 1983, p. 395.

Recommended Reading

Naseer H. Aruri, ed., *Middle East Crucible: Studies on the Arab–Israeli War of October 1973*, AAUG Monograph Series 6, Medina University Press International, 1975.

Lieutenant-General Sir John Bagot Glubb, *A Soldier with the Arabs*, Hodder and Stoughton, 1957.

Noam Chomsky, *The Fateful Triangle: the United States, Israel and the Palestinians*, South End, 1983.

James M. Ennes, *Assault on the* Liberty: *the True Story of the Israeli Attack on an American Intelligence Ship*, Random House, 1979.

David Hirst, *The Gun and the Olive Branch: the Roots of Violence in the Middle East*, Faber and Faber, 1984.

Israel in Lebanon, The Report of the International Commission to enquire into reported violations of International Law by Israel during its invasion of the Lebanon, Ithaca Press, 1983.

Fred J. Khouri, *The Arab–Israeli Dilemma*, 2nd edn, Syracuse University Press, 1976.

Donald Neff, *Warriors at Suez: Eisenhower Takes America into the Middle East*, Simon and Schuster, 1981.

Livia Rokach, *Israel's Sacred Terrorism: a Study Based on Moshe Sharett's Diary and Other Documents*, AAUG, 1980.

Witness of War Crimes in Lebanon, testimony given to the Nordic Commission, Oslo, October 1982, EAFORD and Ithaca Press, 1983.

Dov Yirmiya, *My War Diary: Lebanon June 5–July 1, 1982*, South End, 1983.

The Growth of 'Eretz Israel':
Fulfillment of the Zionist Mission

Israel exists as a result of Zionism. Zionism is an ideology which makes the claim, among others, that God promised to the Jews an area of the Middle East described in Genesis xv, 18. Zionism itself admits that Genesis is, at bottom, the final justification for the state of Israel. The following maps depict the growth of Israel from the area described in the Bible to today.

'Israel' is used with quotes to signify Eretz Israel, the Land of Israel, which is not necessarily the same as the international boundaries shown on most maps.

The shaded areas are territories purchased by any of the Jewish agencies or controlled by the Israeli military.

Map 12   'Eretz Israel' According to Genesis xv, 18

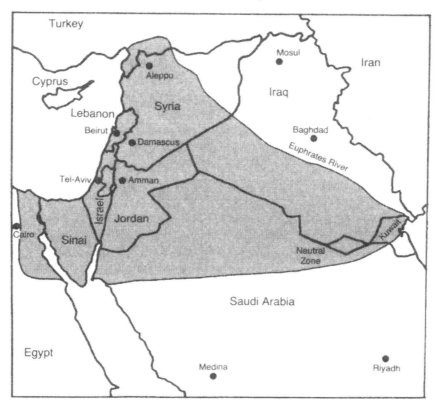

Shown with 1967 ceasefire boundaries.

Map 13 'Eretz Israel' in 1882

Lebanon

Safed

Lake
Tiberias

Haifa

Mediterranean
Sea

Jaffa

Petah Tikva

Nablus

Jordan

Jerusalem

Dead
Sea

Palestine

Land acquired by Zionists for 'redemption'.*

* 'redeemed' land may only be sold to Jews.

Map 14   'Eretz Israel' in 1920

▨ Land acquired by Zionists for 'redemption'.*

* See footnote p. 142.

Map 15   'Eretz Israel' in 1942

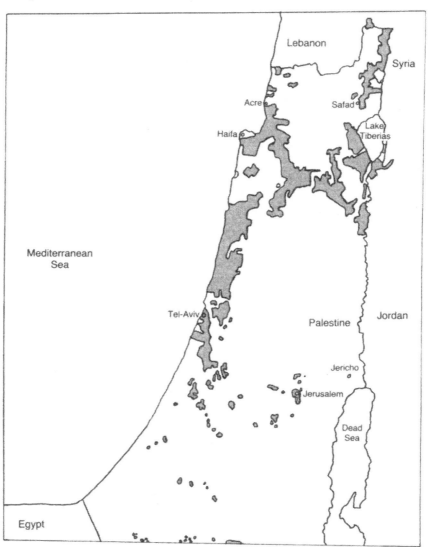

Land acquired by Zionists for 'redemption'.*

* See footnote p. 142.

Map 16   State of Israel in 1949

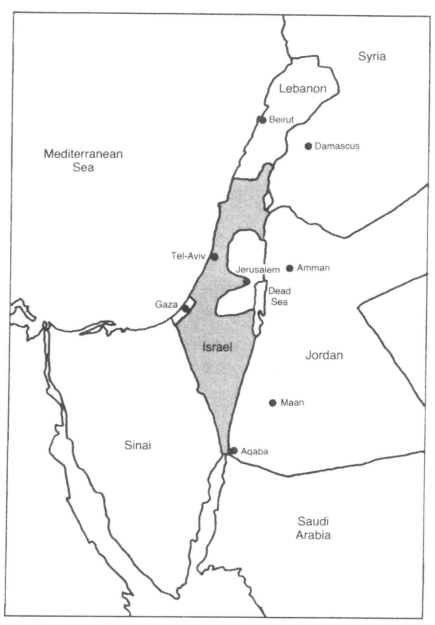

The boundaries are armistice not international boundaries.

Map 17   Israeli Controlled Territory in 1967

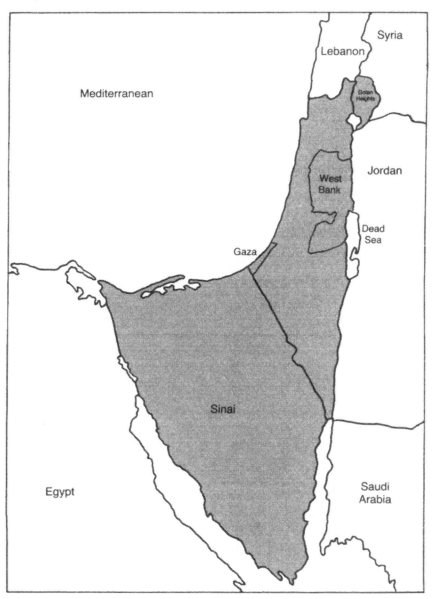

Map 18   'Eretz Israel' in 1988

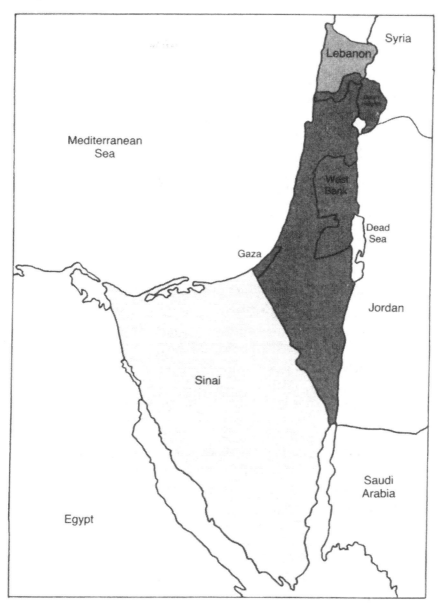

☐ Arab territory from which Israel withdrew in 1982.
▨ Arab territory from which Israel was forced to withdraw in 1985.
■ Israel and Arab territory occupied by Israel in 1989.

Chapter 13

Is Jordan Palestine?*

Zionists claim that a Palestinian Arab state already exists in Jordan and, therefore, Jordan is Palestine – eastern Palestine. They point out that more than half the population of Jordan is Palestinian.

Israel claims that, historically, the territory of 'Palestine' embraced Transjordan (British Palestine Mandate territory east of the Jordan river, that is, today's Hashemite Kingdom of Jordan) and Cisjordan (British Palestine Mandate territory west of the Jordan river, that is, today's Israel, West Bank and Gaza).

Their claim regards Transjordan as part of the area of Palestine which came under the British Mandate and was wrongfully detached by Britain in 1922 from the larger area intended for the Jewish national home as supposedly described in the Balfour Declaration. They claim that Transjordan continued to be regarded by the League of Nations and Britain, the Mandatory power, as legally constituting part of mandated Palestine.

Furthermore, Zionists argue that since the area of Jordan comprises 77 percent of Palestine, as they determine it, and since

---

* I would like to thank the Association of Arab–American University Graduates, Inc. and Sheila Ryan for permission to utilize portions of Ms Ryan's *Palestine is, but Not in Jordan*, Information Paper 24, AAUG, Belmont, 1983, for much of this chapter.

the Palestinians are a majority of the population in Jordan, therefore it is legitimate to say that Jordan is Palestine.

What are the Facts?

What constituted Palestine, in terms of territorial lines on a map, has varied over time and it is misleading to imply that there has always been a recognizable and well-defined area to which the name applied, although there has always been a general area.

During the Ottoman period Transjordan was administered separately from Palestine, the dividing line being the Jordan River. The area east of the Jordan River was part of the Ottoman Turkish *vilayet* (province) of Syria. The area west of the river was administered as three *sanjaks* (sub-provinces), two of which (Acre and Nablus) formed part of the *vilayet* of Beirut, while the third was the independent *sanjak* of Jerusalem. These Ottoman administrative arrangements undermine the Zionist assertion that 'Palestine' meant Transjordan as well (see map 1).

But the most obvious separation between Palestine and Jordan is the very clear natural boundary of the Jordan River itself.

Ottoman rule ended after the First World War and the League of Nations gave the Mandate for the administration of Palestine and Jordan to the British. Although the Mandate incorporated the Balfour Declaration and committed the Mandatory power to facilitate Jewish immigration, the Mandate then proceeded in Article 25 (see appendix 7) to provide discretionary power for effectively removing Transjordan from the operation of the Mandate and putting it under a separate administration. The Article read:

> In the territories lying between the Jordan and the eastern boundary of Palestine as ultimately determined, the Mandatory shall be entitled, with the consent of the Council of the League of Nations, to postpone or withhold application of such provisions of this mandate as he may consider inapplicable to the existing local

conditions, and to make such provision for the administration of
the territories as he may consider suitable to those conditions . . .

In 1923, in accordance with Article 25 of the Palestine Mandate
and with the consent of the Council of the League of Nations,
Britain recognized the existence of an independent government in
Transjordan under the Emir Abdullah.

The Council of the League agreed that the Articles of the
Mandate which dealt specifically with the development of the
Jewish national home should not be applied to Transjordan.
Britain retained its Mandatory responsibility towards the League
and the Emir agreed to be guided by Britain in all matters
concerning foreign relations.

In May 1946 Transjordan attained full independence with the
agreement of Britain, the League of Nations having ceased to exist
on 18 April 1946.

Zionist leaders had reacted angrily in 1922 to the separation of
Transjordan from the area which they believed should be the
'Jewish national home'. They maintained that the national home
for the Jewish people should include, as they put it, the 'whole of
Palestine'.

The Zionist claim that Jordan is Palestine does not hold up for
five reasons. First, their argument, based on one notion (theirs)
of what Palestine comprises, is self-serving. Nothing makes this
1922 map, which was accurate for several months, have a special
authority (see map 19).

Secondly, the population of Jordan was ethnically different from
that of Palestine. The Palestinians were descended from all the
peoples that had invaded or settled in Palestine both before and
after the Arab conquest in the seventh century (see also chapters
1 and 16). The Jordanians were mainly descended from Arab
tribes of the northwestern part of the Arabian Peninsula.

In 1917, at the time of the Balfour Declaration, there were some
540,000 Arabs and 60,000 Jews living in the territory west of the
Jordan River. No reliable figure is available for the population, at
that time, living in Transjordan. In modern times there has never
been any Jewish settlement in Transjordan.[1]

Palestine and Jordan were also distinguishable by the fact that
Transjordan was mostly nomadic while Palestine had 800 villages
and two dozen towns. Transjordan was largely desert and steppe

Map 19   British Mandate for Palestine Including Transjordan – 1922

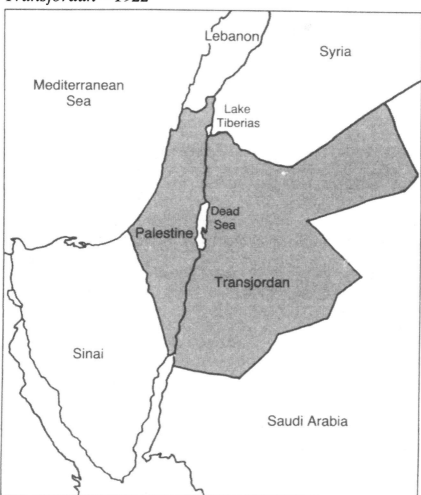

with a narrow strip of cultivable land and with little urban development.

Thirdly, the Balfour Declaration, to which Zionists often refer (see chapter 14) did not promise that all or even part of Palestine should become *the* Jewish national home. It merely declared British *sympathy* with the Zionist goal of creating a Jewish home *in* Palestine. The British government's choice of words was careful and deliberate (see appendix 4).

Fourthly, what is important here is not the Balfour Declaration,

151

which had no legal validity, but the Mandate, which carried the authority of the League of Nations. By virtue of its Article 25 (quoted above) the Mandate clearly provided for the exclusion of Transjordan from the scope of the proposed Jewish national home. The action taken by Britain to exclude Transjordan was duly and properly carried out in accordance with Article 25 and the Zionists had no legal grounds for disputing it.

Originally, the British had artifically joined the west and east banks of the Jordan River (that is, Palestine and Transjordan) both as a matter of convenience in one Mandate and in the hope of getting Jews into the east bank (see map 19). When the British saw that the Palestinians were strongly resisting Zionism they limited the area of application of the Balfour Declaration.

Finally, the Zionist argument that Jordan's population is more than 50 percent Palestinian and that, therefore, a Palestinian state already exists is both disingenuous and cynical. The reason, of course, for the Palestinian presence in Jordan results directly from their expulsion from Palestine in 1948 (see chapter 2) and the West Bank in 1967 by Zionists. Even on the basis of forced dispersal there is no reason why Jordan, with slightly more than 1,000,000 Palestinians, should be preferred as the Palestinian homeland when the area considered to be Israel contains 2,000,000 Palestinians.

Although Israeli Prime Minister Yitzhak Shamir explicitly argued for the 'Jordan is Palestine' position[2] it appears to be a propaganda stunt to mute pressure on Israel to come to terms with the Palestinians. The state of Israel and the World Zionist Organization have never renounced their claim to, and their belief in Jordan being Israel (and not Palestine). The semantical game Zionists play is as follows: if the Jewish national home is in Palestine, and Palestine includes Jordan, then Jordan is Palestine as well. Since Israel is the successor state to all of Palestine then Jordan is Israel.

The Zionist argument about the inclusion of Transjordan within the area of the Palestine Mandate given to Britain has no substance, for it never was the homeland of the Palestinians and was quite properly separated from Palestine and put under a separate Transjordan administration at the outset of the Mandate.

In conclusion, the Zionists' own beliefs concerning Jordan reveals their insincerity and duplicity. They claim that today's Jordan was part of the Palestine Mandate given to Britain, and is therefore part of Palestine, and that it was meant to have been part of the Jewish national home. Therefore, they argue, Jordan is in fact a part of Palestine, 77 percent to be exact. The Zionist claim is not so much that Jordan is Palestine but that Jordan is Israel; that Jordan was wrongfully detached from Palestine (which became Israel in 1948) and rightfully constitutes part of Israel. Presumably, the Israeli argument that Jordan is Palestine may be reworded as follows: Jordan is in reality part of Eretz Israel. Zionism demonstrates its avowed democratic spirit by conceding that Jordan will be allowed to be Palestine. Even if one were to accept the argument, sophistry and all, Jordan might not be allowed to be Palestine for too long. Israeli security needs will surely require an extension of the borders, otherwise the next war might have to be fought on the West Bank.

We are entitled to ask the right to enter and settle in Transjordan.

David Ben-Gurion
Address to the seventeenth Zionist Congress.

Notes to Chapter 13

1. Albert M. Hyamson, *Palestine under the Mandate, 1920–1948*, Methuen, 1950, p. 35.
2. Yitzhak Shamir, 'Israel's Role in a Changing Middle East', *Foreign Affairs*, LX, 4, Spring 1982, pp. 789–801.

Recommended Reading

Nasser H. Aruri, *Jordan: a Study in Political Development (1921–1965)*, Martinus Nijhoff, 1972.

Sir John Bagot Glubb, *A Soldier with the Arabs*, Harper, 1957.

Richard Nyrop, ed., *Jordan: a Country Study*, US Government Printing Office, 1980.

Sheila Ryan and Muhammad Hallaj, *Palestine is, but Not in Jordan*, AAUG, Belmont, 1983.

Chapter 14

The Balfour Declaration

In Palestine we do not propose even to go through the form of consulting the wishes of the present inhabitants of the country.

Lord Balfour
in Doreen Ingrams, comp., *Palestine Papers 1917–1922: Seeds of Conflict*,
George Braziller, 1973, p. 73.

Zionists interpret the Balfour Declaration of 1917 (see appendix 4), and Great Britain's proclaimed support for 'the establishment in Palestine of a national home for the Jewish people', as legitimizing their 'Biblical title' to the land of Palestine (see chapter 15).

Implied in this belief is the myth that the British had the legal right to 'restore' Palestine to its erstwhile and 'true' inhabitants.

Zionists claim that the phrase 'Jewish national home' which appears in the letter of Lord Balfour, the British Foreign Minister at the time, to Lord Rothschild, a leading British Zionist leader, was tantamount to British support for the Zionist goal of a Jewish state. Chaim Weizmann, one of the founders of Zionism, when asked what the Zionists meant by a 'Jewish national home', answered, 'To build up something in Palestine which will be as Jewish as England is English.'[1]

Finally, the Zionists claim that the Balfour Declaration provided international legitimation for the Zionist state in Palestine.

What are the Facts?

First, what is the historical background to the Balfour Declaration?

The Declaration was the culmination of Zionist efforts to secure support for their goals, stated some twenty years earlier at the First Zionist Congress in 1897.

Zionism is a political ideology and a blueprint for action. The stated aim of Zionism was, in the light of their belief that anti-Semitism could never be defeated and eradicated, to 'create for the Jewish people a home in Palestine secured by public law'.[2]

Shortly after the 1897 Zionist Congress, Theodor Herzl, its first president, took steps to obtain public support by meeting the German Kaiser Wilhelm II. In 1901 Herzl attempted to implement a plan whereby the Ottomans would grant the Zionist organization a charter for Palestine in exchange for Jewish assistance to the empire in the solution of its debilitating financial problems. Herzl's diplomatic efforts were all in vain. He died in 1904.

By 1904 Chaim Weizmann, the Zionist leader, moved to England because of his conviction that, among the great powers, Great Britain was most likely to provide support for Zionism. During the following decade he and his associates painstakingly laid the foundations whereby the British would support Zionist objectives or at least not hinder them. Weizmann's vision called for the creation of a Jewish home in Palestine as opposed to Herzl's idea of a home for the Jews.

The negotiations leading up to the Balfour Declaration involved three direct participants: the British government, the Zionists and the non-Zionist British Jews. The Palestinians, who then comprised 91 percent of the population of Palestine, and the Ottoman Turks, who controlled and ruled Palestine, were not party to the negotiations and were not mentioned by name in the subsequent Declaration.

The principal British objective at the time was to win the war against the Germans. This objective required the support of the

United States and Czarist Russia. The British felt that support for a Jewish state would encourage American and Russian Jews to bring pressure on their respective nations more actively to support the British war effort. The German submarine war was taking its toll and the British were desperately seeking support from any quarter. The Zionists offered their support, claiming to be representatives of the 'Jewish people', in return for British support of their goals to establish a state in Palestine. Another reason for British support has been attributed to the anti-Semitism of some British cabinet members, including Balfour. It is worth noting that Herzl himself had earlier attempted to conjure support for his plans among leading British Jews by offering to sponsor and support a plan that would limit the influx of East European Jews into Britain. Leading British Jews felt that the continued influx of their impoverished East European brethren could only lead to increased anti-Semitism in Britain itself. Anti-Semites agree with Zionists that the Jews have no place in their respective societies and therefore have supported or looked favorably on the idea of the establishment of a Jewish state.[3]

The principal Zionist demand was the acquisition of territory and the establishment of a state. Zionist demands were limited by two factors: first, the number of Jews in Palestine in 1917 was a small fraction of the population. Second, the British would negotiate nothing that did not first fit their own imperial plans.

In making their case the Zionists insisted on two important points: first, that the 'national home' be 'reconstituted' so that the impression was given that the Jews had an 'historic right' to Palestine (see chapter 16). Second, the Zionists regarded it as essential that the British government make an unequivocal commitment to carry out the Zionist territorial objective in Palestine. In seeking these objectives, the Zionists deliberately ignored the existence of the Palestinians.

The Jewish community in Britain was opposed to the Zionists. They believed that Zionism would jeopardize the Jewish people in their countries of origin by making demands of loyalty upon them in direct conflict with allegiance to the nations in which they lived. They were worried about the danger of being accused of dual loyalty, or worse, of being disloyal to their own country. Their concern was to maintain the existing rights of the British Jewish community and of Jewish communities in other states.

The anti-Zionist Jews understood that the Zionists' idea of a 'Jewish people' could, in the future, jeopardize Jews in their countries of origin. They knew that Zionism threatened the political rights of Jews through their involuntary inclusion in the claimed 'Jewish people' nationality constituency (see chapter 6).[4] Edwin Montagu, a leader of the British Jewish community, regarded Zionism as a repudiation of Judaism and as a nationalism designed to promote anti-Semitism.[5]

Two important questions arise: first, did the British give Palestine to the Jews? Second, if they did, was it legal for them to do so?

In answering the first question it should be realized that the Declaration was a carefully crafted document, the work of British and Zionist negotiators. Although the Zionists had written most of it, it was given forth under the guise of being an entirely British conception because the British cabinet had approved it. The Balfour Declaration has been viewed as a kind of sacred obligation that the British bestowed upon the Jewish people when, in fact, various Zionists had made the obligation to themselves.[6]

The text itself began with a declaration that the British government viewed with favor the establishment of a Jewish national home in Palestine. The expression 'national home' had no established meaning and was vague. The expression 'viewed with favor' was also vague, meaning not that anything was being given but that the British government would cast a benign eye upon Zionist plans. And when the British said they would use their best endeavours to facilitate the achievement of such an object, namely, the establishment of this national home, this signified that they would either lend a hand or at least not interfere.

The most preposterous nomenclature of the Declaration, though, was the description of the Palestinians who, for all intents and purposes, constituted the population of the country as the 'non-Jewish communities'. The intention was to conceal the true ratio between Arabs and Jews and thereby to make easier the supersession of the former. In the same clause the Declaration addressed itself to the civil and religious rights of the Arabs without defining those civil rights. There was no mention of political rights for the Arabs. The vagueness that runs through the Declaration was quite purposeful.

In conclusion, the Balfour Declaration was not a title, a grant, a promise or a deed but simply a *declaration of intent* on the part of the British government.

In order to answer the second question, as to whether it was legal for Great Britain to give Palestine to the Zionists, the status of the Balfour Declaration in international law deserves analysis.

First, Great Britain, at the time Balfour made the Declaration, possessed no sovereignty in Palestine allowing it to make promises of any kind to any party. The interpretation of the rights described in the Declaration is immaterial. The Balfour Declaration has no basis in international law because, at the time, Palestine was a province of Ottoman Turkey and Britain had no legality to make claims on, about, or promises concerning Palestine.

The Balfour Declaration has been described as a document in which 'one nation solemnly promised to a second nation the country of a third'.[7]

The American diplomat Sol Linowitz wrote:

> The most significant and incontrovertible part is, however, that by itself the [Balfour] Declaration was legally impotent. For Great Britain had no sovereign rights over Palestine; it had no proprietary interest; it had no authority to dispose of the land. The Declaration was merely a statement of British intentions and no more.[8]

Chaim Weizmann's views are important because of his role as a Zionist negotiator: 'The Balfour Declaration of 1917 was built on air', he wrote ten years later.[9]

Secondly, it is immaterial whether the Declaration sought to impose the establishment of a Jewish state or a national home (or even what the difference was between the two concepts). The inhabitants of the land at the time, including the native Jews, all rejected the Balfour Declaration.

It is little known that the Jewish Palestinians (the native non-European Jews of Palestine) also opposed the establishment of a Jewish national home in Palestine. Ronald Storrs, the first British military governor of Jerusalem, wrote: 'The religious Jews of Jerusalem and Hebron and the Sephardim were strongly opposed to political Zionism . . .'[10]

The Zionists have taken it upon themselves to interpret what the British meant by a 'national home'. The definitive interpretation of the Balfour Declaration, however, must remain the prerogative of the British government alone. Repeated official British statements – such as Winston Churchill's White Paper of 1922 and Sir Herbert Samuel's speech in Jerusalem on the King's birthday in 1923 – made it perfectly clear that Britain rejected the Zionist gloss on the Declaration and drew a clear distinction between the concept of a national home and the concept of a national state.

> *Palestine belongs to the Arabs in the same sense that England belongs to the English, or France to the French. It is wrong and inhuman to impose the Jews on the Arabs. What is going on in Palestine today cannot be justified by any moral code of conduct.*
>
> Mahatma Gandhi
> Tendulkar, *Mahatma*, IV, 1938, p. 312.

Thirdly, all Zionist arguments for the validity of the Balfour Declaration are ex post facto validations and have no legal basis. Zionist legal experts often claim that Ottoman Turkish sovereignty over Palestine had been ceded to Great Britain after the First World War. They refer to the Sèvres Peace Treaty where the reference to the Balfour Declaration occurs.

But the Treaty of Sèvres was never ratified by the Ottoman Turks; it was aborted and the final treaty, signed at Lausanne Switzerland between the Turks and the victorious Allied Powers, omitted any reference to Balfour. This omission was important because it meant that when Ottoman Turkey relinquished its sovereignty over Palestine, it did not mortgage the future of Palestine for the establishment of a Jewish state.[11]

The Balfour Declaration was a brief and arbitrary as well as illegal document that remains key in the Arab–Israeli conflict.

The British intentionally and completely ignored the Arabs, who made up 90 percent of the population, by refusing even to mention them by name; they were called the 'non-Jewish communities'. The British were never sincere about the clause concerning the 'rights of existing non-Jewish communities'. As Balfour wrote in a secret memorandum submitted to the British Cabinet in 1919:

> For in Palestine we do not propose even to go through the form of consulting the wishes of the present inhabitants of the country . . .

Zionism be it right or wrong, good or bad, is rooted in age-long traditions, in present needs, in future hopes, of far profounder import than the desires and prejudices of the 700,000 Arabs who now inhabit that ancient land.[12]

Zionism . . . is . . . of far profounder import than the desires and prejudices of the 700,000 Arabs who now inhabit that ancient land.

Lord Balfour
letter to Lord Curzon, 11 August 1919, in Doreen Ingrams, comp.,
Palestine Papers 1917–1922: Seeds of Conflict, George Braziller, 1973,
p. 73.

The Zionists for their part were not always successful in cloaking their real intentions concerning Palestine. Even though they publicly denied their intention of establishing a Jewish state, Chaim Weizmann told a London audience in 1919 that '[The Balfour Declaration] is the key which unlocks the doors of Palestine . . . I hope that the Jewish frontiers of Palestine will be as great as Jewish energy for getting Palestine'.[13]

In conclusion, the Balfour Declaration, regardless of its internal meaning, does not confer legitimacy upon Zionist aspirations regarding Palestine.

In the final analysis the Balfour Declaration is invalid because it violated the principle of self-determination – as far as the Palestinian population was concerned – which was embodied in the covenant of the League of Nations.

In spite of its blatant illegality at every level, the Balfour Declaration has been consistently invoked in order to bolster the Zionist position. It has come to acquire a notoriety and sacredness utterly unjustified. It is worth noting that the Balfour Declaration was not the first instance of the British propensity to barter away Ottoman possessions. In 1915 the British had made a commitment to Hussein Ibn Abdallah, the Sharif of Mecca. That commitment involved the promise of British support for an envisioned independent Arab kingdom that would include Palestine, in exchange for the Sharif's military and diplomatic support of the British against the Ottomans should the latter decide to enter the war on the side of Germany. The British were to renege on every agreement made with Hussein during an exchange that has come to be known as the Hussein–McMahon correspondence. Although the agreement was reached more than a year before the Balfour Declaration and was conducted with a legitimate representative of the national aspirations of the Arab inhabitants of Greater Syria, Zionist interpretation of history would have us view the one but not the other as legally binding.

Notes to Chapter 14

1. Chaim Weizmann, 'The Balfour Declaration', in Mordechai S. Chertoff, ed., *Zionism: a Basic Reader*, Herzl Press, 1975, p. 31.
2. 'The Basle Program', in Walter Laqueur and Barry Rubin, eds., *The Israel–Arab Reader: a Documentary History of the Middle East Conflict*, Penguin, 1984, p. 11. See appendix 5.
3. The English Zionist, Leonard Stein, has provided a careful history of the negotiations leading to the Declaration and the anti-Semitism of the British cabinet. *The Balfour Declaration*, Vallentine, Mitchell, 1961.
4. Sally V. and W. Thomas Mallison, *The Palestine Problem in International Law and World Order*, Longman, 1986.
5. Stein, op. cit., p. 484.
6. J. M. N. Jeffries, 'Analysis of the Balfour Declaration', in Walid Khalidi, *From Haven to Conquest: Readings in Zionism and the Palestine Problem until 1948*, Institute for Palestine Studies, 1971, pp. 173–88; Stein, op. cit.; Nahum Sokolov, *History of Zionism, 1600–1918*, Ktav, 1969.
7. Arthur Koestler, *Promise and Fulfillment: Palestine, 1917–1949*, Macmillan, 1949, p. 4.
8. Sol M. Linowitz, 'Analysis of a Tinderbox: the Legal Basis for the State of Israel'. *American Bar Association Journal*, XLIII, 1957, pp. 522–3.
9. In Mallison, 'The Balfour Declaration', in Abu-Lughod, ed., *The Transformation of Palestine: Essays on the Origin and Development of the Arab–Israeli Conflict*, Northwestern University Press, 1971, p. 85.
10. Ronald Storrs, *Orientations*, Weidenfeld and Nicolson, 1945, p. 340.
11. Henry Cattan, *Palestine and International Law: the Legal Aspects of the Arab–Israeli Conflict*, 2nd edn, Longman, 1973, pp. 51–62.

12. Public Record Office. FO. 371/4183, in Doreen Ingrams, comp., *Palestine Papers, 1917–1922: Seeds of Conflict*, George Braziller, 1973, p. 73.
13. Chaim Weizmann, *Chaim Weizmann: Excerpts from His Historic Statements, Writings and Addresses*, Jewish Agency for Palestine, 1952, p. 48. Zionist historians, being more discreet, omitted these passages from later editions of the book.

Recommended Reading

Alex Bein, *Theodor Herzl: a Biography*, Jewish Publication Society of America, 1943.

Henry Cattan, *Palestine and International Law: the Legal Aspects of the Arab–Israeli Conflict*, 2nd edn, Longman, 1976.

W. T. Mallison, Jr, 'The Balfour Declaration: an Appraisal in International Law', in Ibrahim Abu-Lughod, ed., *The Transformation of Palestine: Essays on the Origin and Development of the Arab–Israeli Conflict*, Northwestern University Press, 1971, pp. 60–111.

Sally V. and W. Thomas Mallison, *The Palestine Problem in International Law and World Order*, Longman, 1986.

Oskar K. Rabinowicz, *Herzl: Architect of the Balfour Declaration*, Herzl Press, 1958.

Chaim Weizmann, *Trial and Error: the Autobiography of Chaim Weizmann*, Harper Brothers, 1949.

Chapter 15

The Bible, Palestine and the Jews

Jewish and Christian Zionists claim that the Jews' exclusive right to the land of Palestine is based on Biblical promises. The fundamental axiom of political Zionism rests on this claim. As Prime Minister Golda Meir once said, 'This country exists as a result of a promise made by God Himself'.[1]

Zionists claim that this promise was made to the Jews. Zionists also make a number of different claims concerning the extent of the 'promised land' (see maps 2–6, 20, pp. 40–1, 102–3, 107 and 171). Finally, they claim that the promise is irrevocable, that the land is theirs forever.

What are the Facts?

First, to whom were the promises made? The promise was given to Abraham in Genesis xii, 7: 'Unto thy seed will I give this land.' Genesis xv, 18 is more explicit: 'Unto thy seed have I given this land, from the river of Egypt unto the great river, the river Euphrates.' (See map 12, p. 141.)

The Zionist claim that this promise was made exclusively to the Jews is incorrect, however. Abraham, through his son Ishmael, is also the father of the Arabs, and therefore the phrase 'to thy seed' inevitably includes the Arabs in this promise. Genesis xxi, 10–12 does not cancel the promises made to Abraham's seed as a whole. The passage reads:

> [Sarah] said to Abraham, Cast out this bondwoman and her son: for the son of this bondwoman shall not be heir with my son Isaac. But God affirmed to Abraham: In all that Sarah saith unto thee, hearken unto her voice: for in Isaac shall seed be called unto thee. And also of the son of the bondwoman will I make a nation, because he [Ishmael] is thy seed.

Woe to men who add house to house, who join field to field till there is room for none but them in all the land.

Isaiah, v, 8

When the covenant of circumcision was made with Abraham and the land of Canaan promised as 'an everlasting possession', it was Ishmael who was circumcised; Isaac had not yet been born. The 'promise' was not made to the Jews exclusively.

Second, what was the extent of the 'promised land'? This question is a little more difficult to determine since there are a number of different references in the Bible. After the birth of Isaac and Ishmael the Book of Deuteronomy (i, 7–8) describes God's command to Moses to occupy the country from the Mediterranean in the west to the Euphrates in the east, and from the Negev desert in the south to the Lebanon in the north. The Israelites did not or could not fulfill this command.

Thirdly, was the promise irrevocable? Zionists, who are not in general religious, point to the promise supposedly made by God in Genesis xiii, 15, 'All the land which you see I will give to you and your descendants for ever,' to ultimately justify the right of the Jews to Palestine. The Hebrew expression *'ad 'olam* has been translated as 'for ever', but its correct meaning is 'until a long time'. The expression meant, according to Deuteronomy xv, 17, for the length of a person's life or to the end of an age. The covenants and promises made by God in the Old Testament were

165

clearly understood to be valid for the foreseeable future and not for eternity.[2]

According to the Biblical scholar, Professor William Holladay, the land was not presented to the Israelites 'as a perpetual right but as a gift, a privilege, something that can be withdrawn if the people are disobedient'.[3] In fact, as all the prophets warned, the privilege was withdrawn because Israel failed to keep the Covenant, and the people went into exile.

Professor Benjamin Beit-Hallahmi of Haifa University has also noted that although 90 percent of Israeli Jews are not religious an overwhelming majority of them believe God gave them Palestine.

Many Jewish and Christian Zionists make vigorous arguments that the creation of the Zionist state of Israel is a fulfilment of Old Testament prophesies. It should be noted that the Biblical promise of the ingathering of all Jews in the Holy Land at the end of days rested on the return of the Messiah without whom the Jews were explicitly forbidden to return. The Christian Messiah arrived 1948 years prior to the establishment of the state and no pious Jew would argue that the Jewish Messiah has already come.

God is neither Israel's real estate agent nor the Arab world's general.

Anthony H. Cordesman, former American official
'The Middle East and the Cost of the Politics of Force', *Middle East Journal*, XL, 1, Winter 1986, p. 8.

There are three further points to be made which Zionists generally do not address. First, it should be stressed that the Zionist claim to ownership of Palestine is based on a selective and self-serving reading of the Old Testament. Most of the founders of Zionism from Herzl to Begin were not religious at all.

Second, the Zionist reading of the Bible is frighteningly literal. The Book of Joshua, so often invoked today in the Israeli army rabbinate, dwells upon the sanctified extermination of conquered populations, putting everyone to 'the edge of the sword . . . both man and woman, young and old' (Joshua vi, 21). This question is quite serious as witness the Israeli invasion of Lebanon in 1982 (see chapter 12).

The Israeli Army rabbinate continually preaches the doctrine of holy war. The central theme was given by a rabbi with the rank of captain:

> We must not overlook the Biblical sources which justify this war [the 1982 war in Lebanon] and our presence here. We are fulfilling our religious duty as Jews by being here. So it is written: the religious duty to conquer the Land from the enemy.[4]

In the early 1970s the Israeli Army rabbinate distributed an appalling booklet explaining the duty of killing non-Jews, even civilians, according to rabbinic law.[5]

What effect might this literal interpretation have on Israeli children in the future? Israeli psychologist G. Tamarin of Tel Aviv University, tested 1,000 children between the ages of eight and fourteen who read the account of slaughter at Jericho given in the Book of Joshua (vi, 20–21). He then asked the question: 'Suppose the Israeli Army occupies an Arab village in battle. Do you think it would be proper, or not, to act against the inhabitants as did Joshua with the people of Jericho?' The number of children who answered 'Yes' varied between 66 percent and 95 percent, according to the school attended or the kibbutz or town where they lived.[6]

Finally, it is fair to ask whether an alleged promise to a wandering shepherd nearly 4,000 years ago (and not written down until 800 years later) in a book accepted as the word of God by a fraction of the world's population, can or should have much legal or political relevance today.

Notes to Chapter 15

1. *Le Monde*, 15 October 1971.
2. Dewey M. Beegle, *Prophecy and Prediction*, Pryor Pettengill, 1978, p. 183.

3. William Holladay, 'Is the Old Testament Zionist?', *Middle East Newsletter* (London), XI, 6, June–July 1968.
4. *Ha'aretz*, 5 July 1982.
5. Noam Chomsky, *Towards a New Cold War: Essays on the Current Crisis and How We Got There*, Pantheon Books, 1982, p. 305. Also see SWASIA, 6 June 1975, National Council of Churches.
6. 'The Zionist State and Jewish Identity', published as *Israca*, 5, January 1973.

Recommended Reading

Elias Chacour, *Blood Brothers: a Palestinian Struggles for Reconciliation in the Middle East*, Chosen Books, 1984.

R. Garaudy, *The Case of Israel: a Study of Political Zionism*, Shorouk International, 1983.

Alfred Guillaume, *Zionists and the Bible*, Institute for Palestine Studies, 1954.

Hassan Haddad and Donald Wagner, eds., *All in the Name of the Bible: Selected Essays on Israel, South Africa, and American Christian Fundamentalism*, Special Report 5, Palestine Human Rights Campaign, 1985.

Grace Halsell, *Journey to Jerusalem*, Macmillan, 1981.

Grace Halsell, *Prophecy and Politics: Militant Evangelists on the Road to Nuclear War*, Westport, Conn.: Lawrence Hill, 1986.

Chapter 16

The Jews' Historic Right to Palestine

Zionists claim that they have an historic right to Palestine which provides the justification for the modern state of Israel. 'The land is the historic home of the Jews,' declared the World Zionist Organization at the 1919 Peace Conference in Versailles.[1] When the state of Israel was proclaimed in 1948 it was 'by virtue of the natural and historic right of the Jewish people'.[2]

Zionists claim that this idea of 'historic right' is linked with the 'promised land' which supposedly confers on all Jews, even if they are not Israeli citizens, a genuine 'divine right' of ownership and domination over Palestine.

What are the Facts?

The justification for this 'historic right' cited by Zionists is the evidence of the Old Testament and the fact that, among many other invaders and inhabitants of Palestine over the millennia, the Jews were also once present.

First, there is no trace found, outside Biblical texts, of the events before the tenth century BC described therein. As for the 'evidence' of the Old Testament it was written by the Jewish patriarchs and therefore the theme of an 'historic right' to the land of Palestine appears only in texts emanating from those who claim to be the beneficiaries thereof.

Do the Zionists perhaps mean that the Jews were the first inhabitants? No, this cannot be the case since there were people, namely the Canaanites, who were there when the Hebrew tribes invaded. Besides, there were also other peoples there before the Jews: the Hittites, the Ammonites, the Moabites and the Edomites.

Do the Zionists mean that the Jews were in some way different and therefore entitled to an exclusive claim to Palestine? This cannot be the case since the Jews, when they conquered Palestine, were just one group of invaders in a long line of conquerors among others (Babylonians, Hittites, Egyptians, Persians, Greeks, Romans, Arabs, Turks).

One of the bases for Zionist territorial claims is the extent of the Kingdom of David and Solomon which lasted for about seventy-three years. Settled populations have inhabited Palestine for some 9,000 years. Much of the land, therefore, which the Zionists claim as exclusively theirs, has been predominantly populated by Jews for less than 1 percent of its history (see appendix 1).

> *If it is proper to 'reconstitute' a Jewish state which has not existed for two thousand years, why not go back another thousand years and reconstitute the Canaanite state? The Canaanites, unlike the Jews, are still there.*
>
> H. G. Wells
> in Frank C. Sakran, *Palestine Dilemma: Arab Rights Versus Zionist Aspirations*, Public Affairs Press, 1948, p. 204.

What, then, is this 'historic right' to Palestine which the Zionists claim?

In about 1200 BC certain Semitic tribes, claiming descent from Abraham, invaded Palestine. By about 1000 BC the Israelites, as they were known, had achieved preeminence under David and Solomon and their kingdom had reached its greatest extent, though the coastal plain had never been taken from the Philistines who had come from Crete at almost the same time as the Hebrew

Map 20   Israel of David and Solomon

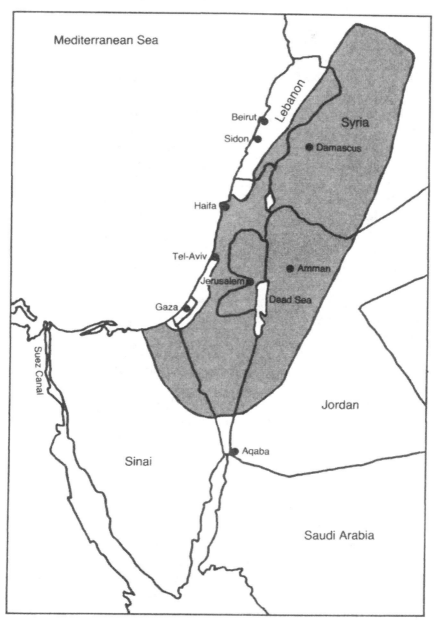

Shown with 1967 ceasefire boundaries.
Source: Sheila Ryan and Muhammad Hallaj, *Palestine is, but Not in Jordan*, Association of Arab–American University Graduates, Belmont, 1983.

171

tribes. (In fact, the land from Gaza to present day Tel Aviv was never, until the middle of the twentieth century, under Jewish control.)

After David, who died in about 970 BC, the Israelite Kingdom declined, dividing, on the death of Solomon, into two parts, Israel, in the northern half, and Judah. About 720 BC the Assyrians overran Israel and in 587 BC Judah was seized by the Babylonians and Jerusalem was destroyed. In both cases most of the population was deported, although the Jews were permitted to return in 540 BC. Around 165 BC the Jews regained a measure of independence which ended when the Romans took Jerusalem in 63 BC.

From AD 70, when the Roman emperor Titus destroyed the Temple, the Jewish community in Palestine practically ceased to exist. A Jewish pilgrim, Benjamin of Tudelas, who visited Palestine in 1170, found 1,440 Jews in the whole country. One hundred years later, a Jewish traveler, Nahum Gerondi, found only two Jewish families in Jerusalem.[3]

When the Christian Crusaders captured Jerusalem in 1099 they burned the Jews in their synagogue. Fortunately, when Saladin, the Muslim conqueror, retook the city in 1187 he allowed the Jews to return.

Although Jews had dreamt nostalgically of being 'next year in Jerusalem' their return to Palestine resulted more from persecution elsewhere. The first Jews to return came from Spain in 1492.[4] They had felt no need to emigrate during eight centuries of coexistence with the Arabs (who, incidentally, were also expelled from Spain along with the Jews), but fled as a result of the intolerance of the Catholic Inquisition.

By 1845 there were only 12,000 Jews in Palestine out of an estimated total population of 350,000. In 1922 the Jews formed slightly more than a tenth of the population of Palestine.[5]

Does the supposed 'historic right' of the Jews to Palestine supersede the rights of the existing native inhabitants? The Zionists seem to believe this since, after all, they declared their state to be a *Jewish* state. Furthermore, they claim that this existing native population is not native but came from outside in the early part of the century or descended from the Arabs who invaded from the Arabian peninsula in the seventh century.

The facts are that modern anthropologists believe that today's Palestinians are descended from the Canaanites, the earliest recorded inhabitants of the land, and the Philistines. Those Arabs who did migrate in the seventh century are also considered Palestinian since 1,200 years of residence certainly qualify them as natives of the land.

The Palestinian people, despite the infusion of other peoples, have remained the natural inhabitants of this land. Certainly each invasion, including the Arabs in the seventh century, created an admixture. But as a prominent American writer has explained,

> The position of the Arabs in Palestine is unique, for unlike all the other foreign conquerors, they did not hold themselves aloof but, instead, made Muslim converts of the natives, settled down as residents, and intermarried with them, with the result that all are now so completely Arabized that we cannot tell where the Canaanites leave off and the Arabs begin.[6]

Professor Maxime Rodinson, a French Jewish historian, has put it similarly:

> A small contingent of Arabs from Arabia did indeed conquer the country in the seventh century. But . . . the Palestinian population soon became Arabized . . . in a way that it was never to become Latinized or Ottomanized. The invaded melted with the invaders.

By the twentieth century, Rodinson writes, 'The Arab population of Palestine was native in all the usual senses of the word.'[7]

In the modern world 'historic titles' are not considered important. For example, in Africa, the Organization of African Unity has abandoned them altogether, rather than plunge the continent into chaos by attempting to redefine the boundaries of, for example, the ancient and extinct Mandingo Empire. As Lord Sydenham remarked in the British House of Lords over sixty years ago: 'If we are going to admit claims based on conquests of thousands of years ago, the whole world will have to be turned upside down.'[8]

If we are going to admit claims on conquest thousands of years ago, the whole world will have to be turned upside down.

Lord Sydenham
Hansard, House of Lords, 21 June 1922.

It is absurd for any one people to make an exclusive claim to the land based on history. The land has been invaded and occupied by so many people that it is impossible for any one group to demand it through historic title. Do the Zionists have a better right than the Canaanites and Egyptians who were there earlier, or the Muslims who were there longest? To paraphrase Roger Garaudy: by what historical manipulation is the international community asked to remember only those episodes in this long history when Jews appear?

Notes to Chapter 16

1. J. C. Hurewitz, *Diplomacy in the Near and Middle East*, II, Van Nostrand, 1956, p. 46.
2. 'State of Israel Proclamation of Independence', in Walter Laqueur and Barry Rubin, eds., *The Israel–Arab Reader: a Documentary History of the Middle East Conflict*, Penguin, 1984, document 26.
3. R. Garaudy, *The Case of Israel: a Study of Political Zionism*, Shorouk International, 1983, p. 35.
4. Using the word 'return' is a bit misleading because the ancestors of these Jews had departed Palestine upwards of a thousand years before in some cases.
5. Great Britain, Government of Palestine, *Statistical Abstract of Palestine 1941*, p. 12.
6. Ilene Beatty, *Arab and Jew in the Land of Canaan*, Henry Regnery, 1957.
7. Maxime Rodinson, *Israel and the Arabs*, Penguin, 1968, p. 216.
8. *Hansard*, House of Lords, 21 June 1922.

Recommended Reading

Ilene Beatty, *Arab and Jew in the Land of Canaan*, Henry Regnery, 1957.

R. Garaudy, *The Case of Israel: a Study of Political Zionism*, Shorouk International, 1983.

Ilan Halevi, *A History of the Jews: Ancient and Modern*, trans. A. M. Berrett, Zed Press, 1987.

Abram Leon, *The Jewish Question: a Marxist Interpretation*, Pathfinder Press, 1970.

Maxime Rodinson, *Israel and the Arabs*, Penguin, 1968.

Chapter 17

Arabs and Jews

Zionists make varying claims as to why Arabs and Jews are fighting in the Middle East. Some argue that the Arabs are anti-Semitic. It was once a popular Zionist argument to claim that the Arab–Israeli conflict is but a continuation of the wars described in the Old Testament. Some Zionists, along with the founders of the movement, claim that Arabs and Jews have some ancient, deep-rooted, ineradicable hatred between them that is the real root of the present conflict.

Zionists have metaphorically identified the modern state of Israel with Israelites fleeing from Egyptian bondage and fighting the Philistines for possession of the Promised Land. The Arabs are identified with the enemies of ancient Israel.

The Zionist view was best expressed by Israel's first Prime Minister, David Ben-Gurion, who wrote in his diaries:

> When we have broken the strength of the Arab Legion and
> bombarded Amman, we would wipe out Transjordan; after that,
> Syria would fall . . . we would thus end the war, and would have
> put paid to Egypt, Assyria and Chaldea on behalf of our ancestors.[1]

Zionists also focus on the several events in more than one

thousand years of Jewish–Muslim coexistence where harm was done to a particular Jewish community; they overlook the times of harmony. Zionists claim that the Jews were consistently persecuted under Arab rule and that this demonstrates that the Arabs are anti-Semitic.[2] Zionists tend to identify Muslims with Arabs and sometimes cite anti-Semitic statements of non-Arab Muslims to bolster the impression that racial hatred is at the bottom of Arab animosity towards Israel.[3]

Israel has often portrayed the Arabs as barbarians wanting to 'throw the Jews into the sea'.

What are the Facts?

In truth, the enmity between the Arabs and Jews is of recent origin. It can be directly traced to the colonizing mission of European Jews who brought with them to the Middle East the philosophy of Zionism which was a reaction to the anti-Semitism prevalent in Europe at the turn of the century.

The Zionist settlement of Arab Palestine, which increasingly was recognized as exclusivist by the native Muslim and Christian Arabs, created the present conflict. The Zionists' self-proclaimed goal was to establish a Jewish state in the land owned and occupied by the Arabs. The Arabs quickly understood that they were to have no place in this proposed Jewish state and therefore resisted its establishment.

I should much rather see reasonable agreement with the Arabs on the basis of living together in peace than the creation of a Jewish state.

Albert Einstein
Out of My Later Years, Littlefield Adams, 1967, in Moshe Menuhin,
The Decadence of Judaism in Our Time, Institute for Palestine Studies,
1969, p. 324.

The classic Zionist characterization of Arab resistance to coloniz-ation as being or nearly being anti-Semitic follows from the logic of Zionism itself. This logic postulates that all non-Jews were, and would be forever, racially anti-Semitic.

Chaim Weizmann, the father of Israel, described this as a 'bacillus', an incurable disease which every non-Jew carried within him, whether he knew it or not.[4] The early Zionists assumed Jews, everywhere and for all time, to be a 'race' who could never be safe from persecution except within a Jewish state. In this light we can see why a Zionist would describe Arab resistance to occupation as motivated by anti-Semitism rather than the real motivation which was the result of an injustice.

The success of Zionism has given rise to the tendency to reinterpret the conflict between Arabs and Zionists as a continuation of medieval Muslim-Jewish religious confrontation. One rarely finds this attitude in pre-Zionist Jewish historians.

A sufficient body of historical evidence exists showing that, in fact, relations between Arabs and Jews were on the whole, relatively amiable before the influx of European Zionist settlers. In *The Jews of Arab Lands* Norman Stillman says that, in medieval times,

> It is not mere coincidence that the flowering of Jewish culture in the Arab world should occur at the very time that Islamic civilization was at its apogee. Day to day contacts between Muslims and non-Muslims were on the whole amicable.[5]

Professor Salo Wittmayer Baron, the renowned Jewish historian, in his magnum opus wrote that 'compared with conditions in other countries, the status of Jews in Islamic lands was fairly satisfactory in both theory and practice'. He went on to say that 'under Islam, the Jews were never treated as "aliens". Hence the absence of any large-scale expulsions of Jews.' Baron concluded that 'Insecure as life generally was in the troubled periods of Islam's decline, there was none of that feeling of personal insecurity which dominated the medieval Jewish psyche in the West.'

The Jew knew, Baron points out, that he would not suffer, because he was a Jew, in the Arab world.[6] This is not to say that there was no persecution of Christians and Jews during particularly unenlightened times of Arab Muslim rule.

The Jews became fully Arabized after the spread of Islam from the seventh to tenth centuries. So did the Christians and other minorities in the Middle East. The Jews followed Muslim intellectual fashions, used the vernacular for their literature and considered Europe as an outpost of barbarism.

The influence of Jews in the Arab caliphate was considerable. When Spain was ruled by the Arab Caliph Abd er-Rahman III, his principle advisor and confidant was a Jew, Hasdai ibn Shabrut, an outstanding figure of this period.[7]

Another Jew, Samuel Hanagid, was the first Spanish Jew to be granted the title 'prince' under the Arab caliphate; he later commanded a great army in the mid-eleventh century.[8]

Zionists claim that anti-Semitism or an ancient animosity motivates the Arabs to 'throw the Jews into the sea' and to genocidal acts. At the time of the June 1967 war it was stridently asserted by Israel's supporters that Egyptian President Gamal Nasser threatened to drive the Israelis into the sea.

These Jews of the Diaspora would like to see in us, for their own reasons, heroes with our backs to the wall. But this wish can in no way change the realities.

Israeli General Ezer Weizmann
Le Monde, 3 June 1972.

This claim, for which there was no evidence at all, was almost universally believed in the West and it had a powerful effect on public opinion in Britain and the United States at that time.

In Britain one Member of Parliament even quoted it during a television program, provoking another Member of Parliament, Christopher Mayhew, to offer £5,000 to any of the millions of viewers who could produce evidence that Nasser had made such a statement. Mr Mayhew repeated the offer later on television, and in the House of Commons[9] and broadened it to include genocidal statements by other Arab leaders. As he explained in a letter to the *Manchester Guardian*:

I made this £5,000 offer with a quite serious intention. I wanted to help to reassure Jewish people that, in spite of much Israeli propaganda to the contrary, responsible Arab leaders are not genocidal. Those who try to suggest otherwise are seriously mistaken and merely help to increase the fear and hatred in the Middle East which does so much to prevent a peaceful settlement.[10]

During the following four years Mr Mayhew received a steady trickle of letters from eager claimants, each one producing some blood-curdling quotation from an Arab leader, usually culled straight from one pro-Israeli publication or another. Mr Mayhew replied to each claimant, explaining that the quotation was mistranslated, wrongly attributed or invented, as the case might be, but always adding that if the claimant was not satisfied he could take him to court.

Eventually, one claimant, a Mr Warren Bergson, did take Mr Mayhew to court. Bergson issued a writ during the October 1974 General Election for Parliament at a time when Mr Mayhew was contesting the constituency of Bath.

In February 1976 the case was heard. Significantly, Mr Bergson was unable to offer evidence for Nasser's alleged statement. Instead, he produced a genocidal threat alleged to have been made by the then Secretary-General of the Arab League, Azzam Pasha, in 1948. When Mr Mayhew produced the original statement in Arabic, however, the claimant was unable to deny that his English version was a flagrant and apparently deliberate mistranslation.

In Britain's High Court of Justice Mr Bergson later acknowledged that, after thorough research, he had been unable to find any statement by a responsible Arab leader which could be described as genocidal. In his settlement statement Mr Bergson regretted 'the inconvenience caused to Mr Mayhew by the issue of this Writ which was widely publicized during the course of his election campaign and apologizes for his suggestion that Mr Mayhew was not a man of integrity because he did not pay £5,000'.

The irony of the claim that the Arabs want to throw the Jews into the sea has not been lost on the Palestinians. While Zionists sought to convince public opinion that their existence was at stake they had, literally, pushed the Palestinians into the sea. Major R. D. Wilson, who served with the British 6th Airborne Division describes the situation in Haifa in 1948: 'Tens of thousands of panic-stricken Arabs streamed out of Haifa . . . The journey was not without its perils since they were open to attack by Jews.'[11]

As photographic evidence shows, Palestinians were driven into the sea at Jaffa late in April 1948. With land routes cut off by

Zionist forces, tens of thousands from the Arab city of Jaffa and neighboring villages fled by boat to Gaza and Egypt; scores were drowned.

There are 3,000 years between the events of the Old Testament and the events of today and 1,300 years between the rise of the Muslim Arabs and today. It is quite true that during this amount of time one can find incidents of massacres of Jews under Muslim Arab rule – as well as massacres of Christians and fellow Muslims. History has also recorded massacres against Hindus, Armenians, Cambodians – and the list goes on. World history is sordid and laced with cruelty of one people against another. Therefore to see in the Arabs an ancient enemy is not only historically inaccurate but anthropologically untenable, not to mention politically self-serving.

To describe all Arab enmity towards Israel as anti-Semitic is misleading. The Arab enmity towards Israel is not based on anti-Semitism but on an injustice done to them by a state that happens to call itself a Jewish state. Had Israel been a Protestant state Arab enmity would not be against Protestants but against the state that describes itself as such and which usurped their land.

It is incorrect to view Arabs and Jews as enemies. In a sense it is incorrect to call the conflict the 'Arab–Israeli Conflict'. The struggle is one between Palestinians and Zionists. It must in conclusion be said that it is ironic that the West today should appear so eager to accept and bemoan so-called Arab and Muslim anti-Semitism. Anti-Semitism does indeed have a long and ugly history, thanks to its mainly Christian European origins. Zionist historians who eagerly date the beginnings of modern Arab anti-Semitism to the 1840 Damascus blood libel, in which Jews were falsely accused of slaughtering gentile children, often omit to mention that this first instance of a Christian anti-Semitic accusation was orchestrated by the French consul in Damascus.

Notes to Chapter 17

1. Michel Bar-Zohar, *The Armed Prophet: a Biography of Ben-Gurion*, Prentice-Hill, 1967, p. 139.
2. This kind of argument is made in many different books, including: Mordechai S. Chertoff, *Zionism: a Basic Reader*, Herzl Press, 1975; Shmuel Ettinger, 'The Modern Period', in *A History of the Jewish People*, H. H. Ben-Sasson, ed., Harvard University Press, 1976. The theme of Arab anti-Semitism has become popular among Zionist apologists wishing to deflect public attention away from the rights of the Palestinian people; for example, Bernard Lewis, *Semites and Anti-Semites: an Inquiry into Conflict and Prejudice*, W. W. Norton, 1986.
3. Leonard J. Davis, *Myths and Facts 1985: a Concise Record of the Arab–Israeli Conflict*, Near East Report, 1984, p. 133.
4. Richard Crossman, *A Nation Reborn: the Land of Weizmann, Bevin and Ben-Gurion*, Hamish Hamilton, 1960.
5. Norman A. Stillman, *The Jews of Arab Lands: a History and Source Book*, Jewish Publication Society of America, 1979, pp. 61, 62.
6. Salo Wittmayer Baron, *A Social and Religious History of the Jews*, 2nd edn, Columbia University Press and Jewish Publication Society of America, 1957, III, *Heirs of Rome and Persia*, p. 172.
7. Cecil Roth, *A Short History of the Jewish People, 1600 BC–AD 1935*, Macmillan, 1936, pp. 155–7.
8. T. Carmi, ed. and trans., *The Penguin Book of Hebrew Verse*, Penguin, 1982, p. 98.
9. *Hansard*, 18 October 1973.
10. *Manchester Guardian*, 9 September 1974.
11. R. D. Wilson, *Cordon and Search: with 6th Airborne Division in Palestine*, Vale and Polden, 1949, p. 193.

Recommended Reading

Salo Wittmayer Baron, *A Social and Religious History of the Jews*, Columbia University Press and Jewish Publication Society of America, 17 vols, 1952–1983.
Norman A. Stillmann, *The Jews of Arab Lands: a History and Source Book*, Jewish Publication Society of America, 1979.

Appendices

1 Rulers of Palestine

Ruler	Date	Length (in years)
Canaanites	first settlers	?
Egypt	indefinite	indefinite
Hyksos	1710–1480 BC	230
Egypt (authenticated)	1480–1350 BC	130
Hittite	1350–1290 BC	60
Egypt	1290–1154 BC	136
Canaanites, Philistines and Jews	1154–1000 BC	154
Jews (David and Solomon)	1000–927 BC	73
Jews (Israel, Ten tribes)	927–722 BC	(205)
Jews (Judah)	927–586 BC	(341)
Jews (widest spread)	1000–586 BC	414
Babylonia	586–538 BC	48
Persia	538–330 BC	208
Greece	330–323 BC	7
Egyptians (Ptolemies)	323–200 BC	123
Seleucids	200–142 BC	57

Jews (Maccabees, partial)		
Seleucids (Tryphon, partial)	142–70 BC	72
Armenia	70–63 BC	7
Rome (Western and Eastern)	63 BC–AD 614	677
Persia	AD 614–628	14
Rome	AD 628–638	10
Arab (Muslim)	AD 638–1085	447
Turks (Seljuk: Muslim)	AD 1085–1099	14
Crusaders (Christian, partial)		
Turks (Seljuk, partial)	AD 1099–1291	192
Arabs (Muslim, partial)		
Egypt (Mameluks)	AD 1291–1517	226
Turks (Ottoman)	AD 1517–1918	401
Great Britain (Military and Mandate)	AD 1918–1948	30
Arabs (Jordan, partial)	AD 1948–1967	19
Jews (partial)	AD 1948–1967	38+
Jews	1967–present	

Source: Ilene Beatty, 'The Land of Canaan', in Walid Khalidi, ed., *From Haven to Conquest: Readings in Zionism and the Palestine Problem until 1948*, Institute for Palestine Studies, 1971, pp. 15–16.

2 Estimated Population of Palestine, 1870–1946

Year	Arabs (%)	Jews (%)	Total
1870	367,224 (98%)	7,000 (2%)	375,000
1893	469,000 (98%)	10,000 (2%)	479,000
1912	525,000 (93%)	40,000 (6%)	565,000
1920	542,000 (90%)	61,000 (10%)	603,000
1925	598,000 (83%)	120,000 (17%)	719,000

1930	763,000 (82%)	165,000 (18%)	928,000
1935	886,000 (71%)	355,000 (29%)	1,241,000
1940	1,014,000 (69%)	463,000 (31%)	1,478,000
1946	1,237,000 (65%)	608,000 (35%)	1,845,000

Figures are rounded.

Sources: The demography of Palestine has become a field of study unto itself due to the lack of accurate data in the nineteenth century. The numbers in this table are estimates constructed from the following sources: Walid Khalidi, *From Haven to Conquest: Readings in Zionism and the Palestine Problem until 1948*, Institute for Palestine Studies, 1971, appendix I; Yehoshua Ben-Arieh, 'The Population of the Large Towns in Palestine during the First Eighty Years of the Nineteenth Century, According to Western Sources', in Moshe Ma'oz, ed. *Studies on Palestine during the Ottoman Period*, Magnus, 1975; Janet L. Abu-Lughod, 'The Demographic Transformation of Palestine', in Ibrahim Abu-Lughod, ed., *The Transformation of Palestine: Essays on the Origin and Development of the Arab–Israeli Conflict*, Northwestern University Press, 1971, pp. 139–63; Alexander Schölch, 'The Demographic Development of Palestine, 1850–1882', *International Journal of Middle East Studies*, XVII, 4, November 1985, pp. 485–505; 'Palestine', *Encyclopedia Britannica*, 11th edn, 1911; 'Palestine', *The Encyclopedia of Islam*, 1964; UN Document A/AC 14/32, 11 November 1947, p. 304; Justin McCarthy, 'The Population of Ottoman Syria and Iraq, 1878–1914', *Asian and African Studies*, XV, 1, March 1981; Kemal Karpat, 'Ottoman Population Records and the Census of 1881/82–1893', *International Journal of Middle East Studies*, XCI, 2, 1978 and Bill Farrell, 'Review of Joan Peters' "From Time Immemorial" ', *Journal of Palestine Studies*, 53, Fall 1984, pp. 126–34.

3 Land Ownership in Palestine, 1882–1946

Year	Arab, Public and State (%)	Jews (%)
1882	99.9	0.09
1890	99.6	0.4
1900	99.2	0.8
1914	98.4	1.6
1920	97.5	2.5
1930	95.5	4.5
1946	94.3	5.7

Sources: Institut National de Statistique, Economic Memorandum, *La Palestine*, Paris, 1948, p. 57; Nathan Weinstock, 'The Impact of Zionist Colonization on Palestinian Arab Society before 1948', *Journal of Palestine Studies*, 6, Winter 1973, pp. 55, 56; Government of Palestine, *A Survey of Palestine*, I, Jerusalem, 1946, pp. 103, 244; Appendix VI, Report of Sub-Committee 2 to the Ad Hoc Committee on the Palestine Question, Document A/AC 32, 11 November 1947, p. 270; Matiel E. T. Mogannam, *The Arab Woman and the Palestine Problem*, Herbert Joseph, 1937, p. 197; Kenneth W. Stein, *The Land Question in Palestine, 1917–1939*, University of North Carolina Press, 1984.

4   The Balfour Declaration, 2 November 1917

Dear Lord Rothschild,

I have much pleasure in conveying to you, on behalf of His Majesty's Government, the following declaration of sympathy with Jewish Zionist aspirations which has been submitted to, and approved by, the Cabinet.

His Majesty's Government view with favour the establishment in Palestine of a national home for the Jewish peoples, and will use their best endeavours to facilitate the achievement of this object, it being clearly understood that nothing shall be done which may prejudice the civil and religious rights of existing non-Jewish communities in Palestine, or the rights and political status enjoyed by Jews in any other country. I should be grateful if you would bring this declaration to the knowledge of the Zionist Federation.

Yours sincerely,
Arthur Balfour

5   The Basle Program, August 1897*

The aim of Zionism is to create for the Jewish people a home in Palestine secured by public law.

In order to attain this object the Congress adopts the following means:

    1. The systematic promotion of the settlement of Palestine with Jewish agriculturists, artisans and craftsmen.

    2. The organization and federation of all Jewry by means of local and general institutions in conformity with the local laws.

    3. The strengthening of Jewish sentiment and national consciousness.

    4. Preparatory steps for procuring of such Government assents as are necessary for achieving the object of Zionism.

6   Article 22 of the Covenant of the League of Nations, 28 June 1919

Article 22. To those colonies and territories which as a consequence of the late war have ceased to be under the sovereignty of the States which formerly governed them and which are inhabited by peoples not yet able to stand by themselves under the strenuous conditions of the modern world, there should be applied the principle that the well-being and development of such peoples form a sacred trust of civilization and that securities for the performance of this trust should be embodied in this Covenant.

The best method of giving practical effect to this principle is that the tutelage of such peoples should be entrusted to advanced nations who by reason of their resources, their experience or their geographical position can best undertake this responsibility, and who are willing to accept it, and that this tutelage should be exercised by them as Mandatories on behalf of the League.

The character of the mandate must differ according to the stage

* This is the official statement of Zionist purpose adopted by the First Zionist Congress in Basle, Switzerland. This congress established the World Zionist Organization.

of the development of the people, the geographical situation of the territory, its economic conditions and other similar circumstances.

Certain communities formerly belonging to the Turkish Empire have reached a stage of development where their existence as independent nations can be provisionally recognized subject to the rendering of administrative advice and assistance by a Mandatory until such time as they are able to stand alone. The wishes of these communities must be a principal consideration in the selection of the Mandatory.

Other peoples, especially those of Central Africa, are at such a stage that the Mandatory must be responsible for the administration of the territory under conditions which will guarantee freedom of conscience and religion, subject only to the maintenance of public order and morals, the prohibition of abuses such as the slave trade, the arms traffic and liquor traffic, and the prevention of the establishment of fortifications or military and naval bases and of military training of the natives for other than police purposes and the defence of territory, and will also secure equal opportunities for the trade and commerce of other Members of the League.

There are territories, such as South-West Africa and certain of the South Pacific Islands, which, owing to the spareness of their population, or their small size, or their remoteness from the centres of civilization, or their geographical contiguity to the territory of the Mandatory, and other circumstances, can be best administered under the laws of the Mandatory as integral portions of its territory, subject to the safeguards above mentioned in the interests of the indigenous population.

In every case of Mandate, the Mandatory shall render to the Council an annual report in reference to the territory committed to its charge.

The degree of authority, control or administration to be exercised by the Mandatory shall, if not previously agreed upon by the Members of the League, be explicitly defined in each case by the Council.

A permanent Commission shall be constituted to receive and examine the annual reports of the Mandatories and to advise the Council on all matters relating to the observance of the mandates.

7 League of Nations Mandate for Palestine (British Mandate) 24 July 1922

The Council of the League of Nations:

Whereas the Principal Allied Powers have agreed, for the purpose of giving effect to the provisions of Article 22 of the Covenant of the League of Nations, to entrust to a Mandatory selected by the said Powers the administration of the territory of Palestine, which formerly belonged to the Turkish Empire, within such boundaries as may be fixed by them; and

Whereas the Principal Allied Powers have also agreed that the Mandatory should be responsible for putting into effect the declaration originally made on November 2nd, 1917, by the Government of His Britannic Majesty, and adopted by the said Powers, in favour of the establishment in Palestine of a national home for the Jewish people, it being clearly understood that nothing should be done which might prejudice the civil and religious rights of existing non-Jewish communities in Palestine, or the rights and political status enjoyed by Jews in any other country; and

Whereas recognition has thereby been given to the historical connexion of the Jewish people with Palestine and to the grounds for reconstituting their national home in that country; and

Whereas the Principal Allied Powers have selected His Britannic Majesty as the Mandatory for Palestine; and

Whereas the mandate in respect of Palestine has been formulated in the following terms and submitted to the Council of the League for approval; and

Whereas His Britannic Majesty has accepted the mandate in respect of Palestine and undertaken to exercise it on behalf of the League of Nations in conformity with the following provisions; and

Whereas by the aforementioned Article 22 (paragraph 8), it is provided that the degree of authority, control or administration to be exercised by the Mandatory, not having been previously agreed upon by the Members of the League, shall be explicitly defined by the Council of the League of Nations;

Confirming the said Mandate, defines its terms as follows:

ARTICLE 1
The Mandatory shall have full powers of legislation and of administration, save as they may be limited by the terms of this mandate.

ARTICLE 2
The Mandatory shall be responsible for placing the country under such political, administrative and economic conditions as will secure the establishment of the Jewish national home, as laid down in the preamble, and the development of self-governing institutions, and also for safeguarding the civil and religious rights of all the inhabitants of Palestine, irrespective of race and religion.

ARTICLE 3
The Mandatory shall, so far as circumstances permit, encourage local autonomy.

ARTICLE 4
An appropriate Jewish agency shall be recognized as a public body for the purpose of advising and co-operating with the Administration of Palestine in such economic, social and other matters as may affect the establishment of the Jewish national home and the interests of the Jewish population in Palestine, and subject always to the control of the Administration, to assist and take part in the development of the country.

The Zionist Organization, so long as its organization and constitution are in the opinion of the Mandatory appropriate, shall be recognized as such agency. It shall take steps in consultation with His Britannic Majesty's Government to secure the co-operation of all Jews who are willing to assist in the establishment of the Jewish national home.

ARTICLE 5
The Mandatory shall be responsible for seeing that no Palestine territory shall be ceded or leased to, or in any way placed under the control of, the Government of any foreign Power.

ARTICLE 6

The Administration of Palestine, while ensuring that the rights and position of other sections of the population are not prejudiced, shall facilitate Jewish immigration under suitable conditions and shall encourage, in co-operation with the Jewish agency referred to in Article 4, close settlement by Jews on the land, including State lands and waste lands not required for public purposes.

ARTICLE 7

The Administration of Palestine shall be responsible for enacting a nationality law. There shall be included in this law provisions framed so as to facilitate the acquisition of Palestinian citizenship by Jews who take up their permanent residence in Palestine.

ARTICLE 8

The privileges and immunities of foreigners, including the benefits of consular jurisdiction and protection as formerly enjoyed by Capitulation or usage in the Ottoman Empire, shall not be applicable in Palestine.

Unless the Powers whose nationals enjoyed the aforementioned privileges and immunities on August 1st, 1914, shall have previously renounced the right to their re-establishment, or shall have agreed to their non-application for a specified period, these privileges and immunities shall, at the expiration of the mandate, be immediately re-established in their entirety or with such modifications as may have been agreed upon between the Powers concerned.

ARTICLE 9

The Mandatory shall be responsible for seeing that the judicial system established in Palestine shall assure to foreigners, as well as to natives, a complete guarantee of their rights.

Respect for the personal status of the various peoples and communities and for their religious interests shall be fully guaranteed. In particular, the control and administration of Waqfs shall be exercised in accordance with religious law and the dispositions of the founders.

ARTICLE 10

Pending the making of special extradition agreements to Palestine, the extradition treaties in force between the Mandatory and other foreign Powers shall apply to Palestine.

ARTICLE 11

The Administration of Palestine shall take all necessary measures to safeguard the interests of the community in connexion with the development of the country, and, subject to any international obligations accepted by the Mandatory, shall have full power to provide for public ownership or control of any of the natural resources of the country or of the public works, services and utilities established or to be established therein. It shall introduce a land system appropriate to the needs of the country having regard, among other things, to the desirability of promoting close settlement and intensive cultivation of the land.

The Administration may arrange with the Jewish agency mentioned in Article 4 to construct or operate, upon fair and equitable terms, any public works, services and utilities, and to develop any of the natural resources of the country, in so far as these matters are not directly undertaken by the Administration. Any such arrangements shall provide that no profits distributed by such agency, directly or indirectly, shall exceed a reasonable rate of interest on the capital, and any further profits shall be utilized by it for the benefit of the country in a manner approved by the Administration.

ARTICLE 12

The Mandatory shall be entrusted with the control of the foreign relations of Palestine, and the right to issue exequaturs to consuls appointed by foreign Powers. He shall also be entitled to afford diplomatic and consular protection to citizens of Palestine when outside its territorial limits.

ARTICLE 13

All responsibility in connexion with the Holy Places and religious buildings or sites in Palestine, including that of preserving existing rights and of securing free access to the Holy Places, religious buildings and sites and the free exercise of worship, while ensuring the requirements of public order and decorum, is assumed by the Mandatory, who shall be responsible solely to the League of Nations in all matters connected herewith, provided that nothing in this article shall prevent the Mandatory from entering into such arrangements as he may deem reasonable with the Administration for the purpose of carrying the provisions of this article into effect; and provided also that nothing in this Mandate shall be construed as conferring upon the Mandatory authority to interfere with the fabric or the management of purely Moslem sacred shrines, the immunities of which are guaranteed.

ARTICLE 14

A special Commission shall be appointed by the Mandatory to study, define and determine the rights and claims in connexion with the Holy Places and the rights and claims relating to the different religious communities in Palestine. The method of nomination, the composition and the functions of this Commission shall be submitted to the Council of the League for its approval, and the Commission shall not be appointed or enter upon its functions without the approval of the Council.

ARTICLE 15

The Mandatory shall see that complete freedom of conscience and the free exercise of all forms of worship, subject only to the maintenance of public order and morals, are ensured to all. No discrimination of any kind shall be made between the inhabitants of Palestine on the ground of race, religion or language. No person shall be excluded from Palestine on the sole ground of his religious belief.

The right of each community to maintain its own schools for the education of its own members in its own language, while conforming to such educational requirements of a general nature as the Administration may impose, shall not be denied or impaired.

ARTICLE 16

The Mandatory shall be responsible for exercising such supervision over religious or eleemosynary bodies of all faiths in Palestine as may be required for the maintenance of public order and good government. Subject to such supervision, no measures shall be taken in Palestine to obstruct or interfere with the enterprise of such bodies or to discriminate against any representative or member of them on the ground of his religion or nationality.

ARTICLE 17

The Administration of Palestine may organize on a voluntary basis the forces necessary for the preservation of peace and order, and also for the defence of the country, subject, however, to the supervision of the Mandatory, but shall not use them for purposes other than those above specified save with the consent of the Mandatory. Except for such purposes, no military, naval or air forces shall be raised or maintained by the Administration of Palestine.

Nothing in this article shall preclude the Administration of Palestine from contributing to the cost of the maintenance of the forces of the Mandatory in Palestine.

The Mandatory shall be entitled at all times to use the roads, railways and ports of Palestine for the movement of armed forces and the carriage of fuel and supplies.

ARTICLE 18

The Mandatory shall see that there is no discrimination in Palestine against the nationals of any State Member of the League of Nations (including companies incorporated under its laws) as compared with those of the Mandatory or any foreign State in matters concerning taxation, commerce or navigation, the exercise of industries or professions, or in the treatment of merchant vessels or civil aircraft. Similarly, there shall be no discrimination in Palestine against goods originating in or destined for any of the said States, and there shall be freedom of transit under equitable conditions across the mandated area.

Subject as aforesaid and to the other provisions of this mandate, the Administration of Palestine may, on the advice of the Mandatory, impose taxes and customs duties as it may consider necessary, and take such steps as it may think best to promote the development of the natural resources of the country and to safeguard the interests of the population. It may also, on the advice of the Mandatory, conclude a special customs agreement with any State the territory of which in 1914 was wholly in Asiatic Turkey or Arabia.

ARTICLE 19

The Mandatory shall adhere on behalf of the Administration of Palestine to any general international conventions already existing, or which may be concluded hereafter with the approval of the League of Nations, respecting the slave traffic, the traffic in arms and ammunition, or the traffic in drugs, or relating to commercial equality, freedom of transit and navigation, aerial navigation and postal, telegraphic and wireless communication or literary, artistic or industrial property.

ARTICLE 20

The Mandatory shall co-operate on behalf of the Administration of Palestine, so far as religious, social and other conditions may permit, in the execution of any common policy adopted by the League of Nations for preventing and combating disease, including diseases of plants and animals.

ARTICLE 21

The Mandatory shall secure the enactment within twelve months from this date, and shall ensure the execution of a Law of Antiquities based on the following rules. This law shall ensure equality of treatment in the matter of excavations and archeological research to the nationals of all States Members of the League of Nations . . .

ARTICLE 22

English, Arabic and Hebrew shall be the official languages of Palestine. Any statement or inscription in Arabic on stamps or money in Palestine shall be repeated in Hebrew and any statement or inscription in Hebrew shall be repeated in Arabic.

ARTICLE 23
The Administration of Palestine shall recognize the holy days of the respective communities in Palestine as legal days of rest for the members of such communities.

ARTICLE 24
The Mandatory shall make to the Council of the League of Nations an annual report to the satisfaction of the Council as to the measures taken during the year to carry out the provisions of the mandate. Copies of all laws and regulations promulgated or issued during the year shall be communicated with the report.

ARTICLE 25
In the territories lying between the Jordan and the eastern boundary of Palestine as ultimately determined, the Mandatory shall be entitled, with the consent of the Council of the League of Nations, to postpone or withhold application of such provisions of this mandate as he may consider inapplicable to the existing local conditions, and to make such provision for the administration of the territories as he may consider suitable to those conditions, provided that no action shall be taken which is inconsistent with the provisions of Articles 15, 16 and 18.

ARTICLE 26
The Mandatory agrees that if any dispute whatever should arise between the Mandatory and another member of the League of Nations relating to the interpretation or the application of the provisions of the mandate, such dispute, if it cannot be settled by negotiation, shall be submitted to the Permanent Court of International Justice provided for by Article 14 of the Covenant of the League of Nations.

ARTICLE 27

The consent of the Council of the League of Nations is required for any modification of the terms of this mandate.

ARTICLE 28

In the event of the termination of the mandate hereby conferred upon the Mandatory, the Council of the League of Nations shall make such arrangements as may be deemed necessary for safeguarding in perpetuity, under guarantee of the League, the rights secured by Articles 13 and 14, and shall use its influence for securing, under the guarantee of the League, that the Government of Palestine will fully honour the financial obligations legitimately incurred by the Administration of Palestine during the period of the mandate, including the rights of public servants to pensions or gratuities.

The present instrument shall be deposited in original in the archives of the League of Nations and certified copies shall be forwarded by the Secretary-General of the League of Nations to all Members of the League.

DONE AT LONDON the twenty-fourth day of July, one thousand nine hundred and twenty-two.

8   Basic Laws of Israel: The Law of Return*

1. Every Jew has the right to immigrate to this country.
2. (a) Immigration shall be by immigrant's visa.

(b) An immigrant's visa shall be given to every Jew who has expressed his desire to settle in Israel, unless the Minister of the Interior is satisfied that the applicant–

(1) is engaged in an activity directed against the Jewish people; or

(2) is liable to endanger public health or the security of the State; or

(3) is a person with a criminal past liable to endanger public welfare.

* Israel Laws 114 (1950) as amended in 1954 and 1970.

3. (a) A Jew who comes to Israel and subsequently expresses his desire to settle may, whilst still in Israel, receive an immigrant's certificate.

(b) The exceptions set out in section 2(b) shall also apply to the grant of an immigrant's certificate, provided that a person shall not be considered as endangering public health on account of an illness contracted after his arrival in Israel.

4. Every Jew who immigrated to this country before the commencement of this Law and every Jew born in the country, whether before or after the commencement of this Law, is in the same position as one who immigrated under this Law.

4A. (a) The rights of a Jew under this Law, the rights of an immigrant under the Nationality Law, 1952 and the rights of an immigrant under any other legislation are also granted to the child and grandchild of a Jew, to the spouse of a Jew and to the spouse of the child and grandchild of a Jew – with the exception of a person who was a Jew and willingly changed his religion.

(b) It makes no difference whether or not the Jew through whom the right is claimed under sub-section (a) is still alive or whether or not he has immigrated to this country.

(c) The exceptions and conditions appertaining to a Jew or an immigrant under or by virtue of this Law or the legislation referred to in sub-section (a) shall also apply to a person claiming any right under sub-section (a).

4B. For the purpose of this Law, 'a Jew' means a person born to a Jewish mother or converted to Judaism and who is not a member of another religion.

5. The Minister of the Interior is charged with the implementation of this Law and may make regulations as to any matter relating to its implementation and as to the grant of immigrants' visas and certificates to minors up to the age of 18.

Regulations regarding sections 4A and 4B require the approval of the Constitution, Law and Justice Committee of the Knesset.

9 Basic Laws of Israel: World Zionist Organization/Jewish Agency (Status) Law*

1. The State of Israel regards itself as the creation of the entire Jewish people, and its gates are open, in accordance with its laws, to every Jew wishing to immigrate to it.

2. The World Zionist Organization, from its foundation five decades ago, headed the movement and efforts of the Jewish people to realize the age-old vision of the return to its homeland and, with the assistance of other Jewish circles and bodies, carried the main responsibility for establishing the State of Israel.

3. The World Zionist Organization, which is also the Jewish Agency, takes care as before of immigration and directs absorption and settlement projects in the State.

4. The State of Israel recognizes the World Zionist Organization as the authorized agency which will continue to operate in the State of Israel for the development and settlement of the country, the absorption of immigrants from the Diaspora and the coordination of the activities in Israel of Jewish institutions and organizations active in those fields.

5. The mission of gathering in the exiles, which is the central task of the State of Israel and the Zionist Movement in our days, requires constant efforts by the Jewish people in the Diaspora; the State of Israel, therefore, expects the cooperation of all Jews, as individuals and groups, in building up the State and assisting the immigration to it of the masses of the people, and regards the unity of all sections of Jewry as necessary for this purpose.

6. The State of Israel expects efforts on the part of the World Zionist Organization for achieving this unity; if, to this end, the Zionist Organization, with the consent of the Government and the approval of the Knesset, should decide to broaden its basis, the enlarged body will enjoy the status conferred upon the World Zionist Organization in the State of Israel.

7. Details of the status of the World Zionist Organization – whose representation is the Zionist Executive, also known as the Executive of the Jewish Agency – and the form of its cooperation with the Government shall be determined by a Covenant to be

* 7 Israel Laws 3 (1952).

made between the Government and the Zionist Executive.

8. The Covenant shall be based on the declaration of the 23rd Zionist Congress in Jerusalem that the practical work of the World Zionist Organization and its various bodies for the fulfillment of their tasks in Eretz-Israel requires full cooperation and coordination on its part with the State of Israel and its Government, in accordance with the laws of the State.

9. There shall be set up a committee for the coordination of the activities of the Government and Executive in the spheres in which the Executive will operate according to the Covenant; the tasks of the Committee shall be determined by the Covenant.

10. The Covenant and any variation or amendment thereof made with the consent of the two parties shall be published in *Reshumot* and shall come into force on the day of publication, unless they provide for an earlier or later day for this purpose.

11. The Executive is a juristic body and may enter into contracts, acquire, hold and relinquish property and be a party to any legal or other proceeding.

12. The Executive and its funds and other institutions shall be exempt from taxes and other compulsory Government charges, subject to such restrictions and conditions as may be laid down by the Covenant; the exemption shall come into force on the coming into force of the Covenant.

10   Basic Laws of Israel: Covenant between the Government of Israel and the Zionist Executive, called also the Executive of the Jewish Agency ·

1. The following are the functions of the Zionist Executive as included in this Covenant:

The organizing of immigration abroad and the transfer of immigrants and their property to Israel; co-operation in the absorption of immigrants in Israel; youth immigration; agricultural settlement in Israel; the acquisition and amelioration of land in Israel by the institutions of the Zionist Organization, the Keren Kayemeth Leisrael and the Keren Hayesod; participation in the establishment and the expansion of development enterprises in Israel; the encouragement of private capital investments in Israel; assistance to cultural enterprises and institutions of higher learning in Israel; the mobilization of resources for financing these activities; the co-ordination of the activities in Israel of Jewish institutions and organizations acting within the limits of these functions by means of public funds.

2. Any activity carried out in Israel by the Executive or on its behalf for the purpose of carrying out the said functions, or part of them, shall be executed in accordance with the laws of Israel and the regulations and administrative instructions in force from time to time, which govern the activities of the governmental authorities whose functions cover, or are affected by, the activity in question.

3. In the organizing of immigration and the handling of immigrants, the Executive shall act on the basis of a plan agreed on with the Government or authorized by the Co-ordinating Board. Immigrants will require visas according to the Law of the Return 5711–1950.

4. The Executive shall, in agreement with the Government, co-ordinate the activities in Israel of Jewish institutions and organizations which act within the limits of the Executive's functions.

5. The Executive may carry out its functions itself or through its existing institutions or those which it may establish in the future, and it may also enlist in its activities the cooperation of other institutions or those which it may establish in the future, and it may also enlist in its activities the cooperation of other institutions in Israel, with the proviso that it may not delegate any of its functions or rights under the Covenant without the agreement of the Government, and shall not authorize any body or institution to carry out its functions, in whole or part, except after prior notification of the Government.

6. The Executive shall be responsible for the mobilization of the financial and material resources required for the execution of

its functions, by means of the Keren Hayesod, the Keren Kayemeth Leisrael and other funds.

7. The Government shall consult with the Executive in regard to legislation specially impinging on the functions of the Executive before such legislation is submitted to the Knesset.

8. For the purpose of co-ordinating activities between the Government and the Executive in all spheres to which this Covenant applies, a Co-ordinating Board shall be established (hereafter called the Board). The Board shall be composed of an even number of members, not fewer than four, half of whom shall be members of the Government appointed by it, and half of whom shall be members of the Executive appointed by it. The Government and the Executive shall be entitled from time to time to replace the members of the Board by others among their members.

9. The Board shall meet at least once a month. It may appoint sub-committees consisting of members of the Board, and also of non-members. The Board shall from time to time submit to the Government and the Executive reports of its deliberations and recommendations. Except as stated above, the Board shall itself determine the arrangements for its sessions and deliberations.

10. The Government must see to it that its authorized organs shall provide the Executive and its institutions with all the permits and facilities required by law for activities carried out in accordance with this Covenant for the purpose of carrying out the Executive's functions.

11. Donations and legacies to the Executive or any of its institutions shall be exempt from Inheritance Tax. All other problems connected with the exemption of the Executive, its Funds and its other institutions, from payment of taxes, customs and other obligatory governmental imposts shall be the subject of a special arrangement between the Executive and the Government. This arrangement shall be formulated in an annex to this Covenant within eight months, as an inseparable part thereof, and shall come into force as from the date of signature of this Covenant.

12. All proposals for alterations or amendments to this

Covenant, or any addition thereto, must be made in writing, and no alteration or amendment of this Covenant, or addition thereto, shall be made except in writing.

13. Any notification to be sent to the Government shall be sent to the Prime Minister, and any notification to be sent to the Executive shall be sent to the Chairman of the Executive in Jerusalem.

14. This Covenant shall come into force on the date of signature.

Signed in Jerusalem, 26 July 1954.

For the Government,   For the Zionist Executive,
Moshe Sharett   Dr Nahum Goldmann
Prime Minister   Chairman
              Berl Locker

11   United Nations General Assembly Resolution 194, 11 December 1948

The General Assembly,
Having considered further the situation in Palestine,

1. *Expresses* its deep appreciation of the progress achieved through the good offices of the late United Nations Mediator in promoting a peaceful adjustment of the future situation of Palestine, for which cause he sacrificed his life; and

Extends its thanks to the Acting Mediator and his staff for their continued efforts and devotion to duty in Palestine;

2. *Establishes* a Conciliation Commission consisting of three States Members of the United Nations which shall have the following functions:

(a) To assume, in so far as it considers necessary in existing circumstances, the functions given to the United Nations Mediator on Palestine by resolution 186 (S-2) of the General Assembly of 14 May 1948;

(b) To carry out the specific functions and directives given to it by the present resolution and such additional functions and directives as may be given to it by the General Assembly or by the Security Council;

(c) To undertake, upon the request of the Security Council, any of the functions now assigned to the United Nations Mediator on Palestine or to the United Nations Truce Commission by resolutions of the Security Council; upon such request to the Conciliation Commission by the Security Council with respect to all the remaining functions of the United Nations Mediator on Palestine under Security Council resolutions, the office of the Mediator shall be terminated;

3. *Decides* that a Committee of the Assembly, consisting of China, France, the Union of Soviet Socialist Republics, the United Kingdom and the United States of America, shall present, before the end of the first part of the present session of the General Assembly, for the approval of the Assembly, a proposal concerning

the names of the three States which will constitute the Conciliation Commission;

4. *Requests* the Commission to begin its functions at once, with a view to the establishment of contact between the parties themselves and the Commission at the earliest possible date;

5. *Calls upon* the Governments and authorities concerned to extend the scope of the negotiations provided for in the Security Council's resolution of 16 November 1948 and to seek agreement by negotiations conducted either with the Conciliation Commission or directly, with a view to the final settlement of all questions outstanding between them;

6. *Instructs* the Conciliation Commission to take steps to assist the Governments and authorities concerned to achieve a final settlement of all questions outstanding between them;

7. *Resolves* that the Holy Places – including Nazareth – religious buildings and sites in Palestine should be protected and free access to them assured, in accordance with existing rights and historical practice; that arrangements to this end should be under effective United Nations supervision; that the United Nations Conciliation Commission, in presenting to the fourth regular session of the General Assembly its detailed proposals for a permanent international regime for the territory of Jerusalem, should include recommendations concerning the Holy Places in that territory; that with regard to the Holy Places in the rest of Palestine the Commission should call upon the political authorities of the areas concerned to give appropriate formal guarantees as to the protection of the Holy Places and access to them; and that these undertakings should be presented to the General Assembly for approval;

8. *Resolves* that, in view of its association with three world religions, the Jerusalem area, including the present municipality of Jerusalem *plus* the surrounding villages and towns, the most eastern of which shall be Abu Dis; the most southern, Bethlehem; the most western, Ein Karim (including also the built-up area of Motsa); and the most northern Shu'fat, should be accorded special

and separate treatment from the rest of Palestine and should be placed under effective United Nations control;

Requests the Security Council to take further steps to ensure the demilitarization of Jerusalem at the earliest possible date;

Instructs the Commission to present to the fourth regular session of the General Assembly detailed proposals for a permanent international regime for the Jerusalem area which will provide for the maximum local autonomy for distinctive groups consistent with the special international status of the Jerusalem area;

The Conciliation Commission is authorized to appoint a United Nations representative, who shall co-operate with the local authorities with respect to the interim administration of the Jerusalem area;

9. *Resolves* that, pending agreement on more detailed arrangements among the Governments and authorities concerned, the freest possible access to Jerusalem by road, rail or air should be accorded to all inhabitants of Palestine;

Instructs the Conciliation Commission to report immediately to the Security Council, for appropriate action by that organ, any attempt by any party to impede such access;

10. *Instructs* the Conciliation Commission to seek arrangements among the Governments and authorities concerned which will facilitate the economic development of the area, including arrangements for access to ports and airfields and the use of transportation and communication facilities;

11. *Resolves* that the refugees wishing to return to their homes and live at peace with their neighbors should be permitted to do so at the earliest practicable date, and that compensation should be paid for the property of those choosing not to return and for loss of or damage to property which, under principles of international law or in equity, should be made good by the Governments or authorities responsible;

Instructs the Conciliation Commission to facilitate repatriation, resettlement and economic and social rehabilitation of the refugees and the payment of compensation, and to maintain close relations with the Director of the United Nations Relief for Palestine

Refugees and, through him, with the appropriate organs and agencies of the United Nations;

12. *Authorizes* the Conciliation Commission to appoint such subsidiary bodies and to employ such technical experts, acting under its authority, as it may find necessary for the effective discharge of its functions and responsibilities under the present resolution;

The Conciliation Commission will have its official headquarters at Jerusalem. The authorities responsible for maintaining order in Jerusalem will be responsible for taking all measures necessary to ensure the security of the Commission. The Secretary-General will provide a limited number of guards for the protection of the staff and premises of the Commission;

13. *Instructs* the Conciliation Commission to render progress reports periodically to the Secretary-General for transmission to the Security Council and to Members of the United Nations;

14. *Calls upon* all Governments and authorities concerned to co-operate with the Conciliation Commission and to take all possible steps to assist in the implementation of the present resolution;

15. *Requests* the Secretary-General to provide the necessary staff and facilities and to make appropriate arrangements to provide the necessary funds required in carrying out the terms of the present resolution.

12   United Nations Security Council Resolution 242, 22 November 1967

The Security Council

Expressing its continued concern with the grave situation in the Middle East,

Emphasizing the inadmissibility of the acquisition of territory by war and the need to work for a just and lasting peace in which every State in the area can live in security,

Emphasizing further that all Member States in their acceptance of the Charter of the United Nations have undertaken a commitment to act in accordance with Article 2 of the Charter,

1. *Affirms* that the fulfillment of Charter principles requires the establishment of a just and lasting peace in the Middle East which should include the application of both the following principles:

    i. Withdrawal of Israeli armed forces from territories occupied in the recent conflict;

    ii. Termination of all claims or states of belligerency and respect for and acknowledgement of the sovereignty, territorial integrity and political independence of every State in the area and their right to live in peace within secure and recognized boundaries free from threats or acts of force;

2. *Affirms further* the necessity

    (a) For guaranteeing freedom of navigation through international waterways in the area;

    (b) For achieving a just settlement of the refugee problem;

    (c) For guaranteeing the territorial inviolability and political independence of every State in the area, through measures including the establishment of demilitarized zones;

3. *Requests* the Secretary-General to designate a Special Representative to proceed to the Middle East to establish and maintain contacts with the States concerned in order to promote agreement and assist efforts to achieve a peaceful and accepted settlement in accordance with the provisions and principles in this resolution;

4. *Requests* the Secretary-General to report to the Security Council on the progress of the efforts of the Special Representative as soon as possible.

Adopted unanimously by the Security Council at the 1382nd meeting.

22 November 1967

13 United Nations General Assembly Resolution 3379 (XXX), 10 November 1975*

The General Assembly,

Recalling its resolution 1904 (XVIII) of 20 November 1963, proclaiming the United Nations Declaration on the Elimination of All Forms of Racial Discrimination, and in particular its affirmation that 'any doctrine of racial differentiation or superiority is scientifically false, morally condemnable, socially unjust and dangerous' and its expression of alarm at 'the manifestations of racial discrimination still in evidence in some areas in the world, some of which are imposed by certain Governments by means of legislative, administrative or other measures',

Recalling also that, in its resolution 3151 G (XXVIII) of 14 December 1973, the General Assembly condemned, *inter alia*, the unholy alliance between South African racism and Zionism,

Taking note of the Declaration of Mexico on the Equality of Women and their Contribution to Development and Peace, proclaimed by the World Conference of the International Women's Year, held at Mexico City from 19 June to 2 July 1975, which promulgated the principle that 'international co-operation and peace require the achievement of national liberation and independence, the elimination of colonialism and neo-colonialism, foreign occupation, Zionism, *apartheid* and racial discrimination in all its forms, as well as the recognition of the dignity of peoples and their right to self-determination',

Taking note also of resolution 77 (XII) adopted by the Assembly of Heads of State and Government of the Organization of African Unity at its twelfth ordinary session, held at Kampala from 28 July to 1 August 1975, which considered 'that the racist regime in occupied Palestine and the racist regimes in Zimbabwe and South Africa have a common imperialist origin, forming a whole and having the same racist structure and being organically linked in their policy at repression of the dignity and integrity of the human being',

Taking note also of the Political Declaration and Strategy to

---

* Resolution 3379 (XXX) adopted by the United Nations General Assembly on 10 November 1975 equating Zionism with racism and racial discrimination.

Strengthen International Peace and Security and to Intensify Solidarity and Mutual Assistance among Non-Aligned Countries, adopted at the Conference of Ministers for Foreign Affairs of Non-Aligned Countries held at Lima from 25 to 30 August 1975, which most severely condemned Zionism as a threat to world peace and security and called upon all countries to oppose this racist and imperialist ideology,

Determines that Zionism is a form of racism and racial discrimination.

2400th plenary meeting 10 November 1975.

14 Important United Nations Resolutions Violated and/or Ignored by Israel, Partial Listing, 1948–75*

Resolution 194 (III) of the General Assembly dated 11 December 1948 concerning the Conciliation Commission, the international regime of Jerusalem, and the right of the Palestinian refugees to return to their homes in Israel.

Resolution 303 (IV) of the General Assembly dated 9 December 1949 concerning the international regime for Jerusalem.

Resolution 237 of the Security Council of 14 June 1967 concerning respect for human rights in the occupied Sinai, Golan Heights, West Bank and Gaza.

Resolution 2252 (ES-V) of the General Assembly dated 4 July 1967 concerning humanitarian assistance and safety of Arabs under Israeli military occupation.

Resolution 2253 (ES-V) of the General Assembly dated 4 July

* Further information on UN resolutions since 1975 can be found in the yearly publication jointly published by the Institute of Palestine Studies and the Center for Research and Documentation, Abu Dhabi, titled *United Nations Resolutions on Palestine and the Arab–Israeli Conflict.*

1967 concerning measures taken by Israel to change the status of Jerusalem.

Resolution 242 of the Security Council dated 22 November 1967 concerning the situation in the Middle East.

Resolution 259 of the Security Council dated 27 September 1968 concerning human rights in the territories occupied by Israel.

Resolution 2443 (XXIII) of the General Assembly dated 19 December 1968 concerning human rights in the territories occupied by Israel.

Resolution 267 of the Security Council dated July 1969 concerning measures taken by Israel to change the status of Jerusalem.

Resolution 271 of the Security Council dated 15 September 1969 concerning arson at Al Aqsa Mosque and the status of Jerusalem.

Resolution 2535 (XXIV) B of the General Assembly dated 10 December 1969 affirming the inalienable rights of the people of Palestine.

Resolution 2546 (XXIV) of the General Assembly dated 11 December 1969 concerning violations by Israel of human rights in the Occupied Territories.

Resolution 2628 (XXV) of the General Assembly dated November 1970 concerning the situation in the Middle East and respect for the rights of the Palestinians.

Resolution 2672 (XXV) C of the General Assembly dated 8 December 1970 concerning equal rights and self-determination of the Palestinians.

Resolution 2727 (XXV) of the General Assembly dated 15 December 1970 concerning violations by Israel of human rights in the Occupied Territories.

Resolution 298 of the Security Council dated 25 September 1971 concerning measures taken by Israel to change the status of Jerusalem.

Resolution 2787 (XXVI) of the General Assembly dated 6 December 1971 concerning the inalienable rights of the Palestinians and other peoples.

Resolution 2799 (XXVI) of the General Assembly dated December 1971 concerning the situation in the Middle East.

Resolution 2851 (XXVI) of the General Assembly dated December 1971 concerning violations by Israel of human rights in the Occupied Territories.

Resolution of the Commission on Human Rights of the Economic and Social Council of the UN dated 22 March 1972 concerning violations by Israel of human rights in the Occupied Territories.

Resolution 316 of the Security Council dated 26 June 1972 condemning Israeli attacks on Lebanon.

Resolution 2949 (XXVII) of the General Assembly dated 8 December 1972 on the situation in the Middle East.

Resolution 2963 A-F (XXVII) of the General Assembly dated 13 December 1972 on the rights of the Palestinians.

Resolution 3005 (XXVII) of the General Assembly dated 15 December 1972 concerning violations by Israel of human rights in the Occupied Territories.

Resolution of the Commission on Human Rights of the Economic and Social Council of the UN dated 14 March 1973 concerning violations by Israel of human rights in the Occupied Territories.

Resolution 332 of the Security Council dated 21 April 1973 condemning Israeli military attacks on Lebanon.

Resolution 337 of the Security Council dated 15 August 1973 condemning Israel for its seizure of a civilian Lebanese airliner.

Resolutions 3089 C and D of the General Assembly dated 7 December 1973 reaffirming the right of the displaced inhabitants to return to their homes and the right of the people of Palestine to self-determination.

Resolution 3092 (XXVIII) of the General Assembly dated 7 December 1973 deploring Israel's practices and violations of human rights in the Occupied Territories.

Resolution of the Commission on Human Rights of the Economic and Social Council of the UN dated 11 February 1974 condemning, inter alia, Israel's policy of annexation, and transfer of population in the Occupied Territories, including Jerusalem.

Resolution 347 of the Security Council dated 24 April 1974 condemning Israel's violation of Lebanon's territorial integrity and sovereignty.

Resolution 3236 (XXIX) of the General Assembly dated November 1974 reaffirming the inalienable rights of the Palestinian people in Palestine.

Resolution 3427 adopted by the General Conference of the UN Educational, Scientific and Cultural Organization in November 1974 concerning the protection of cultural property in Jerusalem.

Resolutions 3240 A, B and C (XXIX) of the General Assembly dated 29 November 1974 expressing concern at Israeli practices affecting human rights in the Occupied Territories and holding Israel responsible for the destruction of the town of Quneitra.

Resolution 3331 (XXIX) of the General Assembly dated 17 December 1974 calling upon Israel to permit the return of the displaced inhabitants and to desist from all measures affecting the physical and demographic structure of the Occupied Territories.

Resolution A and B (XXXI) of the UN Commission on Human Rights adopted on 21 February 1975 concerning Israel's violations of human rights in the Occupied Territories.

Resolution 3414 (XXX) adopted by the General Assembly on 5 December 1975 concerning the situation in the Middle East.

Resolutions 3525 A, B, C and D (XXX) adopted by the General Assembly on 15 December 1975 concerning Israeli practices affecting human rights in the Occupied Territories.

15   US Military and Economic Assistance to Israel, 1948–83, in Millions of Dollars

Year	Economic Aid	Military Aid	Total Aid to Israel	Aid to Israel as % of Total US Aid
1948				
1949				
1950				
1951	0.1		0.1	−1%[d]
1952	86.4		86.4	2.2%
1953	73.6		73.6	1.1%
1954	74.7		74.7	1.3%
1955	52.7		52.7	1.0%
1956	50.8		50.8	−1%
1957	40.9		40.9	−1%
1958	61.2		61.2	1.2%
1959	49.9	0.4	50.3	1.0%
1960	54.8	0.5	55.7	1.1%
1961	48.1		48.1	1.0%
1962	70.7	13.2[c]	83.9	1.2%
1963	63.4	13.3	76.7	1.0%
1964	37.0		37.0	−1%
1965	48.8	12.9	61.7	1.1%
1966	36.8	90.0	126.8	1.8%
1967	6.1	7.0	13.1	−1%
1968	51.8	25.0	76.8	1.1%
1969	36.7	85.0	121.7	1.8%

214

1970	41.1	30.0	71.1	1.0%
1971	55.8	545.0	600.8	7.4%
1972	104.2	300.0	404.2	4.4%
1973[a]	159.8	307.5	467.3	4.7%
1974	88.0	2,482.7	2,570.7	28.6%
1975	393.1	300.0	693.1	9.6%
1976[b]	808.0	1,700.0	2,508.0	27.8%
1977	757.0	1,000.0	1,757.0	22.5%
1978	811.8	1,000.0	1,811.8	20.5%
1979	815.1	4,000.0	4,815.1	34.7%
1980	811.0	1,000.0	1,811.0	18.7%
1981	789.0	1,400.0	2,189.0	20.7%
1982	819.0	1,400.0	2,219.0	24.6%
1983	798.0	1,400.0	2,198.0	24.4%

Source: US Library of Congress, Congressional Research Service.
[a] 1973 onwards includes Soviet Jew Resettlement Funds.
[b] Includes fiscal year 1976 transitional quarter.
[c] Below $50,000.
[d] Minus sign indicates below 1 percent.

16 Palestinian Population, Estimated Size and Distribution, 1982

Total	4,500,000
Distribution	
pre-1967 Israel	550,000
West Bank and East Jerusalem	830,000
Gaza	455,000
Jordan	1,080,000
Lebanon	375,000
Syria	245,000
Other Arab states	790,000
Rest of world	175,000

Source: Edward W. Said, et al., *A Profile of the Palestinian People*, Palestine Human Rights Campaign, 1983, p. 14.

17   Plan Dalet: Zionist Military Operations before the Entry of Arab Regular Armies inside Areas Alloted to the Arab State by the United Nations Partition Resolution, 1 April–15 May 1948

Operation Nachshon

Purpose: To carve out a corridor connecting Tel Aviv to Jerusalem and, by so doing, to split the main part of the Arab state into two. 1 April 1948. *Results*: unsuccessful.

Operation Harel

Purpose: A continuation of Nachshon, but centered specifically on Arab villages near Latrun. 15 April 1948. *Results*: unsuccessful.

Operation Chametz

Purpose: To destroy the Arab villages around Jaffa and so cut Jaffa off from physical contact with the rest of Palestine, as a preliminary to its capture. 27 April 1948. *Results*: successful.

Operation Jevussi

Purpose: To isolate Jerusalem by destroying the ring surrounding Arab villages and dominating the Ramallah–Jerusalem road to the north, the Jericho–Jerusalem road to the east, and the Bethlehem–Jerusalem road to the south. This operation would have caused the whole of Jerusalem to fall and would have made the Arab position west of the River Jordan untenable. 27 April 1948. *Results*: unsuccessful.

Operation Maccabi

Purpose: To destroy the Arab villages near Latrun and, by an outflanking movement, to penetrate into Ramallah district north of Jerusalem. 7 May 1948. *Results*: unsuccessful.

Operation Ben Ami
Purpose: To occupy Acre and purify Western Galilee of Arabs.
14 May 1948. *Results*: successful.

Operation Pitchfork
Purpose: To occupy the Arab residential quarters in the New
City of Jerusalem. 14 May 1948. *Results*: successful.

Operation Schfifon
Purpose: To occupy the Old City of Jerusalem. 14 May 1948.
Results: unsuccessful.

Source: Walid Khalidi, *From Haven to Conquest: Readings in Zionism
and the Palestine Problem until 1948*, Institute for Palestine Studies, 1971,
pp. 856–7.

18   Palestinian Villages Destroyed by Israel, by Districts

Safad and Acre	An-Na'ima	'Iqrit
	As-Salihiya	Khirbat 'Iribbin
Abil al-Qamh	Az-Zawiya	Kafr Bir'im
Az-Zuq al-Fauqani	Buweiziya	Deir al-Qasi
As-Sanbariya	Meis	Sa'sa'
Shauqa at-Tahta	Jahula	Qadas
Mughr ash-Sha'ban	Al-Muftakhira	Buleida
Khisas	Barjiyat	Al-Malikiya
Az-Zuq at-Tahtani	Buleida	'Eitarun
Hunin	Khiyam al-Walid	Deishum
Khalisa	Ghuraba	Salha
Lazzaza	Az-Zib	Fara
Al-Mansura	Al-Bassa	'Alma
Azaziyat	Ma'sub	Ar-Ras al-Ahmar
Ein Fit	Al-Manawat	Marus
Qeitiya	Tarbikha	An-Nabi Yusha'
Al 'Abisiya	Nabi Rubin	Mallaha
Kirbat S'unman	Suruh	Al-'Ulmaniya

Al-Kharrar
Tuleil
Al-Huseinya
Al-Harawi
Jazayir al-Hindaj
Ad-Darbashiya
As-Sumeiriya
At-Tall
Umm al-Faraj
An-Nahr
Al-Chabisiya
'Amqa
Kuweikat
Suhmata
Jiddin
Ghabbatiya
Sabalan
Dallata
Teitaba
Safsaf
Qaddita
'Ammuqa
Meiron
'Ein az-Zeitun
Biriya
Adh-Dhahiriya at-
    Tahta
Sammu'i
Kirad al-Ghannama
Yarda
Weiziya
Qabba'a
Mughr Ad-Druz
Mughr al-Kheit
Fir'im
Ja'una
Mansurat al-Kheit
Az-Zanghariya
Al-Manshiya
Jidru

Ghawarni
Al-Birwa
Ad-Damun
Ar-Ruweis
Mi'ar
Kafar I'nan
Farradiya
Al-Hiqab
Ash-Shuna
Al-Qudeiriya
Yaquq
Ghuweir Abu
    Shusha
Jubb Yusuf
Abu Zeina
As-Samakiya
Tabgha
Tell al-Hinud
Khan al-Minya

Haifa, Tiberias,
Nazareth, Beisan

At-Tira
Balad ash-Sheikh
Yajur
Ash-Shajara
Al-W'ara as-Sauda
Majdal
Hittin
Nimrin
Lubya
Al-Manara
Nasir ad-Din
Nugeib
'Ein Haud
Al-Mazar
Ad-Khirbat Damun
Beit Lahm

Umm al-'Amad
Saffuriya
Ma'lul
Al-Mujeidal
Kafer Sabt
Ma'dhar
Hadatha
Ulam
Samakh
Samra
'Ubeidiya
Jaba'
Ijzim
As-Sarafand
Kafr Lam
'Ein Ghazal
Tantura
Umm az-Zinat
Ar-Rihaniya
Daliyat ar-Rauha
Qumbaza, Khirbat
Qira wa Qamun
Abu Zureiq
Abu Shusha
Ghubaiya al-Fauqa
Ghubaiya at-Tahta
An-Naghnaghiya
Al-Mansi
Waraqani
'Ein al-Mansi
Khirbat Lidd
Indur
Sirin
At-Tira
Danna
Al-Bira
Kaukab al-Hawa
Kafra
Yubla
Khirbat Dalhamiya

At-Taqa
Khirbat Az-Zawiya
Khirbat Umm
   Sabuna
Bureika
Khirbat al-Burj
Qisariya
Khirbat Kabara
Sabbarin
As-Sindiyana
Umm ash-Shauf
Khubbeiza
Al-Buteimat
Qannir
Al-Kafrin
Lajjun
Qumya
Zir'in
Nuris
Jabbul
Al-Hamidiya
As-Sakhne
Al-Murassas
Khirbat al-Jaufa
Tall ash-Shauk
Al-Bawati
Al-Ghazawiya
Zab'a
Arab an-Nufei'at
Khirbat Majdal
Khirbat Manshiya
Ad-Dumeiri
Khirbat Zalafa
Raml Zeita
'Arab al-Fuqara
Ghaziya
Wadi 'Ara
Al-Manshiya
Ashrafiya
Farwana

As-Samiriya
Al-'Arida
Al-Hamra
Al-Khuneizir
Umm 'Ajra
Al-Fatur
As-Safa

Jaffa and Tulkarm

Umm Khalid
Khirbat Bait Lid
Qaqun
Wadi al-Qabbani
Khirbat Zababida
Birkat Ramadan
Miska
Fardisya
Al-Haram
Tabsur
Jalil ash-Shamaliya
Jalil al-Qibliya
Abu Kishk
Kafr Saba
Biyar 'Adas
Khureish
Al-Mas'udiya
Sarona
Ash-Sheikh
   Muwannis
Jammasin al-Gharbi
Jammasin ash-
   Sharqi
Jarisha
Salama
Al-Kheiriya
As-Sawalima
Al-Mirr
Fajja

Majdal Yaba
Al-Muzeiri'a
Rantiya
Al-Muweilih
Al-Yahudiya
Saqiya
Kafr 'Ana
Yazur
Beit Dajan
As-Safiriya
Srafand al-'Amar
Abu al-Fadl
Wilhelma
At-Tira
Deir Tarif
Beit Nabala
Jindas
Al-Haditha
Khirbat
   Adh-Dhuheiriya
Al-Qubeida
Deir Abu Salama

Ramleh

Nabi Rubin
Yibna
Sarafand al-Kharab
Bir Salim
Wadi Hunein
Zarnuqa
Ni'ana
'Aqir
Danyal
Jimzu
Khirbat Zakariya
Barfilya
'Innaba

Beit Shanna
Al-Qubab
Salbit
Abu Shusha
Al-Kunaiyisa
'Arab as-Sukkeir
Al-Mughar
Bashshit
Qatra
Barqa
Yasur
Al-Mansura
Shohma
Umm Kolkha
Al-Mukheizin
Qazaza
Jilya
Sajad
Al-Kheima
Seidun
Deir Muheisin
Khulda
Beit Jiz
Beit Susin
Khirbat Beit Far
Khirbat Ismallah
Sara'
Isdud
Hamama
Julis
Batani Gharbi
Batani Sharqi
Al-Masmiya al-
　Kabira
Qastina
Tall at-Turmus
As-Sawafir ash-
　Shamaliya
As-Sawafir al-
　Gharbiya

As-Sawafir ash-
　Sharqiya
Jaladiya
'Ibdis
Beit Daras
Al-Masmiya as-
　Saghira
Bilin
Ard al-Ishra
At-Tina
Idhnibba
Mughallis
Tall as-Safi
Barqusya
Deir ad-Dubban
Bureij
Zakariya
Ajjur
Beit Nattif
Al-Jura
Khirbat Khisas
Ni'ilya
Hirbya
Majdal
Al-Jiya
Kaukab
Beit Tima
Beit Jirja
Huleiqat
Barbara
Beit 'Affa
Juseir
Hatta
'Iraq Suweidan
Al-Faluja
'Iraq al-Manshiya
Gat
Karatiya
Summeil
Zikrin

Ra'na
Zeita
Kidna
Khirbat Umm Burj
Deir Naknkas
Beit Jibrin
Deir Suneid
Dimra
Sumsum
Bureir
Najd
Huj
Jammama
Al-Qubeiba
Ad-Daweima

Jerusalem

Al-Burj
Bir Ma'in
Khirbat
　Al-Buweiriya
Nataf
Beit Thul
Beit Mashir
Saris
Khirbat 'Umur
'Islin
Ishwa
Kasla
Beit Umm al-Meis
Deir 'Amr
'Artuf
Beit Haqquba
Al-Qastal
Qalunya
Deir Yassin
Lifta
'Ein Karim

Suba	Al-Qabu	At-Tahame
Sataf	Ras az-Zuwuire	Raud Khattab
Khirbat Lauz		Imsura
'Aqqur		Al-Maderiye
Deir ash-Sheikh		Birein
Deit al-Hawa	*Gaza and Beersheba*	Abu Ruthe
Deiraban		Ath-Themele
Sufla	Kaufakha	At-Tahame
Beit 'Itab	Al-Muharraqa	Al-Metrade
Jarash	Bir as-Sab'	Sehel al-Hewa
Ras Abu 'Ammar	Tel al-Milh	Mayet Awad
'Allar	'Imaret Adu Isder	Ruweis al-Beden
Al-Jura	Ad-Daraje	Injeib al-Ful
Al-Maliha	Abu al-Hewawit	'Ein al-Ghidyan
Al-Walaja	Al-Hemade	Umm Reshrush

Source: The designation 'destroyed' refers to Palestinian villages that were depopulated and whose structures were either demolished or transfered to Jewish colonial settlements. This appendix was compiled from Basheer K. Nijim, ed., with Bishara Muammar, *Toward the De-Arabization of Palestine/Israel 1945–1977*, Kendall/Hunt for the Jerusalem Fund for Education and Community Development, 1984. This source provides detailed sectional maps of Palestine locating where each of these villages was located and what their populations had been. It also provides full information on Jewish settlements from the very first settlement, Petah Tikva, in 1878, up until 1977. Appendices 19 and 20 are derived from this source.

19   De-Arabization of Palestine: Arab villages by Subdistrict

Subdistrict	Number of Arab villages before Israel was established	Number of Arab villages demolished by Israel	Arab villages existing today
Safad	83	78	5
Tiberias	29	24	5
Beisan	33	31	2
Nazareth	31	4	27
Jenin	19	6	13
Acre	64	29	35
Haifa	72	45	27
Tulkarm	34	20	14
Ramleh	56	56	0
Jerusalem	41	37	4
Hebron	19	15	4

Source: See appendix 18.

20 *Judaization of Palestine: Jewish settlements by Subdistrict*

Subdistrict	Number of Jewish settlements before Israel was established	Number of Jewish settlements built upon Arab sites	Number of Jewish settlements existing today
Safad	26	30	56
Tiberias	27	11	38
Beisan	24	9	33
Nazareth	20	6	26
Jenin	0	21	21
Acre	9	39	48
Haifa	64	39	103
Tulkarm	54	47	101
Ramleh	25	75	100
Jerusalem	6	33	39
Hebron	1	17	18

Source: See appendix 18.

21 Palestine Liberation Organization Infrastructure

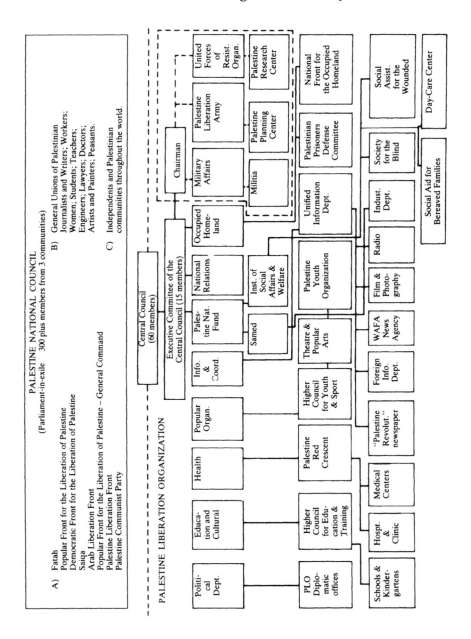

22   The Palestinian Declaration of Independence, excerpts*, 15 November 1988

Palestine, the land of the three monotheistic faiths, is where the Palestinian Arab people was born, on which it grew, developed and excelled. The Palestinian people was never separated from or diminished in its integral bonds with Palestine. Thus the Palestinian Arab people ensured for itself an everlasting union between itself, its land and its history.

Resolute throughout that history, the Palestinian Arab people forged its national identity, rising even to unimagined levels in its defense, as invasion, the design of others, and the appeal special to Palestine's ancient and luminous place on the eminence where powers and civilizations are joined . . . All this intervened thereby to deprive the people of its political independence. Yet the undying connection between Palestine and its people secured for the land its character, and for the people its national genius.

Nourished by an unfolding series of civilizations and cultures, inspired by a heritage rich in variety and kind, the Palestinian Arab people added to its stature by consolidating a union between itself and its patrimonial land. The call went out from Temple, Church and Mosque that to praise the creator, to celebrate compassion and peace was indeed the message of Palestine. And in generation after generation, the Palestinian Arab people gave of itself unsparingly in the valiant battle for liberation. Our people's rebellions are the heroic embodiment of our will for national independence. And so the people was sustained in the struggle to stay and to prevail.

When in the course of modern times a new order of values was declared with norms and values fair for all, it was the Palestinian Arab people that had been excluded from the destiny of all other peoples by a hostile array of local and foreign powers. Yet again had unaided justice been revealed as insufficient to drive the world's history along its preferred course.

And it was the Palestinian people, already wounded in its body, that was submitted to yet another type of occupation over which

---

* An official translation in full can be found in the *Al-Fajr Jerusalem Palestinian Weekly*, 28 November 1988, p. 5.

floated the falsehood that 'Palestine was a land without people'. This notion was foisted upon some in the world, whereas in article 22 of the Covenant of the League of Nations (1919) and in the treaty of Lausanne (1923), the world had recognized that all Arab territories, including Palestine, of the formerly Ottoman provinces, were to have granted to them their freedom as provisionally independent nations.

Despite the historical injustice inflicted on the Palestinian Arab people resulting in their dispersion and depriving them of their right to self-determination, following upon UN General Assembly Resolution 181 (1947), which partitioned Palestine into two states, one Arab, one Jewish, yet it is this resolution that still provides those conditions of international legitimacy that ensure the right of the Palestinian people to sovereignty and national independence.

By stages, the occupation of Palestine and parts of other Arab territories by Israeli forces, the willed dispossession and expulsion from their ancestral homes of the majority of Palestine's civilian inhabitants, was achieved by organized terror; those Palestinians who remained, as a vestige subjugated in their homeland, were persecuted and forced to endure the destruction of their national life.

Thus were principles of international legitimacy violated. Thus were the Charter of the United Nations and its resolutions disfigured, for they had recognized the Palestinian people's national rights, including the right of return, the right to independence, the right to sovereignty over territory and a homeland . . .

The massive national uprising, the *intifada*, now intensifying in cumulative scope and power on occupied Palestinian territories, as well as the unflinching resistance of the refugee camps outside the homeland, have elevated consciousness of the Palestinian truth and right into still higher realms of comprehension and actuality. Now, at last, the curtain has been dropped around a whole epoch of prevarication and negation. The *intifada* has set siege to the mind of official Israel, which has for too long relied exclusively upon myth and terror to deny Palestinian existence altogether. Because of the *intifada* and its revolutionary irreversible impulse, the history of Palestine has therefore arrived at a decisive juncture.

Whereas the Palestinian people reaffirms most definitely its inalienable rights in the land of its patrimony:

— now by virtue of natural rights, and the sacrifices of successive generations who gave themselves in defence of the freedom and independence of their homeland;

— in pursuance of resolutions adopted by Arab summit conferences and relying on the authority bestowed by international legitimacy as embodied in the resolutions of the United Nations Organization since 1947;

— and in exercise by the Palestinian Arab people of its rights to self determination, political independence, and sovereignty over its territory;

— the Palestine National Council, in the name of God, and in the name of the Palestinian people, hereby proclaims the establishment of the State of Palestine on our Palestinian territory with its capital Jerusalem.

The state of Palestine is the state of the Palestinians wherever they may be. The state is for them to enjoy in it their collective national and cultural identity, theirs to pursue in it a complete equality of rights. In it will be safeguarded their political and religious convictions and their human dignity by means of a parliamentary democratic system of governance, itself based on freedom of expression and the freedom to form parties. The right of minorities will duly be respected by the majority, as minorities must abide by decisions of the majority. Governance will be based on principles of social justice, equality and non-discrimination in public rights, men or women, on grounds of race, religion, color or sex, under the aegis of a constitution which ensures the rule of law and an independent judiciary. Thus shall these principles allow no departure from Palestine's ancient spiritual and cultural heritage of tolerance and religious co-existence.

The state of Palestine is an Arab state, an integral and indivisible part of the Arab nation, at one with that nation in heritage and civilization, with it also in its aspiration for liberation, progress, democracy and unity. The state of Palestine affirms its obligation to abide by the charter of the League of Arab States, whereby the coordination of the Arab states with each other shall be strengthened. It calls upon Arab compatriots to consolidate and enhance the emergence in reality of our state, to mobilize its potential and to intensify efforts whose goal is to end Israeli occupation.

The state of Palestine proclaims its commitment to the principles of the UN, and to the universal declaration of human rights. It proclaims its commitment as well to the principles and policies of the Non-Aligned Movement.

It further announces itself to be a peace loving state, in adherence to the principles of peaceful coexistence. It will join with all states and peoples in order to assure a permanent peace based upon justice and the respect of rights so that humanity's potential for well-being may be assured, an earnest competition for excellence be maintained, and in which confidence in the future will eliminate fear for whom justice is the only recourse.

In the context of its struggle for peace in the land of love and peace, the state of Palestine calls upon the United Nations to bear special responsibility for the Palestinian Arab people and its homeland. It calls upon all peace and freedom loving peoples and states to assist in its attainment of its objectives, to provide it with security, to alleviate the tragedy of its people, and to help it terminate Israel's occupation of the Palestinian territories.

The state of Palestine herewith declares that it believes in the settlement of regional and international disputes by peaceful means, in accordance with the UN Charter and resolutions. Without prejudice to its natural right to defend its territorial integrity and independence, it therefore rejects the threat or use of force, violence and terrorism against its territorial integrity, or political independence, as it also rejects their use against the territorial integrity of other states . . .

Therefore, we call upon our great people to rally to the banner of Palestine, to cherish and defend it, so that it may forever be the symbol of our freedom and dignity in that homeland, which is a homeland for the free.

Index